Democracy and Democratization

Dilemmas in World Politics

Dilemmas in World Politics offers teachers and students in international relations a series of quality books on critical issues, trends, and regions in international politics. Each text examines a "real world" dilemma and is structured to cover the historical, theoretical, practical, and projected dimensions of its subject.

BOOKS IN THIS SERIES

Democracy and Democratization: Processes and Prospects in a Changing World, Third Edition
Georg Sørensen

International Human Rights, Third Edition
Jack Donnelly

The United Nations in the Twenty-first Century, Third Edition
Karen A. Mingst and Margaret P. Karns

Global Environmental Politics, Fourth Edition
Pamela S. Chasek, David L. Downie, and Janet Welsh Brown

Southern Africa in World Politics
Janice Love

Ethnic Conflict in World Politics, Second Edition
Barbara Harff and Ted Robert Gurr

Dilemmas of International Trade, Second Edition
Bruce E. Moon

Humanitarian Challenges and Intervention, Second Edition
Thomas G. Weiss and Cindy Collins

The European Union: Dilemmas of Regional Integration
James A. Caporaso

Global Gender Issues, Second Edition
Spike Peterson and Anne Sisson Runyon

Revolution and Transition in East-Central Europe, Second Edition
David S. Mason

One Land, Two Peoples, Second Edition
Deborah Gerner

Dilemmas of Development Assistance
Sarah J. Tisch and Michael B. Wallace

East Asian Dynamism, Second Edition
Steven Chan

THIRD EDITION

Democracy
and
Democratization

*Processes and Prospects in
a Changing World*

GEORG SØRENSEN
University of Aarhus, Denmark

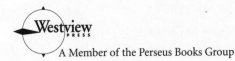

A Member of the Perseus Books Group

Library of Congress Cataloging-in-Publication Data
Sørensen, Georg, 1948–
    Democracy and democratization : processes and prospects in a changing world / Georg Sørensen. — 3rd ed.
        p. cm. — (Dilemmas in world politics)
    Includes bibliographical references and index.
    ISBN-13: 978-0-8133-4380-8 (pbk. : alk. paper)
    ISBN-10: 0-8133-4380-1 (pbk. : alk. paper) 1. Democracy. 2. Democratization. 3. World politics—1989– I. Title.
JC423.S69 2008
321.8—dc22

                                                                2007019903

10 9 8 7 6 5 4 3 2 1

For Lisbet and Mathilde

Contents

List of Illustrations

Boxes

Acronyms

ASEE authoritarian state elite enrichment regime
CCP Chinese Communist party
CSCE Conference on Security and Cooperation in Europe
DDR Deutsche Demokratische Republik
EU European Union
FDI foreign direct investment
GDP gross domestic product
GNP gross national product
HDI Human Development Index
IMF International Monetary Fund
NATO North Atlantic Treaty Organization
NGO nongovernmental organization
NIC newly industrializing country
OECD Organization for Economic Cooperation and Development
PPP purchasing power parities
SAP structural adjustment program
TNC transnational corporation
TPLF Tigrean People's Liberation Front
UN United Nations
UNDP United Nations Development Program

Preface

This third edition of the book thoroughly revises and updates the argument. The ambition remains the same: to evaluate the current prospects for democracy and democratization. There is a new Chapter 3 on democracy in the new millennium. It argues that there has been a shift away from "transition to democracy" toward a "standstill" where a large number of countries remain in the gray area between outright authoritarian and fully democratic. Chapter 4, which discusses the problems involved in promoting democracy from the outside, is also new. The remaining chapters have been revised to include the most recent debates on their respective topics.

I am much indebted to Joan Bloch Jensen, who was an excellent research assistant on this new edition and helped with everything, from collecting recent research in the field to pointing out holes in the arguments, revising tables, and conducting meticulous proofreading. Assistant Professor Svend Erik Skaaning read the entire draft of the third edition and came up with numerous suggestions for improvement. Jonna Kjær once again took care of all the technical details. Executive Editor Steve Catalano from Westview Press warmly supported the third edition with unfailing help and advice; so did Senior Project Editor Carol Smith. Chrisona Schmidt was an excellent copy editor.

I am grateful for positive responses on the first and second editions from professors and students, including feedback from referees and from Chung-in Moon, who made valuable suggestions on the second edition. I also thank friends and colleagues for their help and encouragement. Former series editor George Lopez started this project by inviting me to submit a book proposal on democracy and democratization. Comments from Frances Hagopian and several members of the Dilemmas editorial board helped improve the proposal. Jennifer Knerr and Rachel Quenk, formerly of Westview, were always ready with advice and support as the project moved along. Jørgen Elklit, Hans-Henrik Holm, Hans-Jørgen Nielsen, Ole Nørgaard, and Palle Svensson read the first version of the manuscript, or parts of it, and provided extensive comments that made the first edition a better book. Any shortcomings that remain are my responsibility. Finally, I am grateful, once again, for the constant support and encouragement of my wife, Lisbet.

Georg Sørensen
Berlin, March 2007

Introduction

A statement often repeated nowadays, in both scholarly circles and the mass media, is that democracy has made great progress throughout the world in a brief period of time. In Eastern Europe, totalitarian systems have been replaced by democracies; in Africa, one-party systems headed by a strongman who maintains personal control of the state are challenged by opposition forces exploiting newly gained political liberties; in Latin America, the military dictatorships have crumbled; in many Asian countries, authoritarian systems are moving—or being forced to move—in a democratic direction.

The swift progress of democracy in many countries raised hopes for a better world; the expectations were that democracy would not only promote political liberties and other human rights but would also lead to rapid economic development and increased welfare as well as to international relations characterized by peaceful cooperation and mutual understanding. In this book, we will examine the prospects for these great expectations. A necessary first step is to clarify the concept of democracy. This is done in Chapter 1, which introduces different views of democracy, discusses ways of measuring democracy, and identifies the countries that presently qualify as democratic. Next, we need to know how a transition from authoritarian rule toward democracy unfolds. This issue is the theme of Chapter 2. A model is introduced which demonstrates that the process of **democratization** is a lengthy one involving different phases, including the preparatory phase, the decision phase, and the consolidation phase. Chapter 3 is devoted to the formulation of four propositions, each of which spells out an important characteristic of a democracy's progress and sustainability. The chapter argues that the concept of transition is too optimistic to function concisely as a label covering the current fate of regime change. Actually there has been a shift from "transition" to "standstill" in the sense that many regimes remain in the gray area of semidemocracy or semiauthoritarianism. Chapter 4 discusses the promotion of democracy from the outside with a focus on the delicate balance that outsiders must find between influencing the process of democratization while leaving ultimate control to insiders. Following this groundwork, we are ready to ask about the domestic and international consequences of democracy. Chapter 5 concentrates on possible domestic consequences for economic development, welfare, and human rights. Chapter 6 turns to the international consequences of democracy: Will it pave the way for a more peaceful and cooperative world? Finally, the conclusion briefly considers the future of democracy and democratization.

In one sense it is true, then, that democracy has made great progress in the world in recent years. The way in which democratization has occurred, however, calls into question whether democratic advancement will continue and whether potential positive effects of democracy will be forthcoming. This is the central dilemma surrounding the current transitions toward democracy. The chapters that follow investigate particular aspects of this dilemma. Chapter 3 emphasizes that the processes of democratization in recent years are frail openings with democracy still restricted in many ways and with no guarantees of further democratic progress. Chapter 4 clarifies why the promotion of democracy from the outside is so difficult. Chapter 5 argues that economic development and welfare improvement will not necessarily be forthcoming from fragile democracies. Indeed, there may be a trade-off between democratic stability and welfare progress. Chapter 6 asserts that a more peaceful world as a result of the current democratizations—although a theoretical possibility—is by no means assured. In short, current democratic advancement is taking place in a way that may jeopardize continued democratic progress.

The conclusion briefly considers the future of democracy; it is followed by discussion questions for each chapter and a list of recommended readings.

1

What Is Democracy?

Democracy is a form of government in which the people rule. The concrete way in which democracy should be organized and the conditions and preconditions it requires have been intensely debated for centuries. Indeed, the early contributions to this discussion go back to ancient Greece. I contend that anyone who wants to understand democracy and its present position in the world must have an awareness of the most important debates about the meaning of democracy, a notion of the core features of democracy relevant for today's world, and an understanding of how economic, social, and cultural conditions affect the quality of democracy. Thus I address each of these elements in this chapter. My aim is to introduce the important issues; references are included that direct the reader to sources with in-depth treatments.

The term "democracy" comes from two Greek words: *demos* (people) and *kratos* (rule). The definition "rule by the people" may sound straightforward, but it raises a number of complex issues. The most important ones can be summarized as follows:

- Who is to be considered "the people"?
- What kind of participation is envisaged for the people?
- What conditions are assumed to be conducive to participation? Can the disincentives and incentives, or costs and benefits, of participation be equal?
- How broadly or narrowly is the scope of rule to be construed? What is the appropriate field of democratic activity?

- If "rule" is to cover "the political," what is meant by this? Does it cover (1) law and order? (2) relations between states? (3) the economy? (4) the domestic or private sphere?
- Must the rules of "the people" be obeyed? What is the place of obligation and dissent?
- What roles are permitted for those who are avowedly and actively "nonparticipants"?
- Under what circumstances, if any, are democracies entitled to resort to coercion against their own people or against those outside the sphere of legitimate rule?[1]

Clearly a discussion of democracy must involve not only the *theory* about possible ways of organizing rule by the people but also the *philosophy* about what ought to be (i.e., the best ways of constructing government) and an understanding of *practical experiences* with the ways in which government has been organized in different societies at different times.

Such considerations are often highly interwoven. At the same time, the most significant contributions to deliberations about democracy have one important element in common: They are set against the context of contemporary society as those who have made these contributions perceive it. The debate about democracy therefore has a built-in dynamic: It develops and grows to incorporate new aspects and dimensions when the societal context, or the analyst's perception of it, changes.

Thus Plato's critique of democracy in Athens was set against what he saw as the decline of the city, its defeat in the war with Sparta, and the decay of morality and leadership. In Athens, democracy meant the rule by the poor majority. People could do pretty much as they liked; there was no respect for authority in the family, in the schools, or elsewhere. Eventually, Plato reasoned, laws would not be respected but would be seen as attacks on the freedom of the people. This situation would lead to **anarchy** (the absence of political authority) and chaos, paving the way for tyranny (rule by a single dictator). Plato's solution was to recommend rule by the wise, trained, and educated—the philosophers.[2] Aristotle voiced similar criticisms of democracy, which he also saw as a form of government devoted exclusively to the good of the poor. Developing a position taken by Plato in his later writings, Aristotle argued in favor of room for popular influence, for example, in the making of laws. Such considerations pointed toward a combination of monarchy, aristocracy, and democracy, a "mixed state" where a separation of powers ensured a balance of forces between the main groups in society.[3]

With the decline of Rome, the debate about democracy was put on hold. In the feudal system of the Middle Ages, power was not vested in elected bodies; it was based on rank that could be only attained through inheritance or by force. "No popular movement, however enraged, would think that its aims could be achieved by getting the vote. And in the nations and independent city-states of the later Middle Ages also, power was not to be sought in that way."[4]

A new body of thought about democracy began with the Renaissance and Niccolò Machiavelli (1469–1527), although it did not fully emerge until the nineteenth century. During this time span, ideas about democracy took shape in the context of the development of modern industrial-capitalist society. When liberal democracy began to appear in these countries, new debates opened up about the true content of liberty because liberal values tend to compete. For example, the values of equality and solidarity may compete with the values of individual freedom and autonomy; as Isaiah Berlin famously said, "Total liberty for the wolves is death to the lambs, total liberty of the powerful, the gifted, is not compatible with the rights to a decent existence of the weak and less gifted . . . Equality may demand the restraint of the liberty of those who wish to dominate."[5] In other words, what is the appropriate liberal democratic balance between competing values? Is such a balance even possible?

In more recent times, the process of democratization is happening in many different places around the world, even as globalization and other forces are bringing countries closer together. These developments have sparked new debates about the economic, cultural, and social conditions under which democracy can develop, and about the consequences of globalization for democracy.

Rather than presenting all these debates in detail, I shall identify concepts of the core features of democracy in the modern sense and point out the main areas where these concepts are still debated.

LIBERAL DEMOCRACY AND ITS CRITICS

Liberalism developed in opposition to medieval hierarchical institutions, the despotic monarchies whose claim to all-powerful rule rested on an assertion of divine support. Liberalism attacked the old system on two fronts. First, the liberalists fought for a rollback of state power and the creation of a sphere of civil society where social relations, including private business, nonstate institutions, family, and personal life, could evolve without state interference. "Gradually, liberalism became associated with the doctrine that individuals should be free to pursue their own preferences in religious, economic and political affairs—in fact, in most matters that affected daily life."[6] An important element in this regard was the support of a market economy based on respect for private property.

The second element of early liberalism was the claim that state power was based not on natural or supernatural rights but on the will of the sovereign people. Ultimately this claim would lead to demands for democracy—the creation of mechanisms of representation that ensured that those who held state power enjoyed popular support. Yet the creation of such mechanisms was not a primary concern of early liberalism. The tradition that became liberal democracy was liberal first (aimed at restricting state power over civil society) and democratic later (aimed at creating structures that would secure a popular mandate for holders of state power). Yet liberals had reservations about democracy, fearing that it would impede the establishment of a liberal society.[7] In a sense the development of liberal democratic thinking evolved toward settling the complex relationship between these two elements.

The unfolding thought on liberal democracy has been instructively summarized by C. B. Macpherson in three different models.[8] Instead of presenting these models in detail, I include elements from them in a discussion of more recent debates and critiques with the aim of identifying some of the important issues that have been raised in the different stages of thinking about democracy.

The earliest model of liberal democracy, derived around 1820, builds on contributions from Jeremy Bentham and James Mill. Macpherson called it protective democracy because of the model's preoccupation with protecting citizens from government and ensuring that governors would pursue policies in accordance with the interests of citizens as a whole. Such protection would be secured through universal franchise, since rulers could be removed by voters.

In practice, however, Bentham and Mill accepted severe restrictions on the right to vote, excluding women and large sections of the working classes.[9] Their cause was more liberal than democratic, as they aimed to restrict the political sphere, especially governmental activity and institutions. Civil society should be left to itself, meaning that such issues as "the organization of the economy or violence against women in marriage (rape) are typically thought of as non-political, an outcome of 'free' private contracts in civil society, not a public issue or a matter for the state."[10]

This concern with negative freedom—citizens' freedom from pervasive political authority—was echoed some 150 years later by the so-called New Right or neoliberals. They focused on rolling back regulatory and redistributive activities pursued by the state in the name of general welfare and social justice.

The leading figure of the New Right, Friedrich von Hayek, distinguishes between liberalism and democracy. He calls the former a doctrine about what the law ought to be and the latter a doctrine about the manner of determining what will be the law.[11] For Hayek democracy is of secondary importance. The highest political end is liberty, which can be achieved only if there are strict limits on government activities. Government intervention in civil society must aim at protecting life, liberty, and estate, which basically means creating the best possible framework for the operation of the free market. There is no room, for example, for redistributive measures because they would jeopardize the free choice of individuals in the free market.[12]

In this view democracy is desirable as a mechanism for ensuring that the majority will decide what the law should be. It is vital, however, that democratic majorities respect limitations on government activity. If they do not, democracy will be in conflict with liberty, and if that happens, Hayek is "not a democrat."[13]

In summary, the liberal democratic tradition is primarily concerned with restricting political authority over citizens. Liberty is individual freedom in the realm of civil society. Democracy can be a means of achieving this end but is not the end itself. If there is a democratic core in this way of thinking, it is the principle of the political equality of citizens. We will see that this principle can lead in a different direction from the one taken by the proponents of protective democracy and can result in a more central and positive role for democracy.

John Stuart Mill (1806–1873), the son of James Mill, was more enthusiastic about democracy than his father was. The younger Mill saw democracy as an important element in free human development. Participation in political life could lead toward the "highest and harmonious expansion of individual capacities."[14] At the same time, J. S. Mill shared one of the basic assumptions of the protective democrats: The maximum freedom of citizens requires limitations on the scope of the state's activity. He envisioned representative government in combination with a free market economy.

Thus J. S. Mill followed familiar liberal views concerning restrictions on the scope of government and governmental activity. With regard to enfranchisement, his father had argued for universal franchise, at least in principle. J. S. Mill, however, recommended a system of **plural voting** (which gives some members of the electorate more votes than others) in order to give the "wiser and more talented" more votes than the "ignorant and less able."[15] In two other respects the younger Mill was more democratic than his father. First, in the moral dimension, he saw participation in the political process as a way to liberty and self-development. Second, he directly confronted inequalities in mid-nineteenth-century English society that he considered obstacles to the democratic process. He severely criticized the subjugation of women and pointed to the need for complete equality between the sexes as a precondition for human development and democracy. He was highly critical of extreme inequalities of income, wealth, and power that hindered the human development of the lower classes. Mill's ideas of participation and equality are hard to reconcile with his position concerning a restricted government committed to laissez-faire (which can be interpreted as doing nothing about inequality) and a plural voting system in favor of the well-educated (which is hardly a radical commitment to equality).[16]

Several other thinkers have shared Mill's preoccupation with participation as an important element of democracy and his concern that socioeconomic inequality is a main barrier to democracy and political equality. Jean-Jacques Rousseau (1712–1778) lived almost a hundred years before J. S. Mill. Rousseau's point of departure was a small, preindustrial community. He criticized the notion of representation, saying that citizens should be directly involved in making their laws; otherwise, there is no freedom. "The English people believes itself to be free, it is gravely mistaken; it is free only during the election of Members of Parliament; as soon as the members are elected, the people are enslaved; it is nothing."[17] In other words, real freedom requires direct democracy.

Rousseau's ideas about the role of participation in democracy have often been rejected because they are seen as irrelevant for modern, large-scale society. But C. B. Macpherson and Carole Pateman have argued that Rousseau's ideas are indeed compatible with modern society and that representative government can and should be combined with elements of direct participation if democracy is to be more than merely formal.[18] According to Macpherson and Pateman, structures of participation in local society and in the workplace will vastly improve the quality of representative democracy. A participatory society would make the common man "better able to assess the performance of representatives at the national level, better equipped to take decisions of national scope when the opportunity arose to do so, and better able to weigh up the impact of decisions taken by national representatives on his own life."[19]

Rousseau, like J. S. Mill, felt that socioeconomic inequality would prevent citizens from obtaining equal political rights. In other words, political democracy cannot exist in the presence of socioeconomic inequality. In his critical analysis of capitalism, Karl Marx (1818–1883) related the existence of inequality with the class divisions produced by capitalist society. He held that in a capitalist society a free market and a state based on politically equal citizens are only formalities that hide the reality of rule by the capitalist class. The only way to achieve real political and economic equality and a full democratization of state and society is to abolish the capitalist system and replace it with socialism and ultimately communism.[20] Thus Marx agreed with Hayek that there is a sharp distinction between liberalism and democracy, but he drew the opposite conclusion: In order to achieve liberty and democracy, it is necessary to reject liberal capitalism.

In the debate about the relationship between capitalism and democracy, the liberalist tradition maintains that only a capitalist system can provide the necessary basis for liberty and democracy. The Marxist tradition rejects this view and argues that capitalism must be replaced by socialism as the necessary basis for democracy. The liberal view has prevailed as noncapitalist countries adhering to the Marxist tradition have been unable to construct political systems that can claim to be more democratic than the liberal democracies based on capitalism.

Yet the debate does not end there. Not every capitalist system is democratic. One does not have to be a Marxist to see the obstacles to democracy stemming from economic inequality. Robert Dahl states that modern corporate capitalism tends to "produce inequalities in social and economic resources so great as to bring about severe violations of political equality and hence of the democratic process."[21] Dahl goes on to suggest a system of cooperative control over the economy. This view of the need to extend democratic decision making beyond government to economic and social life has been expressed by others as well.[22]

Thus the current debate about capitalism and democracy is between such thinkers as Hayek, who want to protect life, liberty, and estate by rolling back government intervention in civil society, and a liberal-cum-social democratic group that argues for the necessity of a reformed capitalism with less inequality and more democracy, not only in political affairs but also in social and economic life.[23]

THE MEANING OF DEMOCRACY

It is clear from this brief overview that rule by the people involves many complex elements. Indeed, a full answer to the question of what democracy means today requires a theory of contemporary society supported by substantial normative considerations about the type of people's rule that is desirable, which cannot be pursued here. Instead, I shall illustrate the scope of this debate by outlining two conceptions of democracy with contemporary relevance: one rather narrow, the other very comprehensive.

The narrow concept was formulated by Joseph Schumpeter. For him democracy is simply a mechanism for choosing political leadership. Citizens are given a choice among rival political leaders who compete for their votes. Between elections, decisions are made by the politicians. At the next election, citizens can replace their elected officials. This ability to choose between leaders at election time is democracy. In Schumpeter's words, "The democratic method is that institutional arrangement for arriving at political decisions in which individuals acquire the power to decide by means of a competitive struggle for the people's vote."[24]

At the opposite end of the spectrum is the comprehensive notion of democracy suggested by David Held, who combines insights from the liberal and the Marxist traditions to arrive at a meaning of democracy that supports a basic principle of autonomy:

> Persons should enjoy equal rights and, accordingly, equal obligations in the specification of the political framework which generates and limits the opportunities available to them; that is, they should be free and equal in the processes of deliberation about the conditions of their own lives and in the determination of these conditions, so long as they do not deploy this framework to negate the rights of others.[25]

The enactment of this principle, which Held calls **democratic autonomy**, requires both an accountable state and a democratic reordering of civil society. It foresees substantial direct participation in local community institutions as well as self-management of cooperatively owned enterprises. It calls for a bill of rights that goes beyond the right to cast a vote to include equal opportunity for participation and for discovering individual preferences as well as citizens' final control of the political agenda. Also included are social and economic rights to ensure adequate resources for democratic autonomy. "Without tough social and economic rights, rights with respect to the state could not be fully enjoyed; and without state rights new forms of inequality of power, wealth and status could systematically disrupt the implementation of social and economic liberties."[26]

Between the narrow notion of political democracy suggested by Schumpeter and the comprehensive understanding presented by Held lies the debate about what democracy is and what it ought to be. Looking at democracy this way helps us understand it as a dynamic entity that has been given many different definitions; its meaning remains subject to debate.

This approach can also help us see the possibility of emphasizing different aspects of democracy as we frame our own understanding of the concept. It is not surprising, for example, that conditions in many developing countries have led to an emphasis on the need to meet basic economic rights and equal opportunities for participation, as stressed in Held's comprehensive notion of democracy. Extreme material poverty makes democracy difficult: "When the members of a community suffer from chronic malnutrition and frequent illness, participation in common affairs that is both broad and deep is difficult to maintain. When masses of people suffer from acute hunger or rampant disease, expecting them to achieve genuine democracy is naive."[27] Julius Nyerere, the former president of Tanzania, said that the struggle for freedom in Africa is basically a struggle for freedom from hunger, disease, and poverty.

Industrialized countries, where extreme poverty is not the main problem, can be affected by other impediments to democracy—the lack of economic, social, and consequently political equality stressed by Dahl or perhaps the tough security and surveillance measures adopted by some countries after the September 11, 2001, terrorist attacks. At the same time, most of us would agree that the Western industrialized countries are, in a basic respect, democracies, particularly according to the narrow concept of political democracy provided by Schumpeter.

Is this thought wrong for the protection of the??

One general conclusion that can be drawn from this discussion of the meaning of democracy is that talk of the end of history is inappropriate, even if the authoritarian, noncapitalist regimes of the east have collapsed. [28] (Francis Fukuyama coined this phrase to describe the end point of humankind's ideological evolution and the universalization of Western liberal democracy as the final form of human government.) There is still plenty of room for the development of different variations or models of democracy. *Fukuyama said democracy had won out. He didn't say that it couldn't change.*

This overview of the meaning of democracy does not give us much guidance in determining whether specific countries are democratic. For that purpose we need a precise concept that focuses on democracy as a specific type of political system. In the broad concept suggested by Held, democracy is not only a political but also a social and economic system. Using this broad concept, we would find few (if any) empirical cases of democracy. Viewing democracy as a political system sharpens questions about the relationships between the political system, on the one hand, and the economic and social dimensions, on the other. Although the political system concept of democracy provides the most adequate starting point for the analysis intended here, it is not a normative choice of the "best kind" of democracy.

Dahl identifies government's responsiveness to the preferences of its citizens, considered as political equals, as a key characteristic of democracy. Such responsiveness requires that citizens must have opportunities to (1) formulate their preferences, (2) signify their preferences to their fellow citizens and the government by individual and collective action, and (3) have their preferences weighed equally in the conduct of the government. These three opportunities, in turn, depend on the following institutional guarantees:

1. *Elected officials.* Control over government decisions about policy is constitutionally vested in elected officials.
2. *Free and fair elections.* Elected officials are chosen in frequent and fairly conducted elections in which coercion is comparatively uncommon.
3. *Inclusive suffrage.* Practically all adults have the right to vote in the election of officials.
4. *Right to run for office.* Practically all adults have the right to run for elective offices in the government, though age limits may be higher for holding office than for the suffrage.
5. *Freedom of expression.* Citizens have a right to express themselves without the danger of severe punishment on political matters broadly defined, including criticism of officials, the government, the regime, the socioeconomic order, and the prevailing ideology.
6. *Alternative information.* Citizens have a right to seek out alternative sources of information. Moreover, alternative sources of information exist and are protected by laws.
7. *Associational autonomy.* To achieve various rights, including those listed above, citizens also have a right to form relatively independent associations or organizations, including independent political parties and interest groups.[29]

When these conditions are met, we have a political democracy. It is sometimes referred to as a liberal democracy because of its focus on the form of government. In principle, the seven conditions outlined by Dahl make up my definition of political democracy. [30] The seven conditions cover three main dimensions of political democracy—*competition, participation,* and *civil and political liberties*. Against this background, political democracy can be viewed as a system of government that meets the following conditions:

> *Does the U.S. count? 2-party ...*

- Meaningful and extensive *competition* among individuals and organized groups (especially political parties) for all effective positions of government power, at regular intervals and excluding the use of force
- A highly inclusive level of *political participation* in the selection of leaders and policies, at least through regular and fair elections, such that no major (adult) social group is excluded
- A level of *civil and political liberties*—freedom of expression, freedom of the press, freedom to form and join organizations— sufficient to ensure the integrity of political competition and participation[31]

This is the definition of political democracy that I employ in the present volume.

Our first task in attempting to determine whether a specific country is a democracy is to look for competition, participation, and liberties in that country, not just on the formal level but in real practice. (Many political leaders pay lip service to democratic ideals without meeting them in practice.) This task is complicated by the fact that many countries meet the conditions specified by the three dimensions in varying degrees.

Thus it is necessary to decide on some minimum value with regard to each dimension that a country must meet to qualify as democratic. Furthermore, those that do not qualify may vary substantially in degrees of nondemocracy. For example, Mexico may not have been fully democratic throughout the postwar period, but it was much more democratic than many countries in sub-Saharan Africa. Differentiating degrees of nondemocracy is another substantial task; in the area between full democracy and nondemocracy (or authoritarian rule), there is room for differing types of semidemocracies and semiauthoritarian systems.[32]

Unfortunately, scholars disagree about which dimensions are most important in determining whether there is democracy or about what precise minimum value should be applied for each of the dimensions. Moreover, just trying to analyze the particular conditions specified by the three dimensions can often be difficult (e.g., was an election rigged? do opposition parties get fair possibilities for competing?).

We shall return to attempts to measure political democracy in a moment. It is helpful first to look briefly at processes of democratization based on the concept of democracy just outlined and to indicate the relationship between political democracy as *competition, participation,* and *liberties* and Held's broad concept of democracy.

When democracy is defined in terms of competition, participation, and liberties, we see that the process of democratization—the change of a political system from nondemocratic toward more democratic—can take place in different ways. Dahl identifies two principal routes toward democracy: one focusing on competition, the other on participation.[33] Increased participation (or inclusiveness) means that the proportion of citizens who enjoy political rights and liberties increases. Nondemocratic regimes may exclude a large majority of the population from participation. In democratic regimes the entire adult population enjoys the full range of rights and liberties.

Competition (or liberalization) concerns the extent to which rights and liberties are available to at least some members of the political system. Increasing liberalization means increasing the possibility for political opposition and competition for government power. Figure 1.1 illustrates possible paths from nondemocratic rule toward democracy, each involving a different degree of participation and competition.

Four countries are mentioned in the figure. Denmark is a democracy in which the entire adult population enjoys the full range of rights and liberties. In the former Soviet Union, elections were held regularly and all adults had the right to vote, but no opposition to the ruling Communist party was permitted. There was a high degree of participation but there was no political competition and there were no real liberties, such as freedom of expression, the right to form organizations, and access to alternative sources of information. Therefore, the Soviet Union was not a democracy. The present process of democratization in Russia is first and foremost a process of liberalization, of increased political competition

FIGURE 1.1   **Dimensions of democratization**

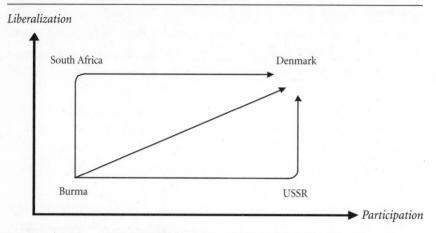

Source: Modified from Robert A. Dahl, *Polyarchy: Participation and Opposition* (New Haven: Yale University Press, 1971), p. 7; and Palle Svensson, "The Liberalization of Eastern Europe," *Journal of Behavioral and Social Sciences* 34 (1991): 56.

backed by real rights and liberties. In South Africa, the situation is different. For many years, a white minority enjoyed the political rights and liberties necessary for political competition, whereas the black majority was excluded from participation. In this case, the process of democratization is primarily one of increasing participation through the inclusion of the black population. Finally, the military dictatorship in Burma offered neither competition nor participation to any part of the population. The processes of democratization will be scrutinized in Chapter 2, where additional concrete examples of different paths toward democracy will be given.

DIMENSIONS OF DEMOCRATIZATION

How does the comprehensive notion of democracy outlined by Held fit into this picture? Held's concept of democracy expands political democracy in two respects: further liberalization and more participation. Once political democracy has been reached, further democratization is possible according to Held's broad concept of democracy. On one dimension, this means additional liberalization. Formal political rights and liberties are worth little if citizens are not secured equal rights in a more substan-

FIGURE 1.2   The movement from political democracy toward democratic autonomy

		Public institutions and governmental processes	Social institutions and economic processes
LIBERALIZATION	Substantive benefits and entitlements	WELFARE DEMOCRACY	DEMOCRATIC AUTONOMY
	Formal rights and liberties	POLITICAL DEMOCRACY	SOCIAL DEMOCRACY

Public institutions and governmental processes   Social institutions and economic processes

PARTICIPATION

Source: Modified from Guillermo O'Donnell and Philippe C. Schmitter, *Transitions from Authoritarian Rule: Tentative Conclusions About Uncertain Democracies* (Baltimore: Johns Hopkins University Press, 1986), p. 13.

tial manner. For example, without a welfare state that prevents extreme material poverty and steep socioeconomic inequalities, poor segments of the population are unable to fully enjoy their political rights. Only with poverty eradicated can formal equal rights be translated into substantial equal rights.   ↳ *Is this even possible?*

It is also possible to extend the other dimension—participation. According to our definition of political democracy, participation concerns government and public institutions. In Held's notion of democracy, participation is extended to social institutions and the economy (note his suggestions about the self-management of enterprises and participation in local community institutions). The movement from political democracy toward Held's notion of democratic autonomy is summarized in Figure 1.2.

The figure demonstrates how the combination of extended liberalization and participation defines the movement from political democracy toward democratic autonomy. Note that this volume does *not* focus on the processes going beyond political democracy but on the processes of democratization depicted in Figure 1.1—the movement from authoritarian rule toward political democracy. Therefore, the terms "democracy" and "political democracy" will be used interchangeably.

We now have (1) a definition of political democracy as participation, competition, and civil and political liberties; (2) a notion of paths of democratization; and (3) a sense of the relationship between political democracy and the much broader and more contested concept of democratic autonomy. The following section looks at attempts to measure democracy, using our definition of political democracy as the starting point.

ATTEMPTS TO MEASURE DEMOCRACY

The measurement of democracy has become its own branch of political science surrounded by an ongoing debate about the best ways of devising and combining indicators. Because of the large number of difficulties in this domain, attempts at estimating the quantity of democracy must be treated with caution. The indexes and overviews are helpful as starting points, but a closer inspection of countries must follow.

There are several studies that attempt to measure the degree of democracy in a large number of countries using Dahl's concept of democracy as a starting point. For example, Tatu Vanhanen's analysis measures democratic progress in 172 countries, from 1850 to 1993.[34] His discussion is rich and nuanced, with many original insights about the causes of democratization. For present purposes, however, we need an index with global coverage that is updated on a regular basis. Therefore, I shall rely on another well-known attempt at measuring democracy, the Freedom House index.[35]

The index employs one dimension for competition and participation (called political rights) and one dimension for civil liberties. For each dimension a seven-point scale is used, so that the highest ranking countries (that is, those with the highest degree of democracy) are 1–1's and the lowest are 7–7's. In other words, the index attempts to reflect the space of semidemocracy or semiauthoritarianism between outright authoritarian (7–7) and fully democratic (1–1) regimes (see Fig. 1.3).

Countries with an average rating between 1 and 2.5 are considered free; those with an average between 3 and 5.0 are partly free; and those with ratings from 5.5 to 7 are considered not free. Although the Freedom House distinction between rights and liberties differs from the breakdown of components in the definition of democracy employed in this volume, both basically cover the same dimensions. Therefore, the Free-

FIGURE 1.3   The Freedom House index for measuring democracy

Classification of countries	Political rights Rating 1-7	Civil liberties Rating 1-7
	Combined average ranking	
Free	1-2.5	
Partly free	3-5.0	
Not free	5.5-7	

Source: Based on R. Bruce McColm, "The Comparative Survey of Freedom: 1991," *Freedom Review* 22, no. 1 (1991): 14.

dom House index can function as an approximate measurement of political democracy for our purposes.

The 2006 Freedom House survey of independent countries identified eighty-nine countries as free. The list, shown in Table 1.1, is ordered according to combined average ratings. Fifty-eight countries are classified as partly free, and another forty-five as not free.[36]

This way of measuring political democracy gives a quick overview of how democracy fares in the world. Always keep in mind that measurements of democracy are imprecise approximations of a complex reality with many different and often contradictory aspects. Consider the way in which Freedom House estimates political rights and civil liberties in each country. For political rights, a series of separate issues concerning (1) electoral processes, (2) political pluralism and participation, and (3) functioning of government, must be estimated. For civil liberties, there are questions concerning (4) freedom of expression and belief, (5) associational and organizational rights, (6) rule of law, and (7) personal autonomy. All in all, twenty-nine different questions are asked, and the answers have to be weighed together.[37]

The Freedom House questions illustrate the potential problems involved in measuring democracy. First, the problem of conceptualization: what are the specific attributes of democracy and how are they related to each other? Second, the problem of best possible estimation or measurement of these attributes; third, the problem of aggregation, that is, of recombining the various measures into an overall evaluation

TABLE 1.1   The Freedom House index classification of free countries, 2006

Average rating: 1

Andorra	Germany	Palau
Australia	Hungary	Poland
Austria	Iceland	Portugal
Bahamas	Ireland	Saint Kitts and Nevis
Barbados	Italy	Saint Lucia
Belgium	Kiribati	San Marino
Canada	Latvia	Slovakia
Cape Verde	Liechtenstein	Slovenia
Chile	Lithuania	Spain
Costa Rica	Luxembourg	Sweden
Cyprus	Malta	Switzerland
Czech Republic	Marshall Islands	Taiwan
Denmark	Micronesia	Tuvalu
Dominica	Nauru	United Kingdom
Estonia	Netherlands	United States
Finland	New Zealand	Uruguay
France	Norway	

Average rating: 1.5

Belize	Israel	Saint Vincent and Grenadines
Bulgaria	Japan	South Africa
Ghana	Mauritius	South Korea
Greece	Monaco	
Grenada	Panama	

Average rating: 2

Antigua and Barbuda	Dominican Republic	Samoa
Argentina	Mali	Sao Tome and Principe
Benin	Mexico	Suriname
Botswana	Mongolia	Vanuatu
Brazil	Namibia	
Croatia	Romania	

Average rating: 2.5

El Salvador	Lesotho	Trinidad and Tobago
India	Peru	Ukraine
Indonesia	Senegal	
Jamaica	Serbia and Montenegro	

Source: Freedom House, *Freedom in the World 2006* (Lanham, Md.: Rowman & Littlefield, 2006).

of democracy. A recent critical analysis of various indices of democracy identifies problems in all three areas, both in the Freedom House index and in other major attempts to measure democracy.[38]

Furthermore, even countries that end up with the best rating (1–1) can be highly dissimilar on important dimensions. Such dissimilarity pertains to variation in institutions and in other aspects, as well as to differences in democratic qualities. We may identify such systems as those of the United States, Botswana, Denmark, Costa Rica, Japan, and Jamaica as democracies, but the specific structures of their political systems, their political culture, and their socioeconomic environments differ substantially. One scholar has suggested making the following distinctions between various types of democratic regimes: presidential versus parliamentary; majoritarian versus representational, two-party versus multiparty, distribution of power among parties, extremist multiparty, and consociational. He defines a consociational democracy as one that has mechanisms serving to promote compromise and consensus among groups in society.[39]

Such differences also indicate substantial variation in the quality of democracy in single countries, even if their ratings are similar. It is only at the level of the individual case (combined with attention to the larger international context) that we can study the interplay between formal freedoms, political processes, and the larger context of socioeconomic and other conditions that affect the quality of democracy. Moreover, if we agree with Held that democracy is made much more difficult by extreme material poverty, then it also becomes relevant to look at socioeconomic conditions as codeterminants of the quality of democracy, even if these conditions are not included in the definition of democracy as a political system. The Human Development Index compiled by the United Nations Development Program (UNDP) provides systematic, comparative information on these conditions.[40]

In sum, actual democracies are dissimilar in important dimensions. In countries like Benin or Malawi, where large parts of the adult population are illiterate and a substantial number of people live below the poverty line, a vigorous democracy is more difficult to achieve than in countries with better socioeconomic conditions. This observation is also relevant for many other African countries, where the situation is similar or even worse, and for such countries as Bolivia, Mongolia, Jamaica, and the Philippines.

Some scholars conclude dramatically that it is impossible to have democracy in any meaningful sense in materially very poor societies.[41] That may be going too far. Socioeconomic conditions do affect the *quality* of political democracy but they do not prevent the development of a democratic system. At the same time, socioeconomic inequalities can impede real political equality in industrialized countries as well. Some data on socioeconomic conditions in industrialized countries is also contained in the UNDP report.[42]

Several projects in recent years have attempted to go beyond the crude Freedom House measure in order to assess the quality of democracy around the world. David Beetham and his colleagues have conducted an "audit of democracy" in the United Kingdom and identified a number of "democratic flaws" in the system.[43] Larry Diamond has coordinated the Quality of Democracy project, which examines eight dimensions on which democracies can vary in quality. The assessment includes social and economic equality and estimates the extent to which public policies correspond to citizen demands and preferences.[44]

The spread of democracy since the end of the cold war has multiplied the variety of more or less democratic systems. This in turn has stimulated a veritable cottage industry of concepts—attempts to produce labels and categories that indicate political systems that have some, but frequently not all and often merely a few, democratic qualities. In other words, the three categories devised by Freedom House (free, partly free, not free) are considered insufficient for describing the current variation in political systems that are more or less democratic. The new concepts are especially directed at countries with some, but far from all, of the characteristics of a political democracy; hence the terms: elite-dominated, frozen, restricted, illiberal, pseudo, hybrid, or electoral democracies, to mention a few. The terms indicate that even if democratic progress has taken place, it is wanting in major respects in many countries. The new democracies analyzed in the next chapter are in the early phases of what may be a long process of transition from authoritarian toward democratic rule. In other words, the ratings these new democracies receive in the indexes are really only snapshots of regimes that are "on the move"—in a process of uncertain transition from one form of regime toward another.

TIME HORIZONS AND LEVELS OF ANALYSIS

Consideration of the meaning and prevalence of democracy must also include the historical dimension. In historical terms, democracy as it has been defined here is a very recent phenomenon. Only four countries—Australia, Finland, New Zealand, and Norway—had extended suffrage to women before World War I. And even if we look for "male democracies" in existence then, we would not find many cases; the constitutional monarchies in nineteenth-century Europe cannot be considered fully democratic because their cabinets were not responsible to elected parliaments in a clear-cut manner.[45]

The semidemocracies of nineteenth-century Europe became fully democratic only in the twentieth century, and several of them, including Italy, Germany, Austria, and Spain, suffered setbacks to nondemocratic rule in the 1920s and 1930s. Consequently it is only for the period after World War II that extended, stable democratic rule existed in the industrialized countries of Western Europe and North America.

The developing countries of Asia, Africa, and Latin America include only a handful of enduring (but not flawless) democracies, among them Costa Rica, India, Venezuela (from 1958), and Jamaica (from 1962). In recent years, transitions toward more democratic rule have taken place in a large number of developing countries and countries of Eastern Europe. The question must be asked whether this phenomenon is a prelude to an era of many more stable democracies than we have seen so far or is merely a fragile flourish that can easily suffer setbacks to nondemocracy. This issue will be addressed in Chapter 2.

The other dimension introduced here concerns levels of analysis. Until now, our discussion about what democracy is and where it can be found has focused on the state: Does this or that country have democracy or not? But this level of analysis is clearly insufficient. There is an international or global level "above" the states and a local level "below" them that must also be taken into account.

How does the *international system* affect prospects for democracy in individual countries? To answer this question, we must analyze dominant trends in the international system and the ways in which they affect specific countries. It is probably universally agreed that the period following World War II saw an enormous increase in all types of exchange between countries, including trade, investment, communication, and travel. In other words, there is a higher degree of globalization and inter-dependence (situations characterized by mutual dependence between countries or among actors in different countries) than ever before.[46]

Against this background, ideas about democracy and human rights have been increasingly diffused. Russian Nobel laureate Andrei Sakharov called the United Nations Declaration of Human Rights the common glue that binds all ideologies together, and state leaders have felt a grow-ing need to appeal to democratic ideas in order to legitimize their rule. There is no doubt that the Helsinki factor—the pressure from the West for more respect for basic human rights in Eastern Europe and the for-mer Soviet Union—has played an important part in the democratic openings there, as we shall see in Chapter 2. Yet leading Western coun-tries such as the United States, France, and Great Britain have not consis-tently supported democracy in all parts of the world. They have, on several occasions, supported nondemocratic leaders in Asia, Africa, and Latin America for reasons of national interest.

At the same time, individual countries to an increasing degree are sub-jected to international forces over which they have little control. This has always been the case, as Dahl points out: "Not just conflict but also trade, commerce, and finance have always spilled over state boundaries. Demo-cratic states, therefore, have never been able to act autonomously, in dis-regard of the actions of outside forces over which they had little or no control."[47] But recent tendencies are more than just replays of this theme. In developing countries, for example, dependence on interna-tional structures has increased in the wake of the debt crisis, which has expanded the power over single countries of such international organi-zations as the International Monetary Fund (IMF) and the World Bank. These countries' frustration over increasing dependency came out clearly in a speech by Julius Nyerere of Tanzania: "When did the IMF be-come an International Ministry of Finance? When did nations agree to surrender their power of decision making?"[48] The IMF would probably respond that the fund acts only on the basis of agreements entered by countries on a voluntary basis.

No clear conclusion emerges from these brief remarks on the effects of the international system on democracy in single countries. I shall return to the issue in the coming chapters, especially in Chapter 4 on the promotion of democracy from the outside. What we may note for now is that actors in the international system can either promote or try to prevent democracy in single countries. Moreover, the dynamics of dependence and interdependence in the international system directly affect the scope of democratic decision making at the national level. In general, one must expect large and socioeconomically strong countries to be much less susceptible to international pressures and challenges than is the case with smaller, socioeconomically weak countries.

Let me turn to the *local level of analysis.* Until now we have assumed that democracy at the level of national government in a country means that democracy also prevails at the local level. Yet this need not always be the case. Examples from India and China illustrate this point.

India is one of a few Third World countries with a long democratic tradition. It adopted a democratic constitution in 1950, and nondemocratic rule prevailed only once, for eighteen months, from 1975 to 1977, during the so-called emergency declared by Indira Gandhi. However, democracy at the national or macrolevel of the political system does not mean that democracy exists in all localities. The Congress party attained its dominant position in India's vast countryside by making alliances that enforced the traditional patterns of domination. Congress dealt with the electorate through "existing patron-brokers who, as landowners and caste-leaders, had no desire to jeopardize their positions by transforming local social structures. In adapting to local conditions, the party thus increasingly became tied to age-old patterns of status and leadership."[49] Against this background, it is not surprising that democratic India has set in motion programs that, although claiming to promote welfare and participation at the local level, have in fact had the opposite effect—making the poor majority even worse off and strengthening traditional structures of dominance and subordination.[50] In the 1990s, intense communal violence, especially between militant Hindus and Muslims, produced a setback for democracy. India's Freedom House classification in 2006 was 2–3 (2006).

In China, political democracy like that found in India was never seriously on the agenda. The Chinese Communist party (CCP) is a Bolshevik party; it did not propose to fight for the interests of all Chinese but only for the interests of workers and poor peasants against internal and external class enemies. Further, the democracy it sought for workers and poor peasants was the democracy of leadership from above combined with some degree of participation from below, and it gave special status to the small faction of the population (less than 1 percent in 1949) who were members of the party.[51]

But it can be claimed that the Communists, within this overall structure of authoritarian socialist rule, also promoted at least some elements of democracy at the local level. They did so through what was called the mass line, which took at least five different forms.[52] First, grassroots and county-level leaders were given a high degree of latitude in ensuring that higher-level instructions were in accordance with local needs, conditions, and opinions. Second, cadres were sent to the villages to work and live alongside the peasants, under similar circumstances, in order to share their experiences and learn from rural life. Third, secret ballot elections were held regularly at village, township, county, and regional levels, providing a democratic and representative character to local government. "The only restriction was the 'three-thirds' principle, according to which one-third of offices were to be filled by CCP members, one-third by non-CCP leftists, and one-third by liberals."[53] Fourth, popular political expression in the form of the "big character poster" (*dazibao,* or wall poster) was encouraged. And, finally, the armed forces were to take part in civilian affairs under rules that required their subordination to civil authority.

These variations do not mean that China is suddenly democratic and India all of a sudden nondemocratic. The core of the matter is that a national framework of democracy does not guarantee real democracy at the local level, and an authoritarian national framework does not completely block democratic elements at the local level.

Yet such contradictions tend to become less pronounced in the long run as democracy at the national level and democracy at the local level tend to reinforce each other. But in the short- to medium run there may be discrepancies between the two. It is important to be aware of these discrepancies in overall assessments of democracy.

CONCLUSION

Democracy means rule by the people. A more precise definition is difficult to formulate because democracy is a dynamic entity that has acquired different meanings over the course of time. Much of this dynamic comes from changes in society and from the different interpretations by analysts of the consequences of these changes for democracy. As societies develop in different ways in today's world, it is not surprising that the meaning of democracy continues to be the subject of debate.

Yet for analytical purposes we need to develop a concept that clearly identifies what democracy essentially is. The core of political democracy has three dimensions: competition, participation, and civil and political liberties. When we study the status of democracy in a specific country, the first step is to look for these three elements. In this context it is helpful to consult one of the indices on democracy (e.g., the Freedom House index), bearing in mind that such overall measurements are imprecise and tentative. In order to make a comprehensive assessment of democracy, one must carefully scrutinize the individual country as well because democratic systems vary greatly in their institutional patterns and along other dimensions. Socioeconomic conditions also affect the quality of democracy. Finally, it is necessary to be aware of the international setting above and the local conditions below the level of national government.

It can be argued that this procedure is too comprehensive and requires analysis of "everything." It is true that all of these stages are seldom completed. The discussion in the present volume is limited to the transition from authoritarian rule to political democracy and to the consequences of democracy. Yet it is important to be aware of the full agenda when evaluating specific cases of democracy in a more comprehensive manner.

2

Processes of Regime Change

What conditions are conducive to the formation of a political democracy? In the first two sections of this chapter I introduce the debate about the effects of general economic, social, and other conditions on the rise of democracy. Some conditions favor democracy more than others, but I shall argue that for a full understanding one must study the interplay between these conditions, on the one hand, and the choices made by political actors, on the other.

Why have so many countries begun a transition toward more democratic conditions in recent years? I argue that no single factor can account for the transitions; they involve a large number of internal and external elements in complex relationships. The movement from authoritarian to democratic rule is a multifaceted, long-term process involving different phases; many of the current transitions are in the early phases of this process. In the final part of the chapter we will examine democratic consolidation.

THE SEARCH FOR DEMOCRACY'S PRECONDITIONS

What pattern of economic, social, cultural, and other conditions is most favorable to the rise and further consolidation of democracy? It was noted in Chapter 1 that the spread of democracy is a relatively recent phenomenon, implying that the conditions brought about by modern industrial society are necessary to produce democracy. This idea was behind Seymour M. Lipset's famous thesis: "The more well-to-do a nation, the greater the chances that it will sustain democracy."[1]

(1) Modernization and wealth generate factors conducive to democracy: higher rates of literacy and education, urbanization, and the presence of mass media. Moreover, wealth provides the resources needed to mitigate the tensions produced by political conflict.[2] A large number of empirical analyses inspired by the Lipset hypothesis have tended to support it. Thus in 1971 Robert Dahl considered it "pretty much beyond dispute" that the higher the socioeconomic level of a country, the more likely it was to be a democracy.[3]

But this expectation does not always hold true. Argentina had many years of authoritarian rule despite a relatively high level of per capita income, as did Taiwan and South Korea. In those two countries, rapid economic development has been accompanied by a fairly equal distribution of income. In his analysis of the major South American cases, Guillermo O'Donnell develops an argument that turns the Lipset thesis on its head: Authoritarianism, not democracy, seems to be the more likely concomitant of the highest levels of modernization. O'Donnell reasons that the process of industrial modernization that took place in several Latin American countries in the 1960s and early 1970s had little to offer the majority of people. In order to pursue this model in the face of popular resistance, the ruling elite needs an authoritarian system.[4]

More recent research has begun to unravel the relationship between economic wealth and democracy in a more detailed way. Adam Przeworski and Fernando Limongi dispute the claim that rising wealth leads to democracy. Some wealthy authoritarian systems remain authoritarian in spite of rising wealth. At the same time, when a country reaches a certain level of wealth, it becomes more likely to sustain a stable democracy. Thus democratic countries with a per capita income of $6,000 or more are extremely unlikely to turn nondemocratic. In sum, there is a relationship between economic wealth and democracy, but it is not a smooth and linear relationship.[5]

A second set of preconditions (the first set, as noted above, being modernization and wealth) often thought to favor democracy concerns (2) **political culture**—the system of values and beliefs that defines the context and meaning of political action. If political culture is tied in with the larger system of culture in a society, is it possible to identify cultural values and beliefs that are especially conducive to democracy?

It has often been asserted that Protestantism supports democracy whereas Catholicism in many cases, especially in Latin America, works against it. In more general terms, some cultures tend to emphasize hierarchy, authority, and intolerance, and consequently are less conducive to democracy. Islam and Confucianism are like Catholicism in this regard. Recent debates have focused on possible incompatibilities between Islam and democracy.[6]

Yet it is difficult to demonstrate a systematic relationship between specific cultural patterns and the prevalence of democracy.[7] Moreover, cultural systems are subject to dynamic change. It may be that Catholicism once worked against democracy in Latin America, but the Catholic Church also played an active role in opposing authoritarian rule in the 1980s.[8]

A third set of preconditions favoring democracy is associated with the social structure of society—the specific classes and groups making up the society. Is it possible to identify groups that consistently favor democracy (e.g., the middle classes, industrial bourgeoisie, workers) and others that consistently work against it (e.g., traditional landowners)?

In his historical account of the roots of democracy and dictatorship, Barrington Moore concludes that "a vigorous and independent class of town dwellers has been an indispensable element in the growth of parliamentary democracy. No bourgeoisie, no democracy."[9] Conversely, landowners tend to support democracy only under special circumstances, such as when small-scale farming is dominant and there is a relatively equal distribution of land. Against Barrington Moore's thesis it must be said that the bourgeoisie does not consistently work for democracy. According to Goran Therborn, democracy has "always and everywhere" been brought about in a popular struggle against the leading sections of the bourgeoisie.[10]

Finally there are **external factors,** the economic, political, ideological, and other elements that constitute the international context for the processes that take place in single countries. It was argued in Chapter 1 that no straightforward conclusion can be made regarding the effect of external factors on democracy. The developing countries of the Third World are most susceptible to external influence, especially by the leading Western countries. Modernization theorists customarily consider this influence beneficial for the promotion of democracy,[11] while dependency theorists draw the opposite conclusion: The inequalities and distortions of the economies and societies of the Third World, brought about by their dependent position in the world economic system, make democracy difficult.[12] For years, many Western countries have established large programs to promote democracy in the world. This has helped move the debate toward the pros and cons of promoting democracy from the outside, a subject that will be taken up in Chapter 4.

Although I have identified four sets of possible preconditions for democracy, Dahl names seventeen variables, classified into seven categories, that are conducive to democracy.[13] Larry Diamond, Juan Linz, and Seymour Lipset employ a similar procedure in the introduction to their study of democracy in developing countries.[14] To all this should be added the diffusion effect—the growth of democracy inspired by democratization elsewhere. Yet for every factor seen as conducive to democracy, counterexamples can be put forward. Moreover, in many countries, different preconditions may exist that point in different directions: For example, cultural factors may be conducive to democracy while economic factors may not be.

The situation is somewhat frustrating. It is possible to point out a number of preconditions that can reasonably be expected to favor or obstruct the possibilities for democracy. But in every case it is also possible to give counterexamples, where the expectations have not held true.

Thus a fixed model or law about democracy cannot be formulated. We cannot say that if x, y, or n preconditions are present, there will be democracy. A law of this kind is unfeasible in the sense that it would leave little or no room for the choices taken by political actors. Such choices make a difference. Juan Linz has noted that in some situations "even the presence of an individual with unique qualities and characteristics—a Charles de Gaulle, for instance—can be decisive and cannot be predicted by any model."[15] In a similar way, many observers give credit to Nelson Mandela for his essential role in South Africa's transition to democracy.

In some cases, as we shall see, democracy can emerge even when none, or only a few, of the preconditions conducive to democracy are present. Economic, social, cultural, and other structural conditions may decrease the likelihood for democracy to occur, but they do not themselves make the policy choice about whether there will be a democratic system. Over the past three decades, democratic openings have taken place in countries where preconditions in terms of modernization and wealth, political culture and institutions, and the social structure of society have been seriously wanting.

However, recognizing the importance of choices taken by political actors does not mean that the search for preconditions is useless. Actors in a given situation are constrained by the structures—the preconditions—that have resulted from the country's development in previous periods. Therefore, the interplay between economic, social, cultural, and other preconditions created in earlier periods and the decisions made by current political actors must be taken into account.

The preconditions set the stage on which the actors play.[16] The preconditions cannot foretell whether the actors will produce democracy or not, but they can provide information about what kind of outcome we can expect from the players. Recent research has emphasized that even if democratic openings can occur in almost any kind of setting, the emergence of stable and consolidated democracy continues to depend on favorable preconditions.[17] For example, even if democracy does not always occur with high levels of economic development, a country's democratic prospects are better at higher rather than lower levels of economic development. Although poor countries with adverse social, economic, and other preconditions may well move toward democracy (as are some African countries), we can expect that the consolidation of democracy will be more rare than in countries with more favorable preconditions. Democracies emerging under such adverse conditions are likely to be highly unstable, frail, and vulnerable. In sum, although the search for economic, cultural, social, institutional, and other preconditions may not yield uniformly predictable results, we can obtain important information about the prospects for democracy, especially in terms of democratic consolidation.

In the final analysis, there is no way around a detailed study of the interplay of actors and structures in concrete settings. First, however, it is useful to discuss in general terms the choices made by political actors.

WHEN DO POLITICAL ACTORS CHOOSE DEMOCRACY?

Democracy does not fall from heaven. It is brought about by individuals and groups—social actors—who fight for it. Adam Przeworski has made a penetrating analysis of the choices taken by the important actors in moving their countries toward democracy.[18] His starting point was the contention that democracy introduces uncertainty in the political process. No single group can be sure that its interests will ultimately prevail. Even the most powerful group, be it local or foreign business, armed forces, bureaucracy, or other privileged elements, must be ready to face the possibility that it can lose out in conflicts with other groups, which means that its interests may not be looked after. In democracies actors may choose policy reforms that attack the power and privilege of dominant groups.

It is not difficult to see why those who are barred from political influence under authoritarian rule struggle for a democratic polity that will give them access to political influence. But why should members of the power bloc supporting authoritarian rule ever opt for a democratic solution that may entail a threat to their interests?

In fact they may strive to keep the authoritarian system. Regime change may only trade one type of authoritarian regime for another. Alternatively, democracy may succeed, even against the wishes of the dominant forces, because the authoritarian regime suffers defeat in a foreign or a civil war or simply disintegrates due to internal division, or because popular forces in favor of democracy prevail.[19]

However, transitions to democracy are rarely based on the complete defeat of the elites behind the previous authoritarian rule. In the vast majority of cases the transition to democracy is based on negotiations with the forces backing the authoritarian regime. The question then becomes: Why should the forces behind authoritarian rule enter such negotiations?

There can be several reasons. There may be a split between hard-liners and soft-liners in the coalition of forces behind authoritarian rule.[20] The latter may seek more democratic forms of rule—perhaps in order to get the upper hand in a conflict with hard-liners—in the face of internal and external pressures and perhaps also due to normative commitments to democracy.

More pragmatic reasons for such a move have to do with problems for which democracy can provide a solution. For example, democracy can help restore the legitimacy of the existing social order, and it can provide an open and regularized system of decision making that can result in a better business environment. According to one scholar, "Another benefit not to be minimized is the international recognition that accompanies democratization. This can yield dividends in the form of inflows of foreign aid and loans."[21]

Elites may support democracy on the basis of self-interest; therefore, it is both fragile and conditional.[22] During the negotiations accompanying transitions toward democracy, the elites try to stack the cards to make sure the democratic institutions that are set up do not threaten their basic interests. This can be done in several ways. Adam Przeworski gives as an example the 1982 Brazilian elections, where "the authoritarian government used every possible legal instrument to secure *a priori* advantage for the pro-government party and to secure to itself the eventual majority in the presidential electoral college."[23] First, the authoritarian rulers allowed the formation of additional parties, with the aim of splitting the opposition; second, they created obstacles that made it difficult for parties that were popular before the authoritarian rulers took over in 1964 to register; third, they made it more difficult for illiterates to cast their ballots, as they were expected to vote against the government.

Przeworski concludes that democratization is possible only "if there exist institutions that provide a reasonable expectation that interests of major political forces would not be affected highly adversely under democratic competition, given the resources these forces can muster."[24] In other words, elite groups will support democracy only insofar as they feel certain that their interests will be looked after. Thus the democratic institutions that are set up as a result of negotiations with elite groups may be restricted in various ways, as in Brazil. The current situation in Russia offers another prominent example of this, as President Vladimir Putin increasingly attempts to control the media and block the emergence of opposition political parties and a strong civil society.[25]

Furthermore, elite groups may require that the policies of the new, democratically based governments build in social and economic conservatism. In summary, when transitions toward democracy result from negotiations with the forces behind the previous authoritarian regime, the new democracy will likely be restricted in various respects, including its ability to enact social and economic reform measures.

A large number of transitions toward democracy in recent years have indeed been of this elite-dominated variety. Although the variations in the actual compromises behind the transitions must be studied, the further development of democracy, as well as prospects for substantial reform benefiting the less privileged, cannot be taken for granted.

WHY THE RECENT SURGE TOWARD DEMOCRACY?

In previous sections we considered the general conditions for democracy and the need to study the interplay between those conditions and the choices made by political actors. In this section, I attempt to answer the question: Why has there been a recent surge toward democracy in so many countries?

More than forty countries made transitions toward democracy between 1974 and 2005. As a result the number of democratic regimes has increased from forty to eighty-nine countries. The transitions began in southern Europe (Greece, Spain, and Portugal). The next wave was in Latin America (Argentina, Uruguay, Peru, Ecuador, Bolivia, Brazil, and later Paraguay) and in Central America (Honduras, El Salvador, Nicaragua, Guatemala, and later Mexico). Then came the transitions in Eastern Europe (Poland, Czechoslovakia, Hungary, Romania, Bulgaria, and the former German Democratic Republic). The most recent wave has been in Africa and in the former Soviet Union. Finally, transitions toward democracy have taken place in Asia over the entire period since the early 1970s (Papua New Guinea, Thailand, Pakistan, Bangladesh, the Philippines, South Korea, Taiwan, Mongolia, and Nepal).

The changes do indeed give evidence of democratic progress in a large number of countries in a relatively short span of time. But some caveats should be taken into account. First, in several countries (e.g., Russia, Bolivia, and Côte d'Ivoire) there have already been reverses toward authoritarian rule; over time, there is a combined process of progress in some countries and setbacks in other countries. Second, several of the countries mentioned are not yet full democracies; they are in the early phases of a transition toward democracy, as I shall argue in further detail later. Finally, it is useful to put democratic progress since 1974 in a larger historical context. Much depends on how the time periods are defined. Progress since 1974 must be seen against the background of democratic breakdowns in earlier periods, especially between the mid-1960s and the early 1970s.

The cases described below underline the fact that there is nothing automatic about transitions away from authoritarianism. Such transitions involve a long sequence of events in which different types of actors stand in the center of the political stage, and the final outcome is not decided beforehand. When we look at transitions in retrospect, explanations for why changes occurred tend to revolve around a search for the obvious: Knowing that an authoritarian regime fell, we can try to stack all the odds that seemed to work against it and in favor of democracy. It is sobering to recall that not many years ago scholars were busily occupied with similar sequences of events going in the exact opposite direction—from more or less genuine democracies toward authoritarian rule. The exercise then was similar to the present one. Knowing that democracy broke down, one could try to stack all the odds that seemed to work against it and in favor of authoritarianism.

In 1984, Samuel Huntington wrote that "it would be difficult to argue that the world was more or less democratic in 1984 than it had been in 1954."[26] Seen from this perspective, democratic progress between 1974 and 1984 merely regained the distance lost by the setbacks of earlier periods. Most of the "new" democracies in Latin America, Eastern Europe, and Asia that have appeared since 1984 are thus in the category of *redemocratization*—returning to more democratic conditions after periods of nondemocratic rule.

No single factor can account for significant moves toward democracy in recent years. There are complex patterns of internal and external elements, of various conditions that interplay with different groups of actors. Ideally, the movements should be untangled country by country, but space does not allow this. Therefore, we will look at events in major regions as well as in some specific countries. Finally, although the question, Why has there been a recent surge toward democracy? really covers two analytically separate issues—the breakdown of authoritarian systems and the move toward democracy instead of toward another authoritarian system—a sharp distinction between these two elements will not be made in the discussion that follows.

The first cluster of transitions took place in the mid-1970s in southern Europe, specifically in Greece, Portugal, and Spain. In all three cases, splits within the authoritarian regimes led to their downfall. At the same time, these countries experienced distinct phases of authoritarian breakdown followed by the establishment of democracy.

In Spain, Francisco Franco made arrangements for authoritarian rule to continue after his death. Admiral Carrero Blanco was to take responsibility for the government and Juan Carlos, a monarch educated under Franco's supervision, was to become head of state. But the scheme was interrupted by the assassination of Carrero Blanco, leaving Juan Carlos with freedom to maneuver when he took over as head of state after Franco died in 1975. Carlos chose to support a process of democratization. In retrospect, it is easy to see internal and external elements conducive to democratic change. Internally, a process of rapid economic growth had strengthened new social groups of workers, members of the middle classes, and students with a quest for political change. It was also becoming clear that membership in the European Union, which Spain badly wanted (as did Greece and Portugal), would require political changes. But in 1975, political democracy was only one of the options open to the main actors, and it took what one observer has called "exceptionally skilled leaders in the regime and the opposition" to negotiate the transition and further consolidate a democratic regime.[27]

In Portugal, dictator Antonio Salazar drained the country of resources by holding on to a Portuguese empire in Africa. Increasing guerrilla activity in the colonies meant that nearly half of the national budget went to defense. Middle-ranking officers fed up with the situation staged a coup in 1974, which led to a period of political experimentation and debate by literally hundreds of new political groups that sprang up after the long period of authoritarian rule. The end result of political democracy appeared only in 1976.

In Greece the transition went faster. A junta mobilized troops in response to the Turkish invasion of Cyprus on July 20, 1974, but it did not even enjoy the full support of its own ranks. When the Joint Chiefs of Staff decided the next day to seek a political solution to the crisis, the return of civilian rule was made possible.

The second important cluster of transitions toward democracy took place in Latin America during the first half of the 1980s. As in southern Europe, the Latin American countries felt pressure for democracy from various organizations in Western Europe and the United States. But internal dynamics had an even greater influence. One important set of reasons concerns problems brought about by the models of economic development that were pursued under authoritarian rule. In many cases, a ruling elite coalition led by the military had used authoritarian rule to promote a strategy of economic development for the benefit of a tiny minority. Production was focused on durable consumer goods for the upper-middle class (cars, consumer electronics, etc.), and no attention was paid to the basic needs of the poor majority. By the early 1980s, these models ran into serious problems. According to one observer, the Latin American countries were "unified by crisis, foreign debt, economic stagnation . . . inflation, rising unemployment and growing social inequalities."[28] The economic crisis did not have purely domestic roots, however. The second round of sharply increasing oil prices hit most Latin American countries hard. One way to cover growing expenditures was to borrow more money from abroad. When the real interest rate on such loans increased dramatically, as occurred during the 1980s, the economic crisis was seriously aggravated.

In some countries, with Brazil as the most important example, the authoritarian regime could draw on a record of strong economic growth despite the fact that benefits were distributed unevenly. However, when the economic crisis set in, the regimes underwent a process of **delegitimation**—they could no longer point to a basis for their right to govern. In other countries (e.g., Argentina and Bolivia), authoritarian rulers could not even point to achievements in terms of economic growth; characterized by corruption and incompetence, their regimes were in even more vulnerable positions.

The problems led to divisions within the authoritarian regimes—the split between hard-liners and soft-liners mentioned earlier. These divisions in turn weakened the authoritarian regime's grip on society and allowed for a process of liberalization with better possibilities for public debate, oppositional activity, and criticism of the political system. As a result, demands for democracy were reinforced and the legitimacy of authoritarian rule was further decreased. At the same time, many social groups in Latin America began to place a high priority on the quest for political democracy. In the days of harsh authoritarianism, there was a tendency for the polarization of forces as well as of outlooks; fascism and socialism were seen by many as the only feasible alternatives for the region. There was no possibility of a middle path. But with liberalization, the notion of political democracy gained new strength; it was supported by bishops and priests, by journalists and professors, and by labor and other social movements.[29]

In several Latin American countries, the process of democratization proceeded slowly, beginning with regime liberalization. In Argentina, however, economic failure inspired the authoritarian military rulers to embark on the Falkland Islands/Islas Malvinas adventure, and the regime collapsed when it lost the war. Yet neither Argentina nor the countries that experienced a more gradual transition have fully consolidated democratic rule, as will be discussed below.

The next region in which dramatic changes toward democracy have taken place is Eastern Europe. Solidarity was founded in Poland in 1980 as workers attempted to improve their economic condition. At first they demanded autonomous unions, not political reform. But it quickly became clear that they would achieve nothing without changes in the political system. Despite splits within the ruling party, agreeing on a model for political reform in Poland seemed impossible. It was not until 1989 that **totalitarian** regimes (authoritarian regimes in which the state attempts to control every aspect of life) began to fall in Eastern Europe. There had been popular uprisings on several previous occasions—in East Germany in 1952, Poland in 1953, Hungary in 1956, and in Czechoslovakia in 1968—but they did not result in political reform. What was different in 1989? One experienced observer points to three basic factors—Gorbachev, Helsinki, and Tocqueville.[30]

The election of Mikhail Gorbachev signaled new Soviet policies toward Eastern Europe. Before Gorbachev came to power, the Brezhnev doctrine, which supported Soviet intervention in Eastern Europe against "unacceptable" regime changes, was in effect. Under Gorbachev, it was changed to the so-called Sinatra doctrine: "Do it your way." Gorbachev's influence can be seen in a telephone call he made in August 1989 urging the Polish Communists to permit the formation of a government led by a member of Solidarity (Tadeusz Mazowiecki). And when he was a guest of honor in East Germany at the country's fortieth anniversary in October 1989, Gorbachev told Erich Honecker that "the problems of DDR [German Democratic Republic] must be solved in Berlin, not in Moscow."[31]

Yet even in the absence of Soviet assistance, the ruling elites of Eastern Europe could have sent troops against the popular demonstrations. Why did they hesitate? The Helsinki factor points to the Western attempt to promote respect for human rights in Eastern Europe through the Helsinki Accords, which in turn opened for some countries the possibility of Western economic assistance. The Helsinki factor worked together with the Tocqueville factor. The latter points to the old ruling elite's loss of belief in its own right to rule, in its own legitimacy:

A few kids went into the streets and threw a few words. The police beat them. The kids said: You have no right to beat us! And the rulers, the high and mighty, replied, in effect: Yes, we have no right to beat you. We have no right to preserve our rule by force. The end no longer justifies the means! In fact, the ruling elites, and their armed servants, distinguished themselves by their comprehensive unreadiness to stand up in any way for the things in which they had so long claimed to believe, and their almost indecent haste to embrace democratic capitalism.[32]

The popular demonstrations themselves still have to be better explained, however. The mounting economic crisis in Eastern Europe meant that the centrally planned economic system was increasingly unable to deliver dynamic performance and satisfy even the most basic needs of the population. A similar situation brought Gorbachev to power in the Soviet Union. The rulers intended to reform and invigorate the system through more intensive cooperation with the West.

But the opening of the system posed a threat to the ruling elite. Without international isolation, the integrated power structure of the totalitarian system became more difficult to sustain. An authoritarian political system and a centrally planned economy based on state ownership are pillars in a mutually supportive system of power, production, and distribution. Tinkering with the system at one point, such as by decentralizing economic control in order to make the enterprises cooperate with foreign firms, creates repercussions in the entire system.[33] The situation puts the ruling elites in a serious dilemma: Their attempts at reforming the system create tensions that threaten their power positions. Yet radical initiatives were necessary to prevent the socioeconomic crisis from running out of control.

The elites proved incapable of devising solutions to this dilemma. Instead, they created a moral dilemma for themselves. The propaganda machinery worked to convince everyone that all was well, but the message sounded increasingly hollow to an educated population well aware of the true state of affairs. Ultimately the gulf between truth and propaganda, between what people thought and what they could say, became intolerable. The demand for truth became as important as the demand for bread, and writers and intellectuals became the driving force in the struggle against the old regimes. The demand for improved material conditions was critical, but no less critical was the demand for freedom of the mind.[34]

The most recent transitions toward democracy have taken place in Africa. When the Berlin Wall fell in 1989, thirty-eight out of forty-five states in Africa south of the Sahara were governed by civilian or military one-party systems in various shades of authoritarianism. No more than eighteen months later, more than half of them had either held competitive multiparty elections or made commitments to do so.[35]

The rapid changes in Eastern Europe were an important catalyst in Africa. On the one hand, those changes signaled that the cold war division, which had helped uphold nondemocratic regimes in both the Western and the Eastern camps in Africa, was coming to an end. On the other hand, they inspired the popular movements that were already mobilizing in Africa.

Thus developments in Eastern Europe stimulated upheavals that were already under way for internal reasons, including severe economic crises, stagnation and increasing foreign debt, corruption, and economic and political mismanagement. There have also been structural changes that have increased the prospects for democratic demands. Urbanization and education have tended to create a population that is less bound by tradition and long-standing political leaders and has less patience for authoritarianism.[36]

With these developments, traditional ideas about specific forms of African governance have lost currency. The two main elements in traditional thinking were decision making by consensus and the concept of one-party democracy. The former grew out of the famous notion of the palaver tree, where people met to discuss issues until they reached a consensus. In this way, a majority could not impose its will on a minority because all individuals participated in the process. Ideally, a consensus reached by everyone would ensure that all individual differences are taken into account. The one-party system is the logical organizational framework for this kind of decision making. Ideally the one-party system should avoid wasting energy on fruitless political competition in an environment that faces urgent tasks of economic and social development. Yet the real functioning of consensus and one-party rule has fallen short of the ideal. Decision making by consensus is not applicable to large, complex societies with many different interest groups; in many cases one-party rule has become a thin veil over authoritarian, corrupt rule by dictators who seek to promote themselves and their own tribes or ethnic groups.[37] The African system of personal rule will be further described later in this chapter.

In many cases, such as in Côte d'Ivoire and Gabon, incumbent leaders saw the writing on the wall and tried to ride with the waves of democratic change instead of being swept aside by them. For example, they gave in to opposition demands for free elections at a time when opposition forces were poorly organized and were not ready to compete with powerful leaders who controlled economic resources and mass media.

One important external factor is the role of the donor countries and agencies that provide the economic aid that is vital for most African states. The pressure from major donors for changes in a democratic direction as a condition for further economic assistance has been steadily increasing over a number of years. It is a piece of advice that few African countries can afford to ignore. Of particular importance is the French position, at least for Francophone Africa, which is heavily dependent on aid from France. (**Francophone Africa** refers to states that were once under French colonial rule and retain special ties with France.) Already in June 1990, the president of France told leaders from Francophone Africa that "the sooner you organize free elections, the better it will be for the youth of your countries who need to express themselves."[38]

Finally, there has been a domino effect in Africa. Once changes begin to occur in some countries, there is an increased likelihood that other countries will move in the same direction. A similar effect can be seen in Latin America, where first Peru and then Ecuador, Argentina, Bolivia, Uruguay, and Brazil moved toward democracy within a decade. In Eastern Europe, democratization caught on even faster in a cluster of countries. At the same time, the domino effect is clearly tied to changes in international conditions that affect several countries simultaneously (e.g., changing donor attitudes toward Africa and new Russian policies toward Eastern Europe). Bear in mind, however, that these external changes have a maximum effect only when they are combined with an internal setting receptive to democracy.

It is more difficult to summarize events in Asia, where the transitions have not clustered in a specific period but have been spread over the past two decades. Furthermore, there have been moves away from democracy and toward authoritarianism, which makes the picture even more confusing. Asian countries have substantially different levels of development and therefore have different economic, social, and political structures. Even so, democracy has moved forward in recent years in the poorest and least developed countries (e.g., Mongolia), in the most well-to-do states (e.g., South Korea and Taiwan), and in countries in between (Thailand and the Philippines). There is hardly a common denominator. Three rather different cases—the Philippines, Nepal, and Taiwan—may demonstrate the socioeconomic factors and political processes at work in the Asian transitions.

The Philippines experienced unstable democracy before Ferdinand Marcos introduced martial law in 1972 as it moved toward industrialization. Yet his ploy was not totally unpopular. Martial law provided a measure of order and stability, violence among oppositional groups decreased, and agrarian reform measures and a streamlined administrative apparatus paved the way for rapid economic growth. By 1980, however, the steam had gone out of the early measures. Rising import prices, not least for oil, a shrinking market for Philippine exports, and increasing foreign debt set the stage for an economic crisis. At the same time, Marcos and his wife, Imelda, together with a small group of cronies, became the subject of increasing criticism because of their monopolistic control of the most important industries. The IMF was not willing to help mitigate the debt problem as long as Marcos refused to shut down the monopolies, an act that would mean turning against his own cronies. In the countryside, the activities of communist guerrillas increased dramatically. Yet Marcos probably could have weathered the storm had opposition leader Benigno Aquino not been killed by his own security forces. The murder rallied opposition forces and produced a movement for reform within the army that was sponsored by Defense Minister Juan Ponce Enrile. The murder also elicited strong criticism from the United States. Marcos attempted to answer his critics by offering a free election. Corazon Aquino won the contest, albeit not with a clear mandate. At this point, Marcos tried to invalidate the election but was unable to do so, lacking internal support from the military and external support from the United States.[39]

In Nepal the basis for democratization differed radically from that in the Philippines. Nepal is a small, poor country whose economy is dominated by agriculture and tourism. Economically and otherwise, it is highly dependent on its giant neighbor, India. In early 1990, the regime in Nepal was an absolute monarchy, as it had been for more than two hundred years. But in that year the king and his government came under pressure from three sides. First, the country had been involved in a year-long deadlock on a trade and transit treaty with India, and the lack of a solution was beginning to create shortages of essential goods in the economy. Second, international aid donors were increasing their pressure for improvements in the human rights situation in the country. Finally, the groups opposing the government were inspired by events in Eastern Europe to increase their drive for political changes, and for the first time opposition forces from the left and the right worked together.

The king and the government initially stood firm, instructing the police to clamp down on demonstrators and banning opposition newspapers. But as the confrontation increased, the king started leaning toward a compromise, and he eventually called on a moderate opposition leader to form a new government. Subsequently the king and the cabinet struggled for control over the process of drafting a new constitution, which was intended to lead to a constitutional monarchy.[40] Recent developments in Nepal have led away from democracy as the king attempts to hold on to extraordinary powers while much of the country is destabilized by a Maoist insurgency.

In Taiwan democratization has been influenced by economic success. For many years, the state pushed and guided economic development. Contrary to the Philippine case, politics in Taiwan has been relatively untouched by corruption and malpractice. Having lost badly to the Communists in the civil war on the mainland, Nationalist leaders were determined to clean up their act and promote rapid economic development on the island. Fifty years of Japanese colonial rule over Taiwan left a strong infrastructure, a productive agriculture, and a population with a comparatively high level of education. Furthermore, the United States was willing to assist Taiwan economically and otherwise as a consequence of the cold war confrontation with communism. The authoritarian regime produced startling economic success but was undermined politically by the same process: Rapid economic development produces stronger social forces outside the state apparatus, including private business, the industrial labor force, and the middle class. These developments tend to put new demands on the state. An important demand in recent years has been for a more democratic society. At the same time, the complex relationship to mainland China continues to play a significant role in the political process.

In conclusion, many of the democratic openings that have taken place could just as easily fall back toward authoritarianism as continue toward more authentic democracy. The early transitions in southern Europe appear to be the most consolidated, whereas the recent democratic openings in Africa are the most fragile, having moved only a short distance away from authoritarianism. The mere passage of time, however, is no guarantee for a continued process of democratization. We will examine several problems facing the current democratic openings after I introduce a model that displays the different phases involved in the transition from authoritarian to democratic rule.

PROCESSES OF TRANSITION AND CONSOLIDATION

The transition from nondemocracy to democratic rule is a complex process involving several phases, although ascertaining where one phase begins and another ends is difficult. In the typical contemporary case, the beginning of the process is marked by crisis within the nondemocratic regime, followed by eventual breakdown. If the transition to democracy begins with some kind of crisis for authoritarian rule that convinces the rulers to leave office, then this phase ends with the installation, based on free elections, of a new government.

But a successful process of democratic transition does not end there. The new regime will often be a restricted democracy, more democratic than the previous regime but not yet fully democratic. Several phases of "democratic deepening" may be necessary before this latter stage is reached. And then the regime still has to be consolidated, which is said to occur when all major political actors see democracy as the "only game in town." There is often considerable overlap between these phases.

Note that the phases outlined here are not necessarily negotiated in a smooth, linear manner. There may be crises and setbacks. And the result of regime change need not necessarily be democracy. The typical pattern for many developing countries has indeed been one of seesawing between a more or less authoritarian system and frail democracy. Moreover, the full process toward consolidated democracy may take a long time, often several decades. In the case of Great Britain, the full process took more than two hundred years.

FIGURE 2.1   Transitions toward democracy: A model

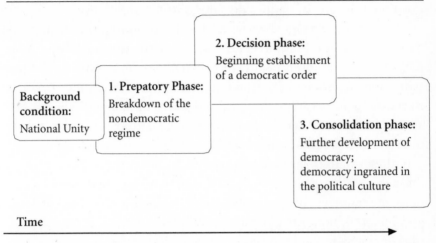

1. Prepatory Phase:
Breakdown of the nondemocratic regime

Background condition:
National Unity

2. Decision phase:
Beginning establishment of a democratic order

3. Consolidation phase:
Further development of democracy; democracy ingrained in the political culture

Time

Source: Based on Dankwart Rustow, "Transitions to Democracy," *Comparative Politics* 2, no. 3 (1970).

A more concrete impression of the phases and problems involved in the transition toward democracy can be attained through a simple model that describes some of the main elements in the transition process (see Fig. 2.1). It is a slightly modified version of a model created by Dankwart Rustow.[41] It cannot be emphasized enough that the transition model introduced below is an analytical device aimed at giving an overview of major elements in a transition process. The model does *not* imply that regime change away from authoritarianism must always lead to consolidated democracy. In most countries with democratic openings, this has not been the case. But we need the model anyway in order to discuss what transition toward democracy is about.

The model has one background condition—national unity—that must be in place before it is possible to conceive of a transition toward democracy. According to Rustow, national unity simply indicates that "the vast majority of citizens in a democracy-to-be . . . have no doubt or mental reservations as to which political community they belong to."[42] There may well be ethnic or other cleavages between groups in the population; it is only when such divisions lead to basic questioning of national unity that the problem must be resolved before a transition to democracy becomes feasible. National unity was an issue in India and Pakistan and is an issue today in Sri Lanka, Kosovo, Russia, and in several

African countries. Democratization demands a settling of the national question: Who are the nations that are going to democratize?

The issue will emerge elsewhere, as well. For example, in China any process of democratization will have to settle the issue of Tibet's claim for autonomy. Empires held together by force must confront the national unity question as a precondition for a process of democratization; rulers and policies cannot change in a democratic manner if the boundaries do not endure. As one observer stated, "The people cannot decide until somebody decides who are the people."[43]

If these matters are not resolved in a democratic manner (e.g., through minority guarantees or local autonomy for the group in question), the result will be the breakdown of democracy combined with repression of the minority group or civil war, as in the case, for example, in Chechnya and Sri Lanka. Again, a return to democracy presupposes that the question of national unity is resolved.

With national unity as the single background condition, the first phase in the transition toward democracy is the *preparatory phase*. It contains first and foremost what Rustow calls a prolonged and inconclusive political struggle. Individuals, groups, and classes challenge the nondemocratic rulers. Democracy may not be their main aim; it can be a means to another end or a by-product of a struggle for other ends, such as a more equal society, a better distribution of wealth, the extension of rights and freedoms, and so forth. The composition of the groups behind the challenge to the rulers varies from country to country and over time periods. As Rustow states, "No two existing democracies have gone through a struggle between the very same forces over the same issues and with the same institutional outcome."[44]

The phases often overlap. In India, for example, the preparatory phase of the struggle for democracy began long before national unity and independence were achieved. The same coalition of forces in the National Congress movement that struggled for national independence struggled for a democratic political system.

Other scholars have analyzed the preparatory phase. Alfred Stepan outlined ten different paths from nondemocratic toward democratic rule.[45] They are differentiated according to the nature of the previous authoritarian regime, the constellation of political and social forces in the various societies, and the different international contexts in which the transitions take place. The contemporary transitions toward democracy include cases of democratization initiated from within authoritarian regimes (e.g., in Latin America) as well as cases mainly triggered by external forces (e.g., in Eastern Europe).

In Chapter 1, two basic dimensions of the process of democratization were identified—liberalization (or competition) and inclusiveness (or participation). According to the comparative study of transitions in Latin America and southern Europe by O'Donnell and Schmitter, the typical beginning of the transition to democracy is a period of liberalization as the incumbent authoritarian rulers extend a measure of civil and political rights to individuals and groups. Space for oppositional political activity (for public competition) is thereby created, albeit within a framework still controlled by the authoritarian regime. This phase began in Brazil, for example, with the suspension of press censorship in 1974. It was overlapped by a later phase of increased participation, which culminated in the election of a civilian president in 1985.[46]

A similar phase of liberalization occurred in several East European countries. It began with single-party pluralism, where the population was allowed to choose among different candidates of the same (Communist) party. But this development was not enough to convey legitimacy on the old rulers. In a following phase, increased opposition led to the introduction of different versions of multiparty systems in Poland, Hungary, and the Soviet Union by the late 1980s.[47]

The second phase of Rustow's model is the *decision phase*, in which there is "a deliberate decision on the part of political leaders to . . . institutionalize some crucial aspect of democratic procedure."[48] Again, that there can be overlap with the previous (preparatory) phase. The decision phase may be split into several subphases. England provides a prime example of this type of incremental democratization. The compromise of 1688 started the process, which was not completed until 1928, when suffrage was extended to women. Even when the time period is shorter, as in Brazil, the decision phase may involve several steps. Indeed, many countries presently in transition toward democracy are stuck in the early phase of the decision step, having made some moves toward democracy but not completing the transition.

If the time period is short, opposition forces have few opportunities to organize themselves into proper actors on the political arena. In Romania, for example, where there was no preceding process of liberalization and where a quick outburst of popular uprising toppled the old regime, a provisional government was formed that was dominated by liberal Communists. The new rulers did not have plans for radical reforms; Romania has moved only slowly and hesitantly toward more democratic conditions.

Thus the pace of transition influences the outcome. So does the institutional legacy of authoritarian rule. To what extent is it possible to build on political parties, interest associations, local governments, and social movements from the period of authoritarian rule? In some cases (e.g., Portugal) institutions were destroyed to the extent that the government following the democratic transition had to start almost from scratch in building new institutions. In other cases, such as Brazil and Peru, structures from previous phases of democratic rule have survived and can be put to use in the transition.[49] In Eastern Europe the new regimes have hardly anything to build on, with the exception of the organizations created in some countries during the liberalization phase. Africa's problems in this regard stem from the fact that in nearly all countries experiences with democracy have been sporadic, and democratic organizations have not been effectively institutionalized.

One important factor influencing the prospects for further democratic development toward consolidation (see below) is the makeup of the leading coalition behind the transition. The crucial distinction is between transitions dominated by the elites who were also behind the old, authoritarian regimes, and transitions in which mass actors have gained the upper hand. The former can be called "transitions from above." As Terry Lynn Karl states, "Here traditional rulers remain in control, even if pressured from below, and successfully use strategies of either compromise or force—or some mix of the two—to retain at least part of their power."[50] In her analysis of Latin American cases Karl stresses that transitions from above are the most frequently encountered type. Transitions from below have not led to stable democracy:

> To date, however, *no* stable political democracy has resulted from regime transitions in which mass actors have gained control, even momentarily, over traditional ruling classes. Efforts at reform from below . . . have met with subversive opposition from unsuppressed traditional elites, as the

cases of Argentina (1946–51), Guatemala (1946–54) and Chile (1970–73) demonstrate.[51]

In Latin America, there have been no transitions from below in the past three decades that resulted in consolidated democracy. At the same time, the distinction between elites and masses must not be overdrawn. Even when elites dominate a transition process, it is also most often shaped by the participation and active influence of popular forces. Karl and Schmitter have argued that several of the transitions in southern and eastern Europe can also be seen as transitions from above, although they stressed that classification is often difficult because of the complex historical patterns in single cases.[52] In the former Soviet Union, for example, elite domination characterized the controlled process of perestroika led by Mikhail Gorbachev; after the unsuccessful August 1991 coup by the old Communist elites, their influence on the transition was substantially reduced.

In sum, democratic openings may lead to restricted democracies that are less capable than a nonrestricted democracy of making reform policies that go against vested elite interests. We will return to this issue in Chapter 3. The final phase of the transition to democracy is the *consolidation phase*. What is consolidation? There is no agreement about the proper definition. The most demanding version states that consolidation is not reached until all the democratic institutions have been formed and the new democracy proves itself capable of transferring power to an opposition party, its most difficult challenge. But this kind of understanding may lead to the assertion that almost no democratic regime can ever be seen as fully consolidated. Therefore, I follow the more modest definition suggested by Juan Linz, who states that a **consolidated democracy**

is one in which none of the major political actors, parties, or organized interests, forces, or institutions consider that there is any alternative to democratic processes to gain power, and that no political institution or group has a claim to veto the action of democratically elected decision makers. This does not mean that there are no minorities ready to challenge and question the legitimacy of the democratic process by nondemocratic means. It means, however, that the major actors do not turn to them and

FIGURE 2.2   Indicators of democratic consolidation

Level	Norms and beliefs	Behaviour
Elite	Most significant leaders of opinion, culture, business, and social organizations believe in the legitimacy of democracy. All major leaders of government and politically significant parties believe that democracy is the best form of government …	Leaders of government, state institutions, and significant political parties and interest groups respect each other's right to compete peacefully for power, eschew violence, and obey the laws, the constitutions, and mutually accepted norms of political conduct.
Organizations	All politically significant parties, interest groups, and social movements endorse … the legitimacy of democracy …	No politically significant party, interest group, movement, or institution seeks to overthrow democracy …
Mass public	More than 70 percent of the mass public consistently believes that democracy is preferable to any other form of government … No more than 15 percent of the public actively prefers an authoritarian form of government.	No antidemocratic movement, party, or organization enjoys a significant mass following …

Source: Adapted from Larry Diamond, *Developing Democracy: Toward Consolidation* (Baltimore: Johns Hopkins University Press, 1999), p. 69.

they remain politically isolated. To put it simply, democracy must be seen as the "only game in town."[53]

Larry Diamond's instructive overview of indicators of democratic consolidation on various levels of analysis is summarized in Figure 2.2.

Seen as a process, consolidation overlaps with the decision phase. The gradual progression of decisions leading from more restricted democracy toward more real democracy can be seen as elements leading toward increased consolidation. The democratic deepening process in the decision phase is an early phase of consolidation. As long as powerful groups and institutions, such as the armed forces in Latin America or the former elites in Eastern Europe, try to circumvent or veto democratically made decisions, democracy is not fully consolidated.[54]

It can be argued that consolidation is not a purely political process but also demands social and economic change. Without changes made to correct the vast inequalities in many societies, there may be decreased political support for democratically elected leaders and a "spiral of delegitimation" of the democratic regime.[55]

The final phase of consolidation is the process whereby democratic institutions and practices become ingrained in the political culture. Not only political leaders but also the vast majority of political actors and of the population come to see democratic practices as part of the right and natural order of things.[56] I will argue in the next chapter that only a minority of the large number of democratic openings discussed here have reached that stage.

From the background condition of national unity, the process of transition from nondemocratic rule to democracy has been described as occurring in three phases, which often overlap in the real world. The preparatory phase is characterized by a political struggle leading to the breakdown of the nondemocratic regime. In the decision phase, clear-cut elements of a democratic order are established, and in the consolidation phase, the new democracy is further developed. Eventually democratic practices become an established part of the political culture. An important marker of the decision phase is elections that are (at least on the whole) free and fair. This makes it important to further study the occurrence and quality of elections.[57] An important marker of consolidation is certainty, which emerges when rules, practices, and institutions framing the political process are developed and also respected by the major political groupings.

Again, there is nothing inevitable about these phases. There is no historical law that defines this transition process as the natural order of things. As already mentioned, the natural order in many developing countries seems to be an uneasy seesaw between semiauthoritarianism and frail democracy. Consequently it cannot be expected that all the countries of the world will sooner or later pass through all of these stages and end up as consolidated democracies.

CONCLUSION

In this chapter we have studied the processes of democratization, first in a general sense and then with a focus on the current transitions toward democracy. We saw that it is impossible to draw up a general law to the effect that democracy will always emerge provided certain preconditions are present. It is more productive to conceive of an interplay between social, cultural, economic, and other conditions, on the one hand, and decisions taken by political actors, on the other.

No single factor can account for the contemporary surge toward democracy. Each case involves a complex pattern of internal and external elements; in each, various conditions interplay with different groups of actors. Furthermore, movements toward democracy in different parts of the world during the past fifteen years must be explained in different ways. The scope of this book does not allow us to unravel the processes country by country, and consequently we looked at events in major regions of the world and reviewed a few specific country examples. We must always keep in mind the danger caused by hindsight: Explaining past events can easily become a search for the obvious because we already know what happened.

In more general terms, the process of transition to democracy can be described with a simple model. The background condition of the model is national unity, and the overlapping phases of the transitions are (1) the preparatory phase, characterized by a political struggle leading to the breakdown of the nondemocratic regime; (2) the decision phase, where clear-cut elements of a democratic order are established; and (3) the consolidation phase, where the new democracy is further developed, and democratic practices eventually become an established part of the political culture.

The phases do not represent a predetermined path that all countries will or must follow. There is no historical law that regimes must move from authoritarian to democratic; a more accurate description of the typical pattern in the developing world is an uneasy fluctuation between authoritarianism and frail democracy. In the next chapter, I will further develop this proposition.

3

From Transition to Standstill

Democracy in the New Millennium

In this chapter I will argue that the term "transition" conveys too much optimism as a label for a process of regime change. What we actually have is a standstill, as a large number of countries remain in the gray area between being outright authoritarian and being fully democratic. "Transition" suggests that these regimes may be on the way to something better, but the evidence indicates that most often they are not; they are more likely to remain semidemocratic or semiauthoritarian. In the rest of this chapter I will further develop this proposition.

I have chosen to identify four characteristic features of regime change in recent democratic openings. Each proposition contains what I believe is an important characteristic of the large majority of these transitions. The discussion of each proposition includes references to concrete examples. The features included are relevant for many or even most of the transitions currently taking place. The few exceptions will be pointed out in due course. The prevalence of these characteristics supports my claim of a shift from democratic "transition" to "standstill."

The first characteristic concerns elections. An increasing number of countries conduct more or less democratic elections, yet they are not democratic in other important respects and many of them are not making any moves in that direction. They remain electoral democracies. The second characteristic concerns lack of "stateness," that is, the institutions and procedures needed for maintaining order and effectively formulating and implementing policies. Many countries exhibit some democratic features while also being **weak states**, sometimes on the verge of collapse.

The third characteristic is **elite domination**; a strongman and his follow-ers or some narrow coalition of elites dominate the political scene and prevent the adoption of policies that go against their vested interests. Al-though these three characteristics overlap in concrete cases, for analyti-cal purposes, it is helpful to discuss them separately.

On the positive side, the process of popular mobilization and organi-zation in the struggle for democracy has reached unprecedented levels. This high degree of mobilization and organization will make it more dif-ficult for the new regimes to revert to authoritarian forms of rule.

ELECTIONS AND DEMOCRACY

Elections tend to be the focus of democratic openings. They are highly visible and often celebrated events; an election appears to be a manifest and certain indicator that the democratic transition is now well under way. Accordingly, holding elections is seen as a core element in the deci-sion phase of the transition model presented in Chapter 2. As one scholar puts it,

> Holding competitive, free and fair "founding elections" based on mass suf-frage can be the key threshold that marks a distinctive shift in the political rules of the game. They may not end the transition; there can still be a re-gression to autocracy and elections certainly do not guarantee consolida-tion. But they certainly signal that regime institutionalization has begun . . . If such elections occur in the context of transitions, they may be signif-icant enough to alter a country's entire political trajectory.[1]

Note that this positive view of the role of elections assumes that elec-tions are "competitive, free, and fair"; they mark the decisive change of the rules of the political game, away from previous authoritarian prac-tices and toward the development of new, democratic practices. They are called **founding elections**. The problem, however, is that many elections are not of this democratically attractive kind. Even highly authoritarian systems, such as the old Soviet Union or present-day North Korea and Cuba, hold elections that certainly do not signal a transition away from authoritarianism. Liberal ideas became dominant after the end of the cold war and the dissolution of the Soviet Union, and authoritarianism has lost legitimacy. Few dictators believe they have an inherent, legitimate right to be dictators. As one observer notes, "To live under autocracy, or even to *be* an autocrat, seems backward, uncivilized, distasteful, not quite *comme il faut*—in a word, 'uncool.'"[2] Clearly the incentive to hold some kind of election in order to demonstrate an element of democratic respectability has increased significantly. Consequently elections do not always function as an indicator of democratization; they also take place in "mixed" or "hybrid" regimes that may retain major authoritarian elements. "The hegemony of liberal democracy as a legitimate regime type has meant that the trend toward democracy has been stealthily accompanied by an even more rapid countertrend towards hybrid regimes."[3]

This state of affairs calls for a more critical view of elections. When are they competitive, free, and fair "founding elections" that mark a transition toward or even a consolidation of democracy, and when are they "demonstration elections" designed to lend a facade of credibility to a regime that is basically authoritarian and wants to remain that way? Of course, a regime can fall somewhere between these extremes. "Good" elections are as much (or even more) about what happens in the preparation leading up to the event as about the political process after the event. "Free and fair elections," says Robert Dahl, are "the culmination of the [democratic] process, not the beginning. Indeed, unless and until the other rights and liberties are firmly protected, free and fair elections cannot take place. Except in countries already close to the thresholds of democracy, therefore, it is a grave mistake to assume that if only the leader of a non-democratic country can be persuaded to hold elections, then full democracy will follow."[4]

Jørgen Elklit and Palle Svensson have summarized the key elements in an acceptable electoral process. On polling day, free and fair elections mean an opportunity for voters to participate in the election, the absence of voter intimidation, and a secret ballot. But there are other key elements that must be in place both before and after polling day. They are summarized in Figure 3.1.

The absence of such elements—often in a context where the election itself is not free and fair—serves to increase the skepticism toward elections as true indicators of democratization. For example, Felix

FIGURE 3.1   Key elements in an acceptable electoral process

Level	Free	Fair
Before polling day	• Freedom of speech • Freedom of assembly • Freedom of association • Freedom from fear in relation to election • Freedom of movement • Absence of impediments to standing for election • Equal and universal suffrage	• A transparent electoral process • An election act with no special privileges to anyone • An independent and impartial electoral commission • Impartial voter education programs • No impediments to inclusion in electoral register • Possible to check provisional electoral register • An orderly election campaign • Equal access to public mass media • No misuse of government facilities in campaign
After polling day	• Legal possibilities of complaint • Independent, impartial courts • Adequate possibilities for resolution of election-related conflicts	• Proper counting and reporting • Proper handling of election material • Impartial reports by media on results • Impartial treatment of election complaints • Acceptance of election results by all involved

Adapted from J. Elklit and P. Svensson, "What Makes Elections Free and Fair," *Journal of Democracy* 8, no. 3 (1997), p. 37.

Houphouet-Boigny, who had been president of Côte d'Ivoire for several decades, took the opposition by surprise in 1990 by suddenly giving in to demands for open presidential and legislative elections. Although there had been no opposition activity for thirty years, the president summoned twenty-six political groups and informed them of the upcoming elections. Opposition requests for additional time to get organized were rejected on the basis that opposition itself had demanded instant elections. Consequently the election was controlled by the president's party, which also largely controlled the media. Both the president and his party scored comfortable victories in an election that was not part of a major process of democratization.

Possible infringements on the democratic election process have been identified by Andreas Schedler. "To qualify as democratic," he says,

> elections must offer an effective choice of political authorities among a community of free and equal citizens. Following Robert Dahl, this democratic ideal requires that all citizens enjoy "unimpaired opportunities", to "formulate" their political preferences, to "signify" them to one another, and to have them "weighed equally" in public decision making. Building upon Dahl, let us delineate seven conditions that must exist if regular elections are to fulfil the promise of effective democratic choice . . . Together, these conditions form a metaphorical chain which, like a real chain, holds together only so long as each of its links remains whole and unbroken.[5]

The seven conditions identified by Schedler and the possible infringements of them are outlined in Table 3.1. There are many other problematic countries in addition to those cited in the examples.

Instead of routinely celebrating elections as part of a successful process of democratization, then, it is necessary to examine them in more detail, also considering the political process before and after polling day. A great number of countries do not meet the seven elements of the chain of democratic choice outlined in Table 3.1.

How can we best characterize the regimes in the vast gray area between consolidated democracy on the one hand and fully authoritarian regimes on the other? As indicated earlier (Chap. 1), this question has led to numerous suggested labels and categorizations. In an early contribution, Guillermo O'Donnell suggested the term "delegative democracy." He first notes that the installation of a democratically elected government is not the same as consolidation of democracy; the election sooner opens "the way to a 'second transition,' probably longer and more complex than the transition from authoritarian rule."[6] Successful consolidation depends on a combination of institutional progress and governmental effectiveness. However, a large number of regimes have achieved neither; they are the delegative democracies. The further characteristics of these regimes are set forth in Box 3.1.

In other words, delegative democracies tend to concentrate power in the presidency and sidestep the political processes involved in going through congress. The democratic notion of representation—a political

TABLE 3.1 The chain of democratic choice

Dimension of Choice	Possible Violation	Examples of Violating Countries
1. **Empowerment:** elections delegate authority	Reserved positions: limiting the scope of elective offices	Morocco
	Reserved domains: limiting the jurisdiction of elective office	Turkey
2. **Freedom of supply:** freedom to form, join, support conflicting parties, candidates, policies	Exclusion of opposition forces: restricting access to electoral arena	Kenya, Zambia, Egypt, Tunisia, Algeria
	Fragmentation of opposition forces: disorganizing dissidence	Iran, Uganda, Peru
3. **Freedom of demand:** ability to learn about alternatives, access plural sources of information	Repression: restricting political and civil liberties	Several countries in Sub-Saharan Africa
	Unfairness: restricting access to media and money	
4. **Inclusion:** equal rights of participation	Legal suffrage restrictions	—
	Practical suffrage restrictions	Mauretania 1990s
5. **Insulation:** free to express electoral preferences	Coercion: voter intimidation	Zimbabwe
	Corruption: vote buying	Philippines, Mexico
6. **Integrity:** one person one vote	Electoral fraud: "redistributive" election management	Haiti, Peru, Zimbabwe, Burkina Faso
	Institutional bias: "redistributive" electoral rules	Kenya, Gambia, Malaysia
7. **Irreversibility:** election winners are given effective power	Tutelage: preventing elected officers from exercising powers	Several countries in Sub-Saharan Africa
	Reversal: preventing victors from taking office	

Source: Adapted from Andreas Schedler, *Journal of Democracy* 13, no. 2 (2002): 39–46.

BOX 3.1 Delegative democracy

Delegative democracies are grounded on one basic premise: he (or eventually she, i.e. Indira Gandhi, Corazón Aquino, and Isabel Perón) who wins a presidential election is enabled to govern the country as he sees fit, and to the extent that existing power relations allow, for the term to which he has been elected. The president is the embodiment of the nation and the main custodian of the national interest, which it is incumbent on him to define. What he does in government does not need to bear any resemblance to what he said or promised during the electoral campaign—he has been authorized to govern as he sees fit . . . Typically, and consistently, winning presidential candidates in DDs present themselves as above all parties, i.e. both political parties and organized interests . . . In this view other institutions—such as Congress and the Judiciary—are nuisances that come attached to the domestic and international advantages of being a democratically elected president. Accountability to those institutions . . . appears as an unnecessary impediment to the full authority that the President has been delegated to exercise.

Source: Guillermo O'Donnell, "Delegative Democracy," *Journal of Democracy* 5, no. 1 (1994), p. 61.

process mediated by negotiations between various parties and interest groups—is replaced by the less democratic notion of delegation, where the all-powerful president decides on his own. O'Donnell argued in 1994 that the purest cases of delegative democracy were Argentina, Brazil, and Peru. Today, it is probably the Hugo Chavez presidency in Venezuela and the Vladimir Putin presidency in Russia that best illustrate delegative democracy. In different ways, both presidents seek to concentrate power and control the political process, rejecting a pluralist notion of democracy "as the representation of diverse interests."[7]

The term **illiberal democracy** was suggested by Fareed Zakaria in a 1997 article and later in a book-length analysis.[8] He emphasizes that democratically elected regimes are frequently "ignoring the constitutional limits on their power and depriving their citizens of basic rights and freedoms. From Peru to the Palestinian Authority, from Sierra Leone to Slovakia, from Pakistan to the Philippines, we see the rise of a disturbing phenomenon in international life—illiberal democracy."[9] In other words, elections may be held but the liberal side of democracy—rule of law, separation of powers, protection of basic rights of speech, assembly, religion, and property—is much less developed. Many countries with elected leaders suffer from a lack of such liberties; these deficiencies may be combined with a flawed electoral process as well. Examples include Albania, Armenia, Bosnia, Burkina Faso, Burundi, Central African Republic, Ethiopia, Gabon, the Gambia, Jordan, Kuwait, Kyrgyzstan, Lebanon, Moldova, Morocco, Senegal, and Venezuela.[10]

Another way of depicting countries in the gray area has been suggested by Thomas Carothers.[11] He first notes that the democratization wave in the past two decades involved nearly one hundred countries; but only a small number of those countries—probably fewer than twenty—are on the way to becoming "successful, well-functioning democracies or at least have made some democratic progress and still enjoy a positive dynamic of democratization."[12] The rest are "neither dictatorial nor clearly headed toward democracy . . . they suffer from serious democratic deficits, often including poor representation of citizens' interests, low levels of political participation beyond voting, frequent abuse of the law by government officials, elections of uncertain legitimacy, very low levels of public confidence in state institutions and persistently poor institutional performance by the state."[13]

Carothers specifically points to two major syndromes that are characteristic of the gray zone; one is "feckless pluralism" and the other is "dominant-power politics." They are set forth in Box 3.2.

Feckless pluralism, according to Carothers, is most common in Latin America (Nicaragua, Ecuador, Guatemala, Panama, Honduras, Bolivia, and, to some extent, Argentina and Brazil) but is also present in the postcommunist world (Moldova, Bosnia, Albania, Ukraine, and, to some extent, Romania and Bulgaria), as well as in Asia (Bangladesh, Mongolia, Thailand) and a few places in sub-Saharan Africa (Madagascar, Guinea-Bissau, Sierra Leone). Dominant power-politics is widespread in three regions: sub-Saharan Africa (Cameroon, Burkina Faso, Equatorial Guinea, Tanzania, Gabon, Kenya, Mauritania), the former Soviet Union (Armenia, Azerbaijan, Georgia, Kyrgyzstan, and Kazakhstan), and the Middle East (Morocco, Jordan, Algeria, Egypt, Iran, and Yemen). At the same time, several countries in this region remain strictly authoritarian.

The core message in Carothers's analysis is that countries in the gray area are most often not under way to becoming more democratic; in that sense, they are not in a process of transition. They are likely to remain in

BOX 3.2   Feckless pluralism and dominant power politics

Feckless Pluralism

Countries whose political life is marked by feckless pluralism tend to have significant amounts of political freedom, regular elections, and alternation of power between genuinely different groupings. Despite these positive features, however, democracy remains shallow and troubled. Political participation, though broad at election time, extends little beyond voting. Political elites from all the major parties or groupings are widely perceived as corrupt, self-interested, and ineffective. The alternation of power seems only to trade the country's problems back and forth from one hapless side to another . . . Overall politics is widely seen as a stale, corrupt, elite-dominated domain that delivers little good to the country and commands equally little respect.

Dominant Power Politics

Countries with this syndrome have limited but still real political space, some political contestation by opposition groups, and at least most of the basic institutional forms of democracy. Yet one political grouping—whether it is a movement, a party, an extended family, or a single leader—dominates the system in such a way that there appear to be little prospect of alternation of power in the foreseeable future. Unlike the countries beset with feckless pluralism, a key political problem in dominant-power countries is the blurring of the line between the state and the ruling party (or ruling political forces). The state's main assets—that is to say, the state as a source of money, jobs, public information (via state media), and police power—are gradually put in the direct service of the ruling party . . . The long hold on power by one political group usually produces large-scale corruption and crony capitalism.

Source: Adapted from Thomas Carothers,
"The End of the Transitions Paradigm,"
Journal of Democracy 13, no. 1 (2002), pp. 9-12.

the gray area and thus retain the less democratic or nondemocratic characteristics outlined here:

what is often thought of as an uneasy, precarious middle ground between full-fledged democracy and outright dictatorship is actually the most common political condition today of countries in the developing world and the postcommunist world. It is not an exceptional category to be defined only

TABLE 3.2   Countries in the gray zone, 2006

Electoral democracies *(Freedom House average score above 2.0 and less than 4.25)*	Electoral authoritarian systems *(Freedom House average score 4.25 and above, but less than 6.5)*
El Salvador, India, Indonesia, Jamaica, Lesotho, Peru, Senegal, Serbia and Montenegro, Trinidad and Tobago, Ukraine, Albania, Bolivia, Colombia, East Timor, Ecuador, Georgia, Guyana, Honduras, Kenya, Macedonia, Madagascar, Nicaragua, Niger, Papua New Guinea, Paraguay, Philippines, Seychelles, Solomon Islands, Sri Lanka, Thailand, Turkey, Guinea-Bissau, Moldova, Mozambique, Bosnia-Herzegovina, Fiji, Sierra Leone, Tanzania, Burundi, Bangladesh, Comoros, Guatemala, Liberia, Malawi, Malaysia, Nigeria, Venezuela, Zambia, Burkina Faso, Tonga	Kuwait, Armenia, Central African Republic, Jordan, Kyrgyzstan, Lebanon, Morocco, Singapore, The Gambia, Uganda, Afghanistan, Bahrain, Congo (Brazzaville), Djibouti, Ethiopia, Yemen, Gabon, Mauritania, Algeria, Angola, Azerbaijan, Bhutan, Brunei, Cambodia, Chad, Egypt, Guinea, Iraq, Kazakhstan, Maldives, Nepal, Oman, Pakistan, Qatar, Russia, Rwanda, Tajikistan, Togo, Tunisia, Cameroon, Congo (Kinshasa), Cote d'Ivoire, Iran, United Arab Emirates, Swaziland, Vietnam

Source: Calculated from Freedom House, *Freedom in the World 2006* (Lanham, Md.: Rowman & Littlefield, 2006). Countries arranged with lowest (i.e. most democratic) scores first.

in terms of its not being one thing or the other; it is a state of normality for many societies, for better or for worse.[14]

What can we say about current regimes in the gray area? Consider the 2006 survey by Freedom House. Countries with an average score of 2.0 or less are considered full-blown liberal democracies, and countries with an average score of 6.5 or more are considered closed authoritarian.[15] Countries between these averages are in the gray area. On this view roughly half of the countries in the world—96 out of 192—are in the gray zone. There are vast differences between them, of course; that is the reason for the many different labels introduced above. If we divided the ninety-six countries into two groups (the middle being an average Freedom House score of 4.25), the half with better scores could be called "electoral democracies," whereas the half with the worse scores could be called "electoral authoritarian systems"; the two groups are identified in Table 3.2.

Although the categorization in the table above is admittedly frayed at the edges, it serves to emphasize that many countries remain in the gray zone and, elections notwithstanding, are more authoritarian than democratic.

In conclusion, Robert A. Dahl lists five conditions that he feels are most favorable for the development of stable polyarchy—stable democratic rule:

- Leaders do not employ coercion, notably through the police and the military, to gain and maintain their power.
- A modern, dynamic, organizationally pluralist society exists;
- The conflictive potentialities of subcultural pluralism are maintained at tolerable levels;
- Among the people of a country, particularly its active political stratum, a political culture and a system of beliefs exists that is favorable to the idea of democracy and the institutions of polyarchy;
- The effects of foreign influence or control are either negligible or positively favorable.[16]

None of these conditions, with the possible exception of the last one, are met in most countries in the gray zone today. Against this background, there is not much hope that the recent democratic openings will progress into consolidated democracies. The argument for using the overall label of "standstill" instead of "transition" is that most of these countries are not on the way to more democracy and will probably remain in the gray zone.

WEAK STATES AND DEMOCRACY

Many states in the gray zone are weak states. They may conduct political processes that are fairly democratic, but any progress toward consolidation of democracy is impeded by the problem of weak statehood. A successful process of democratization requires that these countries develop more "stateness," that is, become stronger states.

The notion of a weak state is an imprecise concept that has been defined variously. For present purposes, we may distinguish between a broad and a narrow concept of state weakness.[17] The narrow concept is of primary interest here, but it is helpful to be familiar with the broad concept as well. States are sovereign territorial entities with a population and a government. In the broad sense, weak states are deficient in three basic respects. First, the economy is defective; there is a lack of a coherent national economy capable of sustaining a basic level of welfare for the population and of providing the resources for running an effective state. Defective economies often depend crucially on the world market because they are mono-economies based on the export of one or a few primary goods and on the import of more sophisticated, technology-intensive products. In sub-Saharan Africa, for example, primary products account for 80–90 percent of total export. At the same time, the weak economy is highly heterogeneous; there are elements of a modern sector but also feudal or semifeudal structures in agriculture. In both urban and rural areas large parts of the population are outside of the formal sectors, living in localized subsistence economies at very low standards.

The second major deficiency in weak states concerns relations between people in society; they do not make up a coherent national community. A national community is a community of sentiment, meaning a common language and a common cultural and historical identity based on literature, myths, symbols, music, and art. Such a community of sentiment is poorly developed in weak states. Instead, ethnic identities connected to tribal, religious, and similar characteristics dominate over the national identity. These ethnic identities are not necessarily primordial in the sense that they reflect ancient characteristics maintained over a long period of time. Precolonial Africa, for example, was not neatly divided into territorially separate entities with clear-cut authority structures; rather, it was a continent of overlapping entities where people had multiple group affiliations. Present-day ethnic groups were created by colonial rulers employing ethnic labeling as a "divide and rule" instrument and then used by postcolonial leaders appealing to ethnic identity to buttress their own power. In the worst cases, the lack of national community can completely block a process of democratization; that is behind Rustow's notion of "national unity" in the above model as a precondition for democratic transition. Even short of that, severe divisions in the population create cleavages and conflicts that impede democratization.

The third major problem in weak states concerns the state apparatus in a direct sense (i.e., the institutions of government at all levels). Weak states lack effective and responsive institutions. This is what is meant by state weakness in a narrow sense. "Effective" means the ability to formulate, implement, and supervise policies. "Responsive" means that the state functions to the benefit of, and with the support of, major groups in society. Effective states have a competent bureaucracy and a political leadership bent on promoting economic, political, and social progress. In organizational terms, a good bureaucracy displays "corporate cohesion of the organization, differentiation and insulation from its social environment, unambiguous location of decision making and channels of authority, and internal features fostering instrumental rationality and activism."[18] This is closely related to demands on the single bureaucrat: he or she must possess general as well as relevant issue competence in order to "analyze problems, formulate feasible solutions and implement them in technically competent ways."[19]

In weak states, the bureaucracy is incompetent and corrupt, and the political leadership does not seek to provide public or collective goods. It *[handwritten: Leads to a loss in legitimacy]* rather seeks to mold the state apparatus into a personal source of income. The spoils of office are often shared by a group of followers making up a network of patron-client relationships in which significant parts of the bureaucracy participate. As a result, the state does not provide public goods in any major way. It is neither effective nor responsive. When the state does not deliver, two consequences follow. First, people turn elsewhere for the satisfaction of material and nonmaterial needs. In sub-Saharan Africa, they have primarily turned to the ethnic communities that are the focal points of a "moral economy." "The moral economy enables individuals in various contexts to rely on nonbureaucratic mutual aid networks and to reciprocate toward those who belong to a common society. Examples include those better off helping relatives and clan members find jobs or pay school fees, as well as regular contributions to weddings and funerals, even for persons with whom face-to-face contact has never been established."[20] The second consequence is that the bond of right and obligation between people and the state does not develop; as a result, bonds of loyalty leading to state legitimacy do not mature. When ethnic communities become the primary focus for the satisfaction of people's needs, loyalties are projected in that direction and ethnic identities are reinforced.

It was hoped that democratic openings over the past two decades would create a new momentum with a positive circle of increased state accountability and efficiency, combined with a population more and more inclined to take on the identity of a national community of citizens. But in many countries the opposite has happened. The early phases of democratization have emphasized ethnic cleavages in the populations. First, democratization increases the possibilities for different ethnic groups to present their views and formulate their demands; the result of that has frequently been more rather than less conflict among groups.[21] Second, the spread of democracy has often meant quick elections, pushed by aid donors wanting to see a democratic transition. But elections organized in a hurry can be a destabilizing event in weak states. According to one scholar,

> Elections appear the wrong place whence to start a process of democratization in a collapsing, conflict-ridden state. In recent years, African elections have typically been organized in a hurry, in some cases before parties have time to consolidate or armed movements agree to disarm. As a result, losers have found it easy to reject election results, and voters have little choice but to choose on the basis of ethnic or religious identity.[22]

Third, state elites may actively enforce links with ethnic groups in their attempt to gain or hold on to power. One analysis found that elections "may actually increase the use of patronage . . . Traditional patron-client relations have often been critical in winning recent elections, indicating that the nature of African politics has not changed despite the new liberalization. Ghana, Nigeria and Kenya have all reported massive overspending as governments sought to reward traditional supporters, notably members of particular ethnic groups and civil servants, to smooth the transitions process or gain votes."[23]

The problems associated with democratizing weak states have led to a different kind of recommendation, one of "stateness first," meaning that "before you can have democracy or economic development, you have to have a state."[24] The problem is, of course, that it is extremely difficult to conduct effective state building over a short span of time, as currently demonstrated in Afghanistan, Iraq, and elsewhere. In a recent book, Francis Fukuyama sets forth the four different elements involved in a process of state building (understood as creating effective and responsive institutions): (1) organizational design and management, (2) political system design concerning institutions at the level of the state as a whole, (3) basis of

TABLE 3.3   Weak states as reported in *Foreign Policy*'s failed states index

1. Sudan	15. Burundi
2. Democratic Republic of Congo	16. Yemen
3. Cote d'Ivoire	17. Sierra Leone
4. Iraq	18. Burma/Myanmar
5. Zimbabwe	19. Bangladesh
6. Chad	20. Nepal
7. Somalia	21. Uganda
8. Haiti	22. Nigeria
9. Pakistan	23. Uzbekistan
10. Afghanistan	24. Rwanda
11. Guinea	25. Sri Lanka
12. Liberia	26. Ethiopia
13. Central African Republic	27. Colombia
14. North Korea	28. Kyrgyzstan

Source: Foreign Policy, *The Fund for Peace*, http://www.fundforpeace.org/programs/fsi/fsindex2006.php

legitimation concerning the perception of state institutions as legitimate by society, and (4) cultural and structural factors concerning the ways in which norms, values, and culture affect the makeup of institutions. [25]

Fukuyama's analysis holds that social and cultural factors, and to some extent legitimation factors, are not easily changed in the short and medium run; nor are they easily transformed by outside forces, such as aid donors. As a result, we must expect problems of state weakness to persist in many countries for some time. These problems mean that attempts at democratization face serious difficulties; state weakness makes it less likely that countries can escape from the gray zone. In the worst case, countries have moved toward complete breakdown.

As noted above, the weak states with the most serious problems are in sub-Saharan Africa. But state weakness can also be found in Asia, in postcommunist systems, in the Middle East, and even in Latin America. Since 2005, *Foreign Policy* together with the Fund for Peace has issued a failed states index based on twelve indicators of weakness. Even if the set of indicators is broader than the definitions of state weakness offered above, we may use the index as an approximate measure of weak statehood in the world. The 2006 version of the index lists twenty-eight countries in the most critical category of countries. They are listed in Table 3.3 in descending order, with the most problematic cases first.

"Stateness" being a precondition for a successful process of democratization, prospects for democratic transition deteriorate when it is lacking.

Even countries that are not on the above list may have significant elements of state weakness. The index includes the twenty-eight countries above in the Alert category; the next category (Warning) contains such states as Egypt, Indonesia, Syria, Kenya, Tajikistan, Russia, Belarus, Iran, Georgia, Ecuador, Venezuela, and the Philippines.

ELITE DOMINATION AND DEMOCRACY

A third major characteristic of many countries in the gray zone is domination by elite groups that interfere in the democratic process in order to protect their interests. In the case of democratic transitions from above, such interference can be part of the actual basis of the whole movement toward democracy. In other words, such groups as the military, traditional economic elites, and leading politicians may insist that the transition toward democracy include acceptance of a set of agreements or political pacts that define vital areas of interest for the elites. An example from Brazil may illustrate this point.[26]

An authoritarian regime led by the military came to power in Brazil in 1964. Some ten years later, a process of liberalization began and culminated in the formation of the new republic with the election of a civilian president in 1985. The return of the civilian regime was orchestrated by the military in alliance with other elite groups. The return to civilian rule was engineered by a series of political pacts, which serve to restrict democracy in several important respects. First, the military retained its influence in the new republic and actually extended it over domestic affairs. The constitutional clauses that serve as the basis for military intervention in domestic affairs remained in place. Even more important, six out of twenty-two cabinet members were uniformed officers.[27]

In addition, the new republic reinforced the Brazilian tradition of clientelism. Frances Hagopian states that "guaranteed access to state resources was the price traditional elites extracted for supporting democratization."[28] The democratic opposition to authoritarian rule led by Tancredo Neves secured access to power by promising state spoils to the traditional elites that had supported authoritarian rule. The elites were given political posts, the right to appoint federal and local state jobs, money for specific projects, and so forth. According to Hagopian, federal and state cabinets are directly based on clientelism. Therefore, these organs do not have the implementation of conceived policies as their main aim. They are geared more toward "diverting their resources to the areas of greatest political return for the ministers and secretaries that head them."[29] Political parties are also affected. They orient their activities toward this system of sharing the spoils and thereby distort the nature of political representation.

With the presidencies of Fernando Cardoso and Lula da Silva, the military and other elite groups have become less directly involved in the political process. But Brazil continues to be plagued by rampant corruption and the lack of major social reform. The military may have left power, but it helped shape "the new political rules in ways that protected conservative, clientelist strongholds through a dysfunctional combination of presidentialism, multipartism and localism."[30]

The power of the old elites in Eastern Europe, the *nomenklatura*, has been compared to the power of the military in Latin America. The Latin American democracies worry about "the *Gorilla* question," and the new democracies in Eastern Europe worry about "the *nomenklatura* question."[31] The countries find themselves in a precarious balance. When the old elites retain a high degree of influence on the transition process, the result is the restricted democracies identified in the Latin American context. If they are cut off from influence, they may utilize whatever remains of their power positions to destabilize the fragile new democracies.[32]

In sub-Saharan Africa, elite domination of the political process is more direct. Power lies with a president—a strongman—who supports a network of political clients by providing access to the state's resources. What is the problem? One plausible answer to this question, provided by Richard Sandbrook and other scholars, points to the lack of legitimacy that characterized postcolonial African states.[33] At independence, there were no strong social forces capable of disciplining political leaders. And the latter had no moral basis or legitimizing ideology from which they could demand compliance of citizens and bureaucrats. Precolonial, traditional legitimacy was no longer a relevant foundation. The type of government that filled this vacuum was a form of **neopatrimonialism.** (Neopatrimonialism must be understood against the background of patrimonialism, a term used by Max Weber to describe any type of government that originates from a royal household and has a ruler who treats matters of state as his or her personal affair. Present-day systems of personal rule in Africa are examples of neopatrimonialism.)

Personal rule is based on personal loyalty, especially toward the leading figure of the regime, the strongman. All important positions in the state, whether bureaucratic, political, military, or police, are filled with his loyal followers—relatives, friends, kinsmen, and tribesmen. Their loyalty to the strongman is reinforced by their sharing of the spoils of office.[34]

The strongman commands a web of informal networks, or **patron-client relationships,** in which two main forms of spoils are distributed. Both emanate from the strongman and his followers' control of the state. They are access to the state's resources in the form of jobs, contracts, favorable loans, opportunities for illegal gain, and so forth, and access to resources not directly controlled by the state but subject to state regulation, such as import permits and business licenses.

The final element in personal rule, in addition to the strongman and clientelism, is an armed force personally loyal to the regime. Because the state lacks legitimacy and many people are excluded from the rewards resulting from clientelism, rulers must resort to coercion or the threat of it for survival. Thus, in determining the degree of democracy in African states, we should focus less on the differences between civilian and military regimes and more on the direct and indirect political influence of the armed forces.[35]

It is against this background that different varieties of frail democracy and authoritarianism have developed in most African states. The study of regime change in Africa has aptly been characterized as "the study of the collapse of the 'tutelary' democratic regimes introduced during decolonization and the emergence of various types of authoritarian regimes."[36] The grafting of more democratic procedures, such as multiparty systems and open presidential elections, is now in the cards or has already been effectuated in many African states. But the consolidation of democracy will require more profound changes in the structure of personal rule take place.[37]

A similar kind of elite domination by a personal ruler or clan has developed in several former Soviet republics. A milder version of it characterizes Georgia; outright authoritarian Belarus is at the other extreme. In-betweens are Armenia, Azerbaijan, Kyrgyzstan, and Kazakhstan. Why do people vote for former Communists? Because they promise to make people rich; "they represent success: more than any other identifiable social group in Eastern Europe, they are seen to have achieved the most in the new regime."[38] Instead of representing the past, former Communists are becoming the architects of the future. The problem is that only a few of the new entrepreneurs hold traditional capitalist virtues, such as hard work, honesty, and responsibility. It is a "corrupt business class which is intimately intertwined with a corrupt political class." The end result is "some forms of robust private entre- preneurship, an enormous, untaxed, gray market, and large companies, some state-owned some private, which enjoy deeply corrupt relation- ships with powerful politicians."[39]

A recent analysis claims that both Russia and Venezuela are turning into "managed democracies" that reject genuine political pluralism and representation of diverse interests:

> Chavez's strategy is to encourage maximum confrontation and political mobilization: the Kremlin's strategy is to encourage maximum confusion and political demobilization . . . Both Chàvez and Putin are masters at em- ploying democratic rhetoric to achieve their political goals; both enjoy popular backing in national opinion polls . . . Each of them heads a regime that in some ways resembles democracy, but in both cases the reality is a near-monopoly of power.[40]

Both Chavez and Putin enjoy access to resources in the form of petro dollars. When the system is based on oil or other mineral rents, the rulers have a much better chance of discounting popular pressure. This is also a major problem in the Middle East, where such oil and mineral rents abound. Arab rulers "gained the means to create a clientelist stra- tum whose backing would help them bypass the need for popular sup- port. Endowed with considerable resources and freed from any possibility of popular pressure, the Arab regimes could ignore public opinion, and did not have to worry about improving their governance or seeking public support."[41] While many such countries remain starkly au- thoritarian, some have moved into the gray zone, including Morocco, Jordan, Algeria, Egypt, Iran, and Yemen.

Elite domination also characterizes many countries in Asia, including Indonesia, Thailand, Malaysia, India, and Cambodia. In these countries landowners and industrialists often yield major political influence; in Pakistan and Bangladesh, for example, the military and religious (Islamist) groups are major players. In Chapter 5 we will examine the economic and social consequences of elite dominance in India.

In sum, various forms of elite domination may impede or even block further democratization of most of the countries in the gray area.

POPULAR MOBILIZATION AND ORGANIZATION IN THE STRUGGLE FOR DEMOCRACY

The three propositions presented so far paint a rather gloomy picture of the current processes of transition toward democracy. But there is also a more promising aspect that concerns popular mobilization and organization. Even when elites dominate the process of transition, there is a large measure of popular activity. Ordinary men and women, workers, students, peasants, and office clerks are taking risks in distributing propaganda against authoritarian regimes, are organizing illegal groups, and in some cases are even directly assaulting the seat of power.[42]

At times different movements come together in a popular upsurge, as diverse social groups join together to form a greater whole, identifying itself as "the people" and demanding democracy and the removal of the old rulers.[43] But the point is that the process of popular mobilization and organization is more than a brief, intense outburst that dies away quickly. It begins during authoritarian rule and continues in a new setting after the first elections have taken place. In that sense, the popular mobilization behind a transition toward democracy includes two different elements: the new social movements that emerged as various types of self-help organizations during authoritarian rule and the overall resurrection of civil society that takes place during the transition.

The term "new social movement" encompasses a wide range of rural and urban associations. In the Latin American context, self-help projects concerning housing, community health care, popular education, consumer and producer cooperatives, and the defense of rural land rights have emerged, as have activities of "protest and conflict, lobbying and pressuring government agencies and politicians."[44] In Africa, similar groups, together with ethnic and kinship associations and regional or hometown groupings, have emerged.[45] The new social movements have often appeared because of the difficulties created by authoritarian rule; the self-help organizations are a strategy of survival. Some organizations in Africa are working outside the formal economy in an attempt to cater to basic needs locally or in cooperation with nearby communities.[46]

During the transition phase these new social movements are joined by human rights groups, amnesty committees, and other civil associations; in some countries in Latin America, the justice and peace commissions of the Catholic Church have played an important role. Their critique of the authoritarian regimes' abuses combined with their demands for democracy help secure basic political, legal, and social rights. Finally, during the transition process organizations of civil society that were suppressed during authoritarian rule often reappear on the political stage, including trade union associations, professional groups (lawyers, engineers, social workers, journalists, and so forth), and university associations.

The emergence of a stronger civil society in the context of the struggle for democracy has a wider perspective. These diverse associations constitute the plural society that is an important precondition for a thriving democracy because they create power centers outside the state. Moreover, their internal organizations create forums for the education of citizens in democratic decision making. In this sense, the associations act as "seedbeds of democracy."[47]

Thus the transition toward democracy creates a more open environment in which the associations of civil society have better possibilities for functioning. But the changes in society raise questions about the relationship between the movements and the emerging political parties. In many cases, the new social movements were organized in direct opposition to the state apparatus and orthodox party politics. Yet becoming active in the political parties seems to be the best way to support nascent democracy.

In Brazil, for example, this issue has divided the grassroots movements. But there is evidence that a large number of activists have gone into party politics since the early 1980s. Some observers have argued that this trend signifies a substantial strengthening of the Brazilian party system because it helps move the parties away from their earlier role as clientelistic machines centered on the advancement of individual leaders. In other words, an institutionalization of the party system is taking place that provides a stronger basis for democracy in Brazil: "The influx of movement activists into the party system . . . brought an ideological coherence and structuring to the system that is entirely novel in Brazilian politics."[48]

The pattern of popular mobilization and organization in the Eastern European transitions has been radically different from that in Latin America. In Eastern Europe, civil society associations were nearly nonexistent before the transitions began (the Church being the only major exception). All aspects of people's lives, from cradle to grave, took place in the context of organizations that were linked with the party-state apparatus. Democratic demands did not come from a medley of different associations, since such associations did not exist. The decisive dividing line was between "them," the party-state elite, and "us," the people. The democratic demands came from the people, and the organizational structures corresponded to this all-encompassing showdown; the popular organizations simply included all of the people—Civic Forum in Czechoslovakia, Neues Forum in East Germany, Solidarity in Poland. But the people's demands were for the right to organize in a civil society, to form associations outside the control and interference of the party-state. This process has now begun, with the socioeconomic changes previously discussed, and it is clearly a long-term undertaking; one scholar has ventured that it is going to take at least a generation.[49]

The flurry of popular activity briefly described here does not apply in equal measure to all current transitions toward democracy. In many cases in Africa and elsewhere, the democratic openings have been a distinctly urban affair, and popular activity has been sporadic. Yet the overall picture is clear: Transitions toward democracy are accompanied by decisive upsurges in popular mobilization and organization. A strengthening of civil society is taking place, which improves the conditions for democracy and simultaneously makes the reversal to authoritarian rule more difficult.

At the same time, however, the transition toward democracy creates a new political environment with new challenges to the popular movements. The rallying point of a common enemy—the authoritarian government—is no longer there. The challenge has shifted from cooperating in a common goal of removing old rulers to working toward institutionalizing democratic competition between the interests and visions of various groups in the population. The demands put on the leading actors to meet this challenge are different from those required during the transition itself. The actors must, according to one observer of Latin America, "demonstrate the ability to differentiate political forces rather than to draw them all into a grand coalition, the capacity to define and channel competing political projects rather than seek to keep potentially divisive reforms off the agenda, and the willingness to tackle incremental reforms . . . rather than defer them to some later date."[50] In other words, popular mobilization and organization in itself improves the prospects for democracy, but the way this popular power is utilized is a decisive element in the difficult process that will determine whether democracy will be consolidated.

CONCLUSION

In this chapter I asserted that "transition" has been replaced by "standstill," leaving countries in the gray area between full democracy and outright authoritarianism. I substantiated this claim by setting forth typical characteristics of those systems. They are electoral democracies, they are severely plagued weak states, and they are often dominated by elites. The only positive characteristic of the transitions is that the process of popular mobilization and organization in the struggle for democracy has reached higher levels than ever before, thereby making reversals to authoritarianism more difficult.

Overall, we must be skeptical about the prospects for many of the new democracies. Strong elite influence in the early stages of the move away from authoritarianism can lead to later instability and stalemate that block further development and strengthening of democracy. Furthermore, the optimal conditions for the consolidation of democracy are not present in the large majority of the new democracies. Finally, the economic and social crisis that exists in these countries makes a smooth passage toward consolidated democracy even more difficult.

Determined groups of actors may well consolidate democracy in some countries, despite the generally adverse conditions. The transition in Spain is an example, as are some of the transitions in Eastern Europe, including Hungary, the Czech Republic, and Poland. But these countries also had the external incentive of a European Community demanding democratization as a membership condition; in the developing world, only a few countries thus present reasonably favorable conditions for democratic consolidation.

The general picture is much gloomier; in most cases, the odds seem to weigh heavily against the further development and consolidation of the frail democratic openings that have taken place in recent years. These openings inspired a wealth of analysis on transitions toward democracy. Unfortunately there is an imminent risk that analysts will next find themselves addressing democratic decay rather than democratic consolidation.

4

◄○►

The Promotion of Democracy
from the Outside

Democracy promotion from the outside has a long history. Already in 1917, President Woodrow Wilson wanted to make the world "safe for democracy." He spoke of "the right of nations great and small and the privilege of men everywhere to choose their way of life and of obedience."[1] Wilson's hopes floundered on the harsh realities of international conflict and war in the following decades. It was only in the context of decolonization after the end of World War II that a more concerted effort got under way. It was sustained by the liberal belief that "all good things go together"; the idea was that an overall process of modernization and development in the newly independent developing countries would lead to democratization almost automatically. Economic growth brings with it a more differentiated social structure, a higher level of education, a stronger middle class, and a more vibrant civil society, all factors that help promote democracy.[2] However, economic growth does not necessarily lead to democracy, as demonstrated by the military regimes that ruled in many Latin American countries in the 1970s and 1980s. That experience resulted in programs directly promoting democracy and human rights.

President Reagan launched a global program for democracy promotion in the early 1980s. He proposed to "foster the infrastructure of democracy, the system of a free press, unions, political parties, universities, which allows a people to choose their own way to develop their own culture, to reconcile their own differences through peaceful means."[3] That led to the establishment of the National Endowment for Democracy. In

BOX 4.1   Democracy assistance in the 1990s

Democracy assistance mushroomed in the early 1990s. With the end of the cold war, the fall of the Berlin Wall, the breakup of the Soviet Union, and the heady acceleration of what enthusiasts were calling the "worldwide democratic revolution", aiding democracy abroad was suddenly of intense interest to U.S. policy makers. U.S. democracy aid extended rapidly in the early 1990s into Eastern Europe, the former Soviet Union, and Sub-Saharan Africa, expanded in Latin America and Asia, and crept into the Middle East. More U.S. actors plunged into the fray and onto the bandwagon. By the mid-1990s, U.S. democracy aid was all over both the developing world and the former communist world and was an accepted part of U.S. foreign aid and foreign policy.

Source: Thomas Carothers, *Aiding Democracy Abroad*
(Washington, D.C.: Carnegie Endowment for International Peace, 1999), p. 40.

the early years the endowment emphasized anticommunism in its operations, a goal that could involve supporting authoritarian, anticommunist regimes as well as programs turned against leftist groups. Thus the democracy-promoting component of the programs was sometimes constrained by other concerns. By the end of the cold war, however, a broader and more global effort to advance democracy became a central element on the agenda of both the United States and other Western democracies. Eastern Europe now became a central area for democracy assistance; many projects are also under way in sub-Saharan Africa and other regions of the Third World.

By the turn of the century, democracy promotion had become a global concern. A new global forum of more than 120 countries, the Community of Democracies, met in Warsaw in June 2000 and adopted the Warsaw Declaration which committed the countries to work together to promote and strengthen democracy. An excerpt from the declaration is set forth in Box 4.2.

More than 120 countries staunchly promoting democracy? Sounds too good to be true. In the next section, we will take up the major skeptical views of democracy promotion from the outside. I will argue that it is possible even if there are barriers. Then we will take a look at the problems and prospects of support for democratic openings with a focus on elections, as well as the considerable challenges of supporting democratic consolidation. The domestic preconditions for democracy are em-

BOX 4.2   The Warsaw Declaration — *120 countries*

The Community of Democracies affirms our determination to work together to promote and strengthen democracy, recognizing that we are at different stages in our democratic development. We will cooperate to consolidate and strengthen democratic institutions, with due respect for sovereignty and the principle of non-interference in internal affairs. Our goal is to support adherence to common democratic values and standards . . . We will encourage political leaders to uphold the values of tolerance and compromise that underpin effective democratic systems, and to promote respect for pluralism so as to enable societies to retain their multi-cultural character, and at the same time maintain stability and social cohesion . . . We will also promote civil society, including women's organizations, non-governmental organizations, labor and business associations, and independent media in their exercise of their democratic rights. Informed participation by all elements of society, men and women, in a country's economic and political life, including by persons belonging to minority groups, is fundamental to a vibrant and durable democracy.

Source: Quoted from the Warsaw Declaration,
http://www.state.gov/g/drl/rls/26811.htm.

---

phasized, as well as the delicate balance that outsiders must find between influencing the process of democratization while leaving ultimate control to insiders.

OUTSIDERS AND DEMOCRACY: A CONTRADICTION IN TERMS?

Democracy promotion from the outside may appear to be a contradiction in terms. If the core of democracy is that government authority is based in the will of the people and that the people's representatives are principally empowered by free and fair elections, how can outsiders assume influence on the process in the first place without risking the charge of being undemocratic? It is true that if foreign actors take over and completely dominate, democracy must suffer. But that is not necessarily what is meant by democracy promotion. If outsiders assist in setting up free and fair elections, if they successfully empower people in civil society by providing education, information, and other means of effective participation, then they can help promote democracy.

The idea that democracy can only grow from within and that external forces must stay out of the picture is problematic in another way. It downplays the extent to which any political system in the world is increasingly dependent on its external surroundings. For many Third World countries, a large portion of their state budget consists of development aid from external donors and their economies deeply depend on links with the world market. The end of the cold war has also demonstrated that political change in one country (or region) is a major influence on political development in other countries or regions (see Chap. 2).[4] Furthermore, what is "domestic" or "internal" as opposed to "international" or "external" is not a given. Most Third World countries acquired their domestic spheres at the time of independence. Before that, they were part of the domestic sphere of their colonial motherland; that experience left them with features more or less conducive to the pursuit of democracy. In sum, we should not exaggerate the notion of a "domestic" sphere in splendid isolation from everything else. It follows that "external" efforts toward democracy promotion are part of a larger pattern of "international" factors that influence developments in the "internal" spheres of countries.

External actors can either help or hinder democracy and democratization in specific countries, leading to the question of whether the emphasis on democracy promotion is primarily rhetoric designed to cover the pursuit of narrow national interests.[5] During the cold war, the superpowers were first and foremost looking for allies in the Third World, caring little whether their partners were democratic or not. The logic of power and national interest prevailed in the sense that the United States supported nondemocratic regimes in Latin America, the Middle East, and elsewhere; that the Soviet Union would support nondemocracy in the Third World was less surprising given its status as a totalitarian dictatorship.

As already noted, the end of the cold war removed the constraint of superpower competition and strengthened a policy trend already under way in the United States and other Western countries: an emphasis on support for democratization and human rights. Other national interests are not completely out of the picture, of course; they never are. The question is whether the new context is more conducive to real democracy promotion. Many observers answer affirmatively while others re-

BOX 4.3   Low-intensity democracy

All over the world, the United States is now promoting its version of "democracy" as a way to relieve pressure from subordinate groups for more fundamental political, social and economic change. The impulse to "promote democracy" is the rearrangement of political systems in the peripheral and semi-peripheral zones of the "world system" so as to secure the underlying objective of maintaining essentially undemocratic societies inserted into an unjust international system. The promotion of "low-intensity democracy" is aimed not only at mitigating the social and political tensions produced by elite-based and undemocratic status quos, but also at suppressing popular and mass aspirations for more thoroughgoing democratization of the twenty-first century international order.

Source: Adapted from William I. Robinson, *Promoting Polyarchy:*
Globalization, US Intervention, and Hegemony
(Cambridge: Cambridge University Press, 1996), p. 6.

---

main skeptical.[6] Some charge that the United States continues to follow the same policies it always has—support for friendly elites in other countries—with a new twist: The elites must support the basic rules of a liberal democratic game. In his thorough analysis William I. Robinson contends that the United States supports low-intensity democracy, as explained in Box 4.3.[7]

A similar charge of promoting "low-intensity democracy" has been put forward against France in the context of its policies in Francophone Africa.[8]

With the terrorist attacks of September 11, 2001, a new dimension has been added to the project of democracy promotion. On the one hand, the attacks led the United States to focus on its use of foreign aid to "promote freedom and support those who struggle non-violently for it, ensuring that nations moving towards democracy are rewarded for the steps they take."[9] On the other hand, the attacks renewed the specter of the cold war in the sense that the "war on terror" may necessitate friendly relationships with nondemocratic regimes in Pakistan, Egypt, and elsewhere. In the long term, there is no doubt that the establishment of more democratic political systems will help combat extremism and terrorism (Box 4.4). In the short and medium term, however, processes of democratization

BOX 4.4   Ways democracy can mitigate extremism

- *Avenues for peaceful change of government.* The public can remove leaders and bring about a change of policies without risking widespread political crisis.
- *Channels for dissent and political discussion.* Citizens are less likely to feel powerless.
- *Rule of law.* No need to resort to violence in order to resolve disputes.
- *Civil society.* Meaningful opportunity to affect change in your own country.
- *Free flow of information.* Help construct more responsive policies.
- *Strong states.* No need to rely on repression and an extensive military apparatus to control the population.
- *Sustainable economic and social development.* Democracy is essential to human development.
- *Needed values and ideals.* Stable and free nations do not breed the ideologies of murder.

Adapted from Jennifer L. Windsor, "Promoting Democratization
Can Combat Terrorism," *Washington Quarterly* 26, no. 3 (2003): 46-47.

can exacerbate conflict and tensions within societies. Democratization changes the prevailing power structure, threatening the political status and gains of established elites, who then seek to protect their position and access to power. In doing so, they may appeal to religious or ethnic differences to mobilize support or to create a climate of disorder and violence that discourages any further change in favour of maintaining the status quo.[10]

Furthermore, conflict and tension may also emerge as a reaction against democracy promotion efforts by Western countries.

Where do these skeptical voices leave efforts at democracy promotion? First, the charge of one-sided support for elite-dominated democracies may be somewhat overdrawn, because the distinction between elite domination and mass domination is less straightforward than it seems. Some administrations receive support from both the elites and a majority of the population, as demonstrated in Brazil, Chile, and South Africa; this broad support is reflected in their politics. Moreover, democracy introduces an element of uncertainty into the political process (see Chap. 2) by opening channels for popular pressure on the rulership that can point away from "low-intensity democracy." Even elite-dominated de-

mocracies may be pushed in the direction of more effective reform measures and in that sense become more responsive to mass needs.

Second, in some countries (e.g., Egypt) there is a need to clarify policies of democracy promotion. "U.S. foreign policy has multiple, sometimes contradictory objectives in Egypt and throughout the Middle East.
In the past, democracy advocates within USAID have felt constrained by
the policy dictate of a State Department and a White House that were
simply not interested in promoting democracy through U.S. diplomatic
or assistance efforts."[11]

Taking this into consideration, I believe a soft version of the elite support thesis applies. Western countries are most likely to support regimes
that (1) exercise leadership that is oriented toward cooperation with the
leading Western countries; (2) are liberal on economic policies, including support for economic openness toward the world market; (3) respect
private property and have an effective system of commercial law. Within
such a framework, substantial democracy promotion from the outside is
surely possible, even if there can be cases where support for "friendly
elites" is an overriding concern.

CREATING DEMOCRATIC OPENINGS

The tendency to focus on elections as a core element in a process of democratization was examined in the previous chapter. As active resistance
to authoritarian rulers intensified in many countries, it was perhaps logical that donors would support these processes by helping set up and
conduct free and fair elections. The hope was that they would become
founding elections, signaling that the transition toward democracy was
under way. Since elections involve a number of technical and administrative issues that are well-suited tasks for donors, they are appropriate
candidates for external assistance. The twelve steps of the electoral
process are identified in Box 4.5.

In this context, electoral aid has typically focused on five categories:
(1) electoral system design, (2) administration, (3) voter education, (4)
election observers, and (5) election mediation (i.e., helping hold a
fragile electoral process together and ensuring that election results are
respected).[12] External assistance is highly relevant here and is likely to

BOX 4.5   The twelve steps of the electoral process

1. Establishment of the legal framework for the electoral process
2. Establishment of adequate organisational management structures for managing the electoral process
3. Demarcation of constituencies and polling districts
4. Voter education and voter information
5. Voter registration
6. Nomination and registration of political parties and candidates
7. Regulation of the electoral campaign
8. Polling
9. Counting and tabulating the vote
10. Resolving electoral disputes and complaints
11. Election result implementation
12. Post-election handling of election material

Adapted from Jørgen Elklit, "Electoral
Institutional Change and Democratization," p. 40.

be effective. Clearly donors have helped improve a large number of elections in the past decades. Yet in many cases elections have not achieved the founding election quality referred to earlier. Are donors to blame for that?

In the early days of democracy aid, election assistance may have lapsed into "equipment dumps or a 'we will just do it for you' approach."[13] More recently, serious problems have arisen when political leaders ignored the task of election administration or even sought to undermine a decent electoral process. An example of this is provided in Box 4.6.

Yet self-seeking politicians in new democracies do not bear full responsibility for fragile elections. Donors tend to set up election systems modeled on their own systems that may be financially and politically unviable in the new context. In the words of two experienced commentators,

Poor countries need democracy, but the democratic institutions and processes they can afford are limited, different from those in use in the established industrial democracies, and probably less than ideal. In trying to promote democracy, donors need to consider the cost much more than they do now. Unfortunately, many democratization programs ignore the issue of affordability and long-term sustainability. Inspired by the sudden

BOX 4.6   Zambia's 1996 election sabotaged

The United States and other major donors, concerned about the backsliding in Zambia's transition, established a full range of aid programs to support the election. President Frederick Chiluba, however, was determined to run the elections his way, doing everything necessary to ensure his continued rule. He manipulated the drafting of constitutional amendments to exclude his only major opponent, insisted on using a controversial foreign company to handle the voter registrations system despite widespread lack of confidence in that system, treated state television as his personal campaign tool, and persecuted domestic power groups that dare to criticize. The many international aid programs bearing on the election . . . did not stop Chiluba from doing what he pleased with the elections.

Source: Thomas Carothers, *Aiding Democracy Abroad*
(Washington, D.C.: Carnegie Endowment for
International Peace, 1999), p. 130.

democratic transitions in Eastern European countries, donors approached democracy assistance much in the same way they had initially approached economic assistance—as a heroic, short-term effort to get countries through a sudden takeoff to democracy. If outside help could push a country over initial hurdles and into a democratic transition, donors did not need to worry about the sustainability of their projects. . . . The idea that most (or even many) countries would experience such a takeoff has long since been abandoned. Even the most sanguine democracy promoters now admit that successful elections are at best a first, reversible step that must be followed by the long, hard slog of consolidation.[14]

Election costs initially may not appear to be serious barriers to democratization, but in the context of poor countries they are big items on the budget. In South Africa in 1994, election costs came to some $200 million; the 1999 elections were even more expensive. Mozambique's 1994 elections cost $64.5 million, close to 4.5 percent of Mozambique's GDP. Even if the donors provided most of the funding ($59.1 million), this situation illustrates how donors helped set up elections that are not economically viable in the long run.[15] When the first-round, generously funded, high-profile elections are followed by second-round, lower profile elections with reduced funding, the quality of elections will suffer. In other words, high-cost elections are not sustainable in the long run, as

BOX 4.7   Cost and quality of elections

There are numerous examples of political parties, civic groups, and electoral institutions ceasing to exist after the prominent first election, which demonstrates that sophisticated technical assistance cannot compensate for a real will to reform on the part of the recipient country. After the 1994 election in Mozambique, the country did little to update its voter registry; as a result, a major new voter-registration exercise had to be undertaken in preparation for the local elections in 1998 . . . When external funding is not provided for later elections, the technical quality of the contest invariably suffers. The dangers of a transition from first elections lavishly funded by foreign donors to polls that are more in line with the country's capacity were seen in 1996 in Nicaragua. The path-breaking 1991 elections received considerable foreign assistance and went smoothly. The 1996 election budget was much smaller, due to a precipitous decline in international assistance. Partly as a result of this decline, the elections were poorly organized, with slow delivery of voter-identification documents and ballot papers, delays in printing ballots, and problems tallying votes.

Source: Marina Ottaway and Theresa Chung,
"Toward a New Paradigm," *Journal of Democracy* 10, no. 4 (1999): 102.

explained in Box 4.7. Poor-quality elections may lead to problems for the larger process of democratization because people's confidence in the political system may decline.

Donors can strive to introduce elections that are less technically sophisticated and cost less. There has also been a tendency to overwhelm elections with too many external observers who fly in to monitor them. Although such mistakes are being corrected; election quality ultimately depends on the "real will to reform on the part of the recipient country" (Box 4.7). That might be a much more troublesome issue to deal with. New elections often have to confront the "Chiluba problem" (Box 4.6) of unwilling rulers conspiring to remain in power, elections or not. The early phase of democratic openings and elections depends heavily on the quality of the political culture and existing institutions.

As noted in Chapter 3, elections organized in a hurry are not conducive to a stable process of secure democratization. Some commentators have concluded that elections should be postponed until a more comprehensive process of social change has taken place. "Development first, democracy later," says Robert Kaplan.[16] The demand for "stateness first," as expressed by Francis Fukuyama (Chap. 3), does not does not guarantee the creation of better preconditions for democracy and democratization. Taiwan and South Korea are examples of authoritarian rule that did involve a broad process of social change, including the creation of more effective states. But they are exceptions rather than the rule. In most cases, authoritarianism has not promoted the development of stronger states. The issue, then, is less one of postponing elections for long periods and more ensuring the best possible preparation for elections that can become solid and sustainable elements in a durable process of democratization. That this is no easy task has already been demonstrated.

THE GREATEST CHALLENGE: DEMOCRATIC CONSOLIDATION

Although external support for elections presents difficult problems, the greatest challenge for external donors is the further consolidation of democracy. We saw above that democracy aid in the 1990s was frequently focused on the elections themselves. In the 1980s, international focus tended to be on the strictly liberal aspects of liberal democracy, that is, devising a limited role for the state in an economy guided by market principles and open to international exchange. That was the version of liberal democracy behind the first generation of structural adjustment programs (SAPs). This view is not openly expressed in World Bank publications because the bank sees itself as a neutral, nonpolitical player. Even so, the state is viewed as a problem or a constraint rather than a positive player in its own economic, social, and political development. The SAPs aimed at minimizing the role of the state in society, liberalized markets, and privatized public enterprise.

Structural adjustment had some positive effects, especially in improving the conditions for agricultural production. The balance between market and state had tipped too much in favor of the state in a number of countries, and adjustment can play a constructive role in such cases.[17] But most of the time, the possible beneficial effects tended to be cancelled out by the short- and medium-term negative effects of rapidly increasing prices, rising unemployment, cutbacks in public services, and so on. In an analysis of Latin America, one scholar termed the result "market authoritarianism," referring to the emergence of political and economic

BOX 4.8   **Major tasks of democratic consolidation**

Sector	Sector Goal	Type of Aid
State institutions	Democratic constitution	Constitutional assistance Rule-of-law aid
	Independent, effective judiciary and other law-oriented institutions	Legislative strengthening
	Competent, representative legislature	
	Responsive local government	Local government development
	Prodemocratic military	Civil-military relations
State/Society nexus	Strong national political parties	Political party building
Civil society	Active advocacy NGOs	NGO building
	Politically educated citizenry	Civic education
	Strong, independent media	Media strengthening
	Strong, independent unions	Union building

Source: Adapted and modified from Thomas Carothers,
Aiding Democracy Abroad (Washington, D.C.: Carnegie Endowment
for International Peace, 1999), p. 88.

systems with some of the institutions and procedures of liberal democracy but little to offer the poor majority whose everyday problems of mere survival remain a low priority on the political agenda. [18]

Given the problems with both the election model and the market model of democratization, recent efforts have taken a broader view of the political and economic issues at stake in processes of transition. They seek to promote a state that is democratic in the sense of being responsive, legitimate, and under the rule of law; but the intention is also to promote a state that is developmentalist in the sense of being able to advance a process of economic and social development. Seen from the point of view of development, a strong state has the following capacities: institutional, technical, administrative, and political, where the latter includes legitimate authority and responsive and representative government. [19] From the point of view of democratization, this leads to the democratic consolidation emphasis. The tasks in this regard are summarized in Box 4.8.

Democratic opening and democratic consolidation overlap, as some of the tasks in the box may belong to the former as well as the latter. Certainly the challenges facing a solid process of democratic consolidation are numerous and complex. Note that each of the major items specified in the box contains its own menu of items that must be addressed in order to meet the challenge of consolidation.[20] And to this should be added the promotion of social and economic development in the context of democratic consolidation. This is a long-term undertaking with many problems and setbacks, especially given the relatively poor conditions for democratic consolidation identified in Chapter 3.

For an account of the various tasks of democracy consolidation the reader is referred to Thomas Carothers's detailed analysis.[21] We will now turn our attention to the precarious balance outside democracy promoters must establish between controlling, steering, and deciding about the appropriate road forward, versus leaving decisive control and command of the democratization process to insiders. The other item concerns the decisive importance of domestic preconditions for a successful process of democratization.

In a number of cases, outsiders have taken control of the democratization process in the countries where they operate. This is especially the case in war-torn societies with a high degree of violent domestic conflict. When Lord Paddy Ashdown took over as High Representative in Bosnia in 2002, he made the following statement:

> I have concluded that there are two ways I can make my decisions. One is with a tape measure, measuring the precise equidistant position between three sides. The other is by doing what I think is right for the country as a whole. I prefer the second of these. So when I act, I shall seek to do so in defence of the interests of all the people of Bosnia and Herzegovina, putting their priorities first.[22]

The problem is that when outsiders, even well-meaning ones, try to promote democracy by doing what they think is right, domestic political processes are not allowed to operate. Although the technical trappings of democracy may be installed, they are devoid of political substance because all the key decisions are taken by outsiders. The dilemma is highlighted in a recent analysis by David Chandler:

This high-handed approach [by Paddy Ashdown, GS], which has marked the ten years of international regulation in the tiny postwar Bosnian state, is at the centre of the neo-Wilsonian state-building dilemma discussed here: the dilemma that imposing 'good governance' policy practices, alleged to be in the interests of all, inevitably means restricting the importance of the political sphere of political party competition and policymaking by elected representatives. This dilemma is increasingly posed in the post–cold war era as international actors have a much freer hand to impose conditions on, as well as directly intervene in, states that have failed or are judged to be at risk of failure.[23]

Even if Bosnia, Kosovo, East Timor, Afghanistan, and Iraq are extreme cases in the sense that outsiders have greater control than is usually the case, the situation illustrates a core dilemma facing outsiders. If they do too little, the process of democratization may not go anywhere; if they do too much, the process suffers in other ways that may be just as serious. The greatest challenges are presented by societies subjected to military intervention, because outsiders are bound to be dominant in core areas and the transfer to local control is complicated if violent conflict persists.

The optimum situation for democracy promotion would be cases where outsiders can provide strong incentives for insiders to move in the direction of consolidating democracy. Such was the case with Eastern European countries aspiring to become members of the European Union. Because the political forces in Eastern Europe saw EU membership as an attractive prospect, they were eager to meet the demands for democracy consolidation that the EU had set up. Once membership is actually achieved, this incentive weakens. Some commentators find that this helps explain the present consolidation problems in certain Eastern European countries.[24]

The other general item to be touched on here concerns the primary importance of domestic conditions for a successful democratization process. In some developing countries—generally those at the higher levels of economic development—both political and economic reforms are doing reasonably well. Yet a few countries have achieved political and economic success despite potentially grave problems such as a high potential for ethnic conflict and a low level of economic development at

[margin note: less than optimum]

the time of independence. If we can explain why these countries have been successful in spite of the adverse conditions they face, we may have some indications about how to get around the problems discussed above. This information is important for donors because it identifies domestic conditions conducive to a successful process of democratization.

Two obvious candidates for further scrutiny in this respect are Botswana and Mauritius. On independence in 1968, Mauritius was a poor sugar economy with deep ethnic cleavages in the population; Botswana was a cattle economy with a population divided into eleven different tribes. The country had the good fortune of discovering diamonds, but several other African countries with rich mineral deposits have been unable to convert that potential into broader development. How could Mauritius and Botswana succeed economically and simultaneously establish functioning political democracies? An analysis by Barbara and Terrance Carroll answers that question. They identify the following factors behind the political and economic success of the two countries: (1) talented political leaders who were personally committed to democratic government and economic development; (2) the creation of a competent, politically independent state bureaucracy with personnel policies based largely on merit but with a composition that is reasonably representative of their societies; and (3) the development of a public realm that is capable of imposing at least modest checks on the actions of the state and is characterized by a balance between universalistic and particularistic norms and by a pragmatic recognition of the important representative role of tribal or ethnic organizations and institutions.[25]

Yet the analysis by Carroll and Carroll begs new questions. Where do talented leaders committed to democratic government and economic development come from? As they indicate, success cultivates success. Once a competent leadership has been established and demonstrates a decent track record, chances are good that capable leadership will continue. But what about that crucial turnaround phase, where success is by no means secure and leadership may turn out to be narrow-minded, egoistic, and self-serving? What is it that brings forward the Mandelas instead of the Mugabes and the Mobutus? The hopeful answer that such leadership is more or less automatically created by holding elections has not been confirmed by events. Furthermore, good and honest leaders are not enough, especially if they are committed to bad policies. Julius Nyerere of Tanzania is an honest man who has done much good for the country, but his policies of a state-led economy and a basically nondemocratic polity produced disastrous results.

As for the second item, a good bureaucracy, it is clear that early decisions were made in both Botswana and Mauritius not to sacrifice competence for "nativization" of the public service and to base recruitment on merit. At the same time, however, Carroll and Carroll stress that the Weberian ideal of an impartial public service probably should be abandoned when it comes to developing countries with many different ethnic groups in the population. In the two countries examined, care has been taken to make the bureaucracy representative of subgroups in society without sacrificing merit. Such a representative bureaucracy "is more likely to consider a wide range of views and interests in making decisions. Indeed, the simple existence of a representative bureaucracy is often taken by the public as evidence that the state is responsive and legitimate."[26]

The third item above concerns the need for a civil society to constrain the state. In many poor Third World countries there is no civil society in the traditional Western sense of the word. At very low levels of development, there is no business class, no middle class, not even a well-defined peasant class. Partly as a consequence of this, there are few autonomous, strong secondary organizations based on universal membership criteria. According to an analysis by Göran Hydén, "the prime contemporary challenge is how to restore a civic public realm. The trend of postindependence politics in most African countries has been to disintegrate the civic public realm inherited from the colonial powers and replace it with rivaling communal or primordial realms, all following their own informal rules."[27] Yet the good news from Botswana and Mauritius is that these communal and primordial realms can act as "a modest check on the power of the state."[28] In other words, under favorable circumstances traditional social forces can perform some of the functions we would normally expect in the presence of a more fully developed civil society. Some societies can sustain democracy even with weak civil societies and continuing ethnic divisions.

Perhaps the main message from these countries is the importance of competent leadership combined with some measure of institutional in-

BOX 4.9   Main findings of the 2006 democracy audit

- Lack of democratic awareness. People's knowledge about democracy is far too limited.
- Lack of democracy between elections. Democracy manifests itself mainly at election times. In the period between elections, popular participation and influence is very limited and consultations with civil society rarely take place.
- Lack of confidence. There is a significant lack of confidence in the democratic practices, institutions, and actors alike. Suspect election practices; hollow party manifestos; personalities rather than policies guiding the political space; promises but no action, are some of the expressions featuring prominently.
- Lack of poverty eradication. Poverty has not been significantly reduced and in some countries even increased. Democracy is not delivering what most people are looking for.

Source: Adapted from *Mellemfolkeligt Samvirke: The State of Democracy— Empower the Poor!* (Copenhagen: Mellemfolkeligt Samvirke, 2006). Findings based on a survey of the countries in which the NGO is active.

novation and an active civil society. The latter point squares with a recent analysis by a Danish NGO that conducted a "democracy audit" that identified a number of serious problems in the context of democratizing developing countries; they are listed in Box 4.9.

Against this background, the Danish NGO proposes a number of measures and recommends massive investment in

- Strengthening an understanding of how democracy functions among the poor and marginalized
- Strengthening local organizations as channels of influence among the poor and marginalized
- Strengthening, through support to decentralized, open, and transparent governance, the ability of government institutions to understand and address the needs of the poor and marginalized

This is an example of what is meant by a complex, long-term undertaking. There is no simple and quick way to further the consolidation of democracy. And once concrete projects are designed, new challenges are bound to emerge. For example, the above recommendations include

BOX 4.10   **Donor-funded democracy NGOs**

Most donor-funded democracy NGOs are essentially "trustee organizations" that act on behalf of largely silent constituencies. Even in democracy NGOs that have a strong membership base, a small group acts on behalf of a more passive constituency, delivering goods and services—civic education, political representation and advocacy—training that they believe to be in the group's interest. Civic-education NGOs deliver knowledge that leaders believe others need; women's organizations lobby on behalf of rural women who are rarely consulted; and legal-reform groups promote change of which the beneficiaries are mostly unaware. . . . The problem is that in emerging democracies foreign donors will not fund these trustee organizations ad infinitum, and this raises serious questions about their sustainability, given the recipient country's lack of resources.

Marina Ottaway and Theresa Chung,
"Toward a New Paradigm," *Journal of Democracy* 10, no. 4 (1999): 107.

strengthening civil society organization designed to promote the influence of the poor and marginalized. However, once external donors begin sponsoring such organizations, there is a tendency for them to emerge out of the blue in order to get a cut of the external assistance. Rather than bottom-up organizations with active and mobilized constituencies, they tend to be top-down organizations,

> usually formed at the initiative of just a few people, with programs and activities molded above all by what donors are willing to fund. If these organizations have a membership, it tends to be small and assemble after the NGO has been formed. Most importantly, it is not the membership that determines the organization's policies, but the leaders, together with the funders and the NGOs from donor countries that won the contract to 'strengthen civil society' in a particular country.[29]

Box 4.10 further characterizes these organizations.

The analysis by Ottaway and Chung proposes that external donors pay more attention to cost and sustainability. Donors need to move toward a demand-led approach, "concentrating on projects that already have the support of organized constituencies." That would mean supporting organizations with a membership ready to actively support the organization's work and to pay at least some modest dues toward covering the costs of

BOX 4.11   Democracy promotion according to Thomas Carothers

Accepting that most democracy promotion efforts do not bring about rapid or decisive change does not imply that the United States should downgrade or abandon its commitment to advancing democracy abroad. It means that democracy promotion must be approached as a long-term, uncertain venture. Policy makers must be prepared to stick to the goal for decades, to weather reversals, and to find ways to question and criticize their own methods as they go along without throwing the enterprise into disarray. The challenge, in short, is to build a cautious, realistic understanding of capabilities into the commitment. Basing a call for a democracy-oriented foreign policy on an assumption of vast American influence over other countries' political fortunes only sets up the policy edifice for a fall.

Source: Thomas Carothers, *Aiding Democracy Abroad*
(Washington, D.C.: Carnegie Endowment for International Peace, 1999), p. 351.

the organization. Possible candidates for support are labor unions, professional associations, producer groups, and women's organizations that can positively demonstrate the commitment of their members. A move in this direction would also mean that democratization is supported from the bottom up in contrast to a top-down process of reforming national institutions and practices. There are some indications that Western democracy assistance is moving in this direction, signaling that democracy promotion is increasingly seen as a long-term undertaking. [30]

CONCLUSION

This chapter has sketched the complex problems involved in supporting a process of democratization from the outside. To begin with, donors may have other interests than pure democracy promotion, and they may support models and practices that are less than suitable for the recipient countries. Even so, outsiders are able to substantially support a process of democratization. But the process is difficult and the main job must be left to insiders. Democracy cannot be taught; it can only be learned. [31] Thomas Carothers instructively summarizes the challenges to democracy promotion from the outside in Box 4.11. He specifically discusses U.S. democracy promotion, but his observations have general relevance for all donors.

Against this background, it is not too surprising that quantitative analyses covering a large number of countries report merely a small impact of democracy aid on democratization.[32] According to recent reports more troubles lie ahead, since an "assault on democracy assistance" is emerging in a number of countries.[33] There is special resistance toward programs that seek to empower civil society. Such reactions characterize many countries where "transition" has been replaced by "standstill" (Chap. 3). Gershman and Allen identify the following ways of impeding democracy assistance:

- Constraints on the right to associate and the freedom to form NGOs
- Impediments to registration and denial of legal status
- Restrictions on foreign funding and domestic financing
- Ongoing threats through use of discretionary power
- Constraints on political activities
- Arbitrary interference in the internal affairs of NGOs
- Harassment by government officials
- Establishment of "parallel" organizations of ersatz NGOs
- Harassment, prosecution, and deportation of civil society activists[34]

None of these problems make external support for democracy promotion impossible. Gershman and Allen's analysis also suggests an appropriate response to the new challenges.[35] However, conditions for promoting democracy from the outside have not been improving, even if democratic openings have occurred in a large number of countries. Both insiders and outsiders face formidable challenges in supporting a viable process of democratic consolidation. This chapter has emphasized the importance of domestic conditions conducive to the promotion of democracy. Three elements of such domestic conditions were emphasized above: (1) political leaders committed to the promotion of democracy, (2) a politically independent, merit-based state bureaucracy, and (3) a vibrant civil society capable of imposing checks on the state. The major problem for democracy promotion (and even for the general progress of democracy) is that these three conditions are not present in a large number of countries in the gray zone.

5

◄◦►

Domestic Consequences
of Democracy

Growth and Welfare?

Is democracy really worth the trouble? Does it pave the way for improvement in areas of life other than those narrowly connected with political freedom? For the people of the countries currently undergoing transition toward more democratic rule, this issue is crucial. In this chapter we will look at the consequences of democracy for economic development, defined as growth and welfare. The relationship between democracy and human rights is also examined. Whereas democracy was treated as a dependent variable in Chapter 2 as we looked for conditions favorable to the rise of democracy, it is treated as an independent variable in this chapter, where we are looking at its effects on economic development. We will consider the question of whether democracy, once it is attained, will be able to fulfill expectations of improved performance in terms of economic growth and welfare. The scholars who have addressed this issue are not all optimists; some even see a trade-off between political democracy on the one hand and economic development on the other. The main standpoints in the theoretical debate are outlined, and the empirical studies addressing the question are surveyed.[1] I reject the notion of a general trade-off between democracy and economic development, and I demonstrate why economic development and welfare improvement will not necessarily be forthcoming from the new democracies.

THE DEBATE ON DEMOCRACY AND DEVELOPMENT

Many scholars see an incompatibility between democracy and economic growth for both economic and political reasons. The economic reasons relate to the fact that growth requires an economic surplus available for investment. Such a surplus can be either invested or consumed. Hence the only way to increase the surplus available for investment is to reduce consumption. The argument is that a democratic regime will not be able to pursue policies of curbing consumption (holding down real wages) because the consumers are also voters, and they will punish the politicians at the ballot box as soon as they get the chance. Therefore, in a democratic system, political leaders have to cater to the short-term demands of the population. In the words of an Indian economist: "Under a system in which lawmakers . . . seek the approval of the electorate, the politician cannot afford . . . to follow any policies which will not produce tangible benefits for the electorate by the time the next election comes around."[2]

Accordingly, there is an incompatibility in the short- and medium run between economic growth (investment) and welfare (consumption): You cannot have your cake and eat it too. Those who have economic reservations about democracy focus on the tendency for democratic leaders to be persuaded by the electorate to promote too much welfare and consequently too little growth. Their actions jeopardize the whole basis for welfare promotion in the long run.

Those with political reservations about democracy take as their starting point the fact that economic development is best promoted when there is a high degree of political stability and order.[3] Democracy is counterproductive in this regard because it opens the already weak institutions of developing countries to pressure from different groups in society. Instability and disorder are the result, especially in countries with a massive potential for conflict stemming from numerous religious, ethnic, regional, and class divisions. Policies for change that promote long-run national development can best be advanced by governments insulated from the crisscrossing political pressures of a democratic polity. In that sense, authoritarianism is best suited for the promotion of change.[4]

Another argument scholars have made to show that authoritarian rule is better suited than democracy to promote economic development is based on the fact that increasingly the odds are being stacked against the successful promotion of development, and thus the demands for comprehensive state action to promote development have increased dramatically over time. There is more competition from the world market and a higher internal urgency for development than was the case when the industrialized Western countries went through the early phases of development. Indeed, the processes of development then and now are qualitatively different. And in this century there has been no case of successful economic development without comprehensive political action involving massive state intervention in the economy. Such concerted state action is difficult, if not impossible, under democratic conditions.[5]

The current tasks of nation building are indeed formidable. "It is almost inconceivable how the process can be managed without recourse to dictatorship," exclaimed one scholar, and his words succinctly summarize the position of those seeing an incompatibility between democracy and economic development. [6] At the same time, it must be stressed that the trade-off is temporary. Political order and governmental authority are needed during the early, difficult stages of economic development. Only at a later stage do participation and distribution become relevant. The position was summarized neatly by Gabriel Almond and G. Bingham Powell: "State building and economy building are logically prior to political participation and material distribution, since power sharing and welfare sharing are dependent on there being power and welfare to share."[7]

Critics of the viewpoint that there is a trade-off between democracy and economic growth challenge all of the above arguments. They counter the economic argument about democracy hurting growth as follows. Although it is true that a specific amount of economic surplus can be either invested or consumed but not both, the conclusion that there is thus a sharp contradiction between growth and welfare is not as straightforward as it seems. For example, public expenditure in such areas as health and education constitutes investment in human capital, which simultaneously improves welfare for large groups in the population. Indeed, many economists advocate a strategy of development that emphasizes basic human needs because in that area it is possible to have growth and welfare simultaneously.[8] If we can have simultaneous growth and welfare, the argument in favor of authoritarianism because of democracy's tendency to promote too much welfare weakens severely. Indeed, the choice may be not between growth and welfare but between two different kinds of investment policy—one that supports welfare and one that does not. And it can be argued that a democratic government is more likely to promote the former policy and an authoritarian government, the latter.[9]

Next, the critics turn the argument that democracy cannot secure order and stability on its head by pointing out that authoritarianism can mean arbitrary rule and undue interference in citizens' affairs. Only a democracy can provide the predictable environment in which economic development can prosper. Moreover, political and economic pluralism reinforce each other. Without basic civil and political liberties, citizens will not feel secure to pursue economic goals.[10] In that sense, there is a mutually reinforcing relationship between democracy and economic development.

Finally, there is the argument concerning the need for comprehensive and concerted state action in order to promote economic development. Although strong state action may be needed, it cannot be taken for granted that a strong state capable of taking a leading role in economic development efforts is necessarily a nondemocratic state. In other words, a strong state and an authoritarian state are not synonymous. A strong state has an efficient and noncorrupt bureaucracy, a political elite willing and able to give priority to economic development, and well-designed policies for pursuing development goals. A strong state in this sense is not necessarily authoritarian.[11] The argument concerning democracy's effects on economic development are summarized in Figure 5.1.

In sum, the view of the critics is not so much that democracy is invariably better suited for promoting economic development than is authoritarian rule (for there may be cases in which authoritarian rule has helped produce a faster rate of growth during certain periods). Rather, the view is that the arguments presented by those advocating a trade-off between democracy and development are not strong enough to support a general claim of the superiority of authoritarianism for economic development. In other words, democracy and development cannot be seen as generally incompatible even if cases of fast growth under authoritarian conditions exist. Some countries with harsh authoritarian rule have

FIGURE 5.1   Democracy: Does it promote or impede economic development?

	Democracy impedes economic development	Democracy can promote economic development
Economic reasons	Democracy is unable to reduce consumption in favor of investment. Thus, economic growth suffers.	Democratic investment in basic human needs is good for economic growth.
Political reasons	Democracy increases the pressure on weak institutions. Concerted state action is more difficult. The state is weak.	Democracy provides a stable political environment and the basis for economic pluralism. Democracy means legitimacy: A strong state is often also a democratic state.

not shown the economic development benefits identified by the trade-off advocates.

So is there a trade-off between democracy and development? Several analyses have been conducted in an attempt to answer this question, yet inconclusively.[12] Robert Marsh surveyed the performance of ninety-eight countries between 1955 and 1970 and concluded that "political competition/democracy does have a significant effect on later rates of economic development; its influence is to *retard* the development rate, rather than to facilitate it. In short, among the poor nations, an authoritarian political system increases the rate of economic development, while a democratic political system does appear to be a luxury which hinders development."[13] Yousseff Cohen reached a similar conclusion following his study of economic growth in a number of Latin American countries.[14]

Dirk Berg-Schlosser, in his analysis of African regimes, stated that authoritarian systems have a "strong positive effect on the overall rate of GNP growth,"[15] but he emphasized that democratic (polyarchic) regimes have done better than should be expected: "Thus polyarchic systems fare quite well both in terms of GNP growth and the improvement of the basic quality of life. They also have the best record concerning normative standards (protection of civil liberties and freedom from political repression)."[16] Dwight King reached a similar conclusion in his

study of six Asian countries: "If performance is evaluated in terms of material equality and welfare rather than growth, and is examined diachroni-
cally over the past decade and within differentiated population groups
(rural, landless, and near landless), democratic-type regimes (Malaysia,
Sri Lanka) have performed better than bureaucratic-authoritarian ones
(Indonesia, Philippines, Thailand)."[17]

In another early study G. William Dick examined the growth record
of seventy-two countries between 1959 and 1968. He categorized the
countries according to their form of government: authoritarian, semicompetitive, or competitive. He readily admitted that the data are not
unambiguous, but he maintained that the "results certainly do not support, and tend to refute, the view that authoritarian countries are universally capable of achieving faster economic growth in the early stages of
development than countries having competitive political systems."[18]

Thus, as mentioned earlier, no clear answer to the trade-off question
emerges from these studies, and there is little help to be had from the review of additional analyses, as general surveys of the field have demonstrated.[19] The question inevitably arises of whether it is a meaningful
exercise to seek a definite answer through these largely quantitative
analyses of large numbers of cases covering limited periods of time.
Dick's contribution provides a good example of the problems involved.
First, it does not seem reasonable to base such an analysis on a period
covering less than a decade. The economic performance of developing
countries varies substantially over time, and nine years is not a representative period. Second, whereas a small number of cases would not be
representative, a large number of cases invariably present problems with
regime classification. The best growth performers in Dick's analysis are
the so-called semicompetitive countries. According to the definition he
used and data from 1970, Algeria, Ethiopia, South Africa, and Nicaragua
under Anastasio Somoza are classified not as authoritarian but as semicompetitive. But one could easily argue that such regimes should be considered authoritarian, and then the whole basis for Dick's conclusion
would disappear.

The other contributions are plagued by similar problems. What we learn
from these analyses is that a large number of countries are not clearly
identifiable as democratic or authoritarian and that countries switch
among the categories, being semidemocratic yesterday, authoritarian to-

day, and semidemocratic tomorrow. Each time they make a stop in one of the categories, they lend their economic performance data, often covering only a few years, to a different argument in these investigations.

If the overwhelming methodological problems could be solved, would it then be possible to come up with a universally relevant answer to the trade-off question? I contend that it is impossible to arrive at a law-like statement concerning the effects of regime form on economic development. When theorizing the relationship, we need to be less ambitious in the middle range. Instead of attempting to make universal statements about the relationship between regime form and economic development, we should look for systematic relationships between development outcomes and *different types* of democratic and authoritarian systems, and we should study outcomes in comparable pairs of democratic and authoritarian cases.

Both of these pathways are tried out in the sections that follow. We will look first at a pair of comparable cases, one authoritarian and one democratic, and then at different types of authoritarian and democratic systems.[20]

INDIA VERSUS CHINA

India and China are large, populous, and until recently predominantly agrarian countries. Both had a rather low level of social and economic development in 1950, following India's independence in 1947 and the Chinese revolution in 1949. Today, India has a long tradition of democratic rule, whereas China has been under socialist authoritarianism since the Communist victory in 1949. India's democracy may be less than perfect and some democratic elements may have been present in China (see Chap. 1), but the overall difference is clear. Thus we have a democratic country and an authoritarian country that have had stable regime forms for more than five decades and have a number of basic traits in common, including similar levels of development in 1950. They are good candidates for comparing development outcomes of democratic and authoritarian regimes.

Economic development as defined here includes two elements, growth and welfare. Let us first look at the economic growth of China and India,

TABLE 5.1   Economic growth in China and India

Indicators	China		India
GDP per capita 2005 (constant 2000 US$)	1,445.	❯	586
Real GDP (constant 2000 US$) PPP$[a]	5,878	❯	3,118
Annual growth rate, GDP per capita (%)			
1965–1980	6.9	❯	3.6
1980–1990	10.2	❯	5.8
1991–2005	9.8	❯	3.9
Industrial growth (% per annum)			
1965–1980[b]	12.1	❯	5.5
1980–1990	11.1	❯	7.1
1991–2005	12.2	❯	6.4
Agricultural growth (% per annum)			
1950–1980[c]	3.1	❯	2.3
1980–1990	5.9	❯	3.1
1991–2005	3.9	❯	2.5

[a]PPP (purchasing power parities): An attempt to measure real GDP in terms of domestic purchasing powers of currencies, thereby avoiding the distortions of official exchange rates.

[b]Figures for China are for 1953–1982; those for India are for 1956–1979.

[c]Figures for China are for 1952–1977.

Sources: United Nations Development Programme, *Human Development Report, var. years* (New York: Oxford University Press); World Bank, *World Development Report, var. years* (New York: Oxford University Press); Pranab Bardhan, *The Political Economy of Development in India* (Delhi: Oxford University Press, 1984); Jürgen Domes, *The Government and Politics of the PRC: A Time of Transition* (Boulder: Westview, 1985).

shown in Table 5.1. We must bear in mind that growth statistics are seldom fully reliable, and there is also a problem with comparability.[21]

Although the exact magnitudes of the growth rates are in question, we have no reason to doubt that the overall growth rate in China has been substantially higher than in India. On one important dimension the difference is not dramatic—agricultural growth between 1950 and 1980. Before discussing this point further, let me make a few more general remarks on the growth figures.

The data in Table 5.1 seem to fully confirm the trade-off argument insofar as authoritarian China has achieved much higher growth rates than has democratic India. Those who believe that there is a trade-off between democracy and economic growth would probably contend that the authoritarian Chinese regime has consistently held down consumption and given first priority to investment. Moreover, the regime has been able to avoid disorder and instability while consistently pursuing a strategy of rapid change.

There is some truth to those contentions: Except during the 1980s, the Communist leadership has invariably put investment before consumption. During the twenty years from 1956 through 1976, high rates of investment were made possible only by curbing consumption to a level that, in the rural areas, was hardly above subsistence.[22] But there is more to the story. Elements other than the mere curbing of consumption contributed to the high growth rates. Most importantly, the regime initiated far-reaching reforms in industry and agriculture that made economic surpluses available for investment. The surpluses had previously accrued to private landowners and capitalists. At the same time the reforms increased productivity, especially in agriculture. Several analysts have pointed out that the lack of such basic reforms is responsible for a large, unrealized growth potential in Indian agriculture.[23] It was a main thesis in Barrington Moore's contribution that big landowners and moneylenders in India appropriate a large part of the agrarian surplus and spend it unproductively.[24] A number of scholars have echoed that opinion, and in fact the taxation of agricultural income in India has been extremely low.[25] At the same time, the strategy of the Green Revolution adopted in some areas of India from the mid-1960s aimed at increasing production through the use of modern inputs, such as chemical fertilizers, pesticides, irrigation, and new crop varieties. The strategy has increased productivity in Indian agriculture, but over time the contribution from agriculture toward industrial growth has been wanting.

Yet there are some less attractive elements in the Chinese growth record that must also be discussed. The power of the authoritarian regime to organize rapid economic growth also involves the power to commit horrible mistakes and even persevere in such mistakes, as occurred during the so-called Great Leap Forward initiated in 1958, which was supposed to boost production to the extent that China could be among the highly industrialized countries in ten years. The leap was a failure in industry and a disaster in agriculture; the production of food grain dropped in 1959 to the level of 1953. Only in 1978 did the per capita output of food grain reach the level of 1956.[26] Industrial output increased dramatically at first but then dropped sharply in 1961–1962.

Behind the rise in output was a complete lack of consideration for quality and for the cost of resources; behind the decline was increasing organizational chaos and misallocation of resources. In what can be seen only as an extreme arrogance of power, Mao Zedong, for reasons of personal pride, held on to the strategy of the Great Leap even after it had proven catastrophically wrong.[27]

The Stalinist growth strategy that was employed in China must also be questioned from a more general perspective. It gave top priority to heavy industry while holding agriculture in an iron grip, allowing few possibilities of increasing both investment and consumption in agriculture.[28] This explains the substantial difference between Chinese industrial and agricultural rates of growth before 1980. It also helps explain why agricultural growth in China before 1980 was only slightly higher than in India (if it actually was higher, given the uncertainty of the data).

The Stalinist strategy was changed after Mao's death. His successor, Deng Xiaoping, pushed for reforms in industry and agriculture aimed at decentralization and a more prominent role for market forces. Such reforms are behind the improved rates of growth in agriculture since 1980, but implementing similar reforms in industry proved complicated. China is currently in a phase of transition. Few people are interested in reverting to the old centralized economic and political structure; yet it is difficult to move toward a more decentralized, market-based system because the institutional preconditions need to be created. These include a set of rules for conducting competition and for defining what is legal and illegal. Indeed, there is a lot of "official speculation" because these rules are not clear.[29] In short, the transformation toward another system is far from smooth and easy.

Having surveyed economic growth in China and India, let us now turn to the other aspect of economic development, welfare. There is no single best indicator for the level of welfare, but the United Nations Development Program (UNDP) has in recent years published the *Human Development Report*, which ranks countries according to some of the best indicators. Drawing primarily on these data, Table 5.2 outlines welfare achievements in China and India.

Even when we allow for some uncertainty in the data, there is no doubt about the general tendency: China has achieved a substantially higher level of welfare according to these indicators than has India. China's rat-

TABLE 5.2   Welfare in China and India

Indicators	China	India
Life expectancy at birth, 2005 (years)	71.6	63.3
Adult literacy rate, 2004 (% ages 15 and above)	91	61
Under-age-five mortality rate, 2003 (per thousand)	37	87
Human Development Index rank[a], 2005	0.755	0.602

[a]The Human Development Index (HDI) is composed of three indicators: life expectancy, education, and income. For each indicator, a worldwide maximum (1) and minimum (0) are identified, and each country is then ranked according to its position. The combined average of the three positions is the HDI; the closer it is to 1, the better the ranking. See United Nations Development Programme, *Human Development Report 2006* (New York: Palgrave Macmillan), p. 394.

Source: United Nations Development Programme, *Human Development Report 2006*, http://hdr.undp.org/hdr2006; World Bank, *World Development Report 2006*.

ing in the composite Human Development Index is much better than India's (the rate of improvement for China since 1975 is higher as well). Note that the figures in the table are averages for the population as a whole. The situation for the poor is much worse. The percentage of the population living in **absolute poverty,** that is, at a minimum level of subsistence or below, is over 35 in India, and this percentage has basically remained unchanged since that country's independence. With a population increase from 360 million to more than 1 billion between 1950 and 2003, there has been, of course, a dramatic increase in the number of very poor people. The corresponding percentage of the population living in absolute poverty in China is 17.[30]

These data go squarely against the expectation that democratic regimes will give in to the electorate's demands for tangible benefits and will thus give priority to immediate welfare demands rather than the long-term goals of investment and growth. The pertinent question is, of course, the following: Why has democratic India not done more for welfare?

Improved welfare for the masses has always received high priority in the development goals of Indian governments. But it is a long way from political rhetoric to actual welfare progress. First, good wishes must be translated into concrete political initiatives, and even in this early process we see a reduction in the rhetorical "welfare impulse." Second, to the extent that political measures are actually taken, there is a lack of implementation, especially in the rural sector. Welfare measures are perceived as a threat to the elite, who then fight to keep them from being carried out. Programs concerning the redistribution of land, tenancy regulations, minimum wage regulations, and the protection of the rural poor have all been subject to such resistance.[31] And when implementation does take place, there are often leakages in the delivery pipeline. Funds end up in the hands of corrupt officials or middlemen; benefits are diverted at the end of the pipeline in favor of nontargeted, upper-income recipients.[32]

These are some of the mechanisms behind the lack of welfare progress in India. Their existence can be explained by looking at the structure of socioeconomic and political power that forms the basis of democracy in that country. Since independence, the Congress party has been dominated by three groups: the urban professionals, the bourgeoisie in industry and trade, and the rural landowning elite. It is, roughly speaking, the interests of these groups that have been looked after in the development policies of administrations led by the Congress party.[33]

Therefore, if we ask who have been the primary beneficiaries of the development policies conducted by the Indian state since independence, three groups emerge. First, there is the Indian bourgeoisie (or industrial capitalist class). With their control of a powerful nucleus of monopolistic undertakings, the bourgeoisie has enjoyed a protected domestic market and has benefited from a large public sector supplying the industrial infrastructure and other basic inputs at low prices; public financial institutions have provided a cheap source of finance, and the level of taxation has never constituted a serious burden.

Second, there are the rich farmers. They have benefited from price supports on farm products and from a wide range of subsidized inputs (e.g., fertilizer, power, and water). Moreover, the threat of land reform has been held in check, and there has been no significant taxation of agricultural income and wealth.

The third group is the bureaucracy—the professionals and white-collar workers in the public sector. The benefits to this group have come from the substantial expansion of the public sector, partly by direct intervention in the economy in the form of public enterprises and partly through indirect controls; the bureaucracy has the power to grant licenses, subsidies, and other favors sought by the private sector.

In sum, Indian governments have presided over this coalition constituting roughly the top 20 percent of the population. It is a dominant coalition, and its position is reinforced because the government policies further, in the long run, the interests of its members.[34] The development policies of the state have never significantly been outside of the orbit of what is acceptable to the dominant coalition. The mass of poor people is too unorganized, divided, and politically weak to radically change this state of affairs.

Why, then, is there a better welfare situation in China, in spite of an authoritarian government pushing economic growth? On the one hand, the reforms in agriculture promoted not only growth but also welfare. According to one estimate, the poorest fifth of rural households increased its share of the overall income from 6 percent to 11 percent as a consequence of the agrarian reform.[35] On the other hand, a number of measures were taken that were aimed directly at welfare improvement. Three areas stand out in this respect—health, education, and public distribution systems. The average health situation in the country was substantially improved by the system of public health care created in the 1950s and expanded to cover the rural areas during the 1960s. In addition to preventive care, the usual domain of public health care, this system also includes curative health care.[36] With regard to education, 93 percent of the relevant age-groups attended primary school already in 1983, and even if more than one-third of the pupils from the rural areas drop out, the level of education has been considerably improved. Finally, the social security system in China includes the distribution of food through public channels that have extensive coverage.[37]

Yet there are also welfare elements in India's favor. Democratic India has avoided policy excesses, such as China's Great Leap Forward, that can lead to catastrophic situations. There has been no severe famine in India since independence. Warning signals of such disasters are quickly relayed through a relatively free press, and the democratic government is prompted to take swift countermeasures. The situation is different in China. There was, for example, no free press to expose the failures of the Great Leap Forward and the severe famine that followed in its wake. The famine is estimated to have killed between 16.5 and 29.5 million people. At the same time, the more open political system in India has not provided protection against endemic undernutrition. Jean Drèze and Amartya Sen stated that "every eight years or so more people die in India because of its higher regular death rate than died in China in the gigantic

famine of 1958–61. India seems to manage to fill its cupboard with more
skeletons every eight years than China put there in its years of shame."[38]

In summary, the overall results in the growth and welfare aspects of
economic development put authoritarian China ahead of democratic
India. Radical reforms in China paved the way for economic development that has provided a decent level of living for the large majority. The
reforms could not have been implemented without a strong leadership
bent on pushing such policies, perhaps even to the point of using coercion against opponents. But these radical reforms have also involved
conflicts and mistaken policies that have led to human suffering and loss
of life. Moreover, the other side of the strong, determined leadership is
that it has promoted a system in which there is a blatant lack of basic
civil and political rights.

In India the democratic government has, by and large, protected the
basic civil and political rights of the people. Policy excesses have been
avoided, as have human catastrophes such as large-scale famines. And
the economic growth rates have been at a stable and respectable level.
But democracy has also maintained a highly unequal social structure
headed by a dominant elite whose members resist far-reaching change
that would benefit the poor. The lack of progress on the welfare dimension in India has led to human suffering and loss of life, not
through spectacular disasters like in China but through the quiet, con-
tinuous suffering of the 35 percent of the population who are in absolute poverty.

TYPES OF AUTHORITARIAN SYSTEMS

Comparing India and China helps shed a more nuanced light on the theoretical debate over economic development outcomes of democratic
and authoritarian regimes. Yet the debate obviously cannot be settled on
the basis of one pair of cases. The comparison says nothing about the relationship between India and China and other examples of authoritarian
and democratic regimes. Even if the India-China contrast does not give
high marks to Indian democracy, it is necessary to know more about different types of authoritarian and democratic systems and how India and
China fit into this larger picture before further conclusions can be

FIGURE 5.2   **Types of authoritarian systems and their consequences for economic development**

Regime type	Aspects of economic development		Country example
	Growth	*Welfare*	*Country example*
Authoritarian developmentalist regime	+	+	Taiwan under authoritarian rule; China
Authoritarian growth regime	+	-	Brazil under military rule
Authoritarian state elite enrichment regime	-	-	Zaire under Mobutu

drawn. I shall argue in the following sections that China is not very typical of the large group of authoritarian systems. China belongs, together with a few other countries, to a rather exclusive group of authoritarian developmentalist regimes that have been capable of promoting both economic growth and welfare. When we look at development outcomes, the large number of authoritarian systems belong to two less attractive groups: Either they push growth but not welfare or, even worse, they push neither. Regimes in this latter group do not have economic development as their main aim. Their ultimate goal is to enrich the elite that controls the state. These three main types of authoritarian systems are outlined in Figure 5.2 and are further described below.

AUTHORITARIAN DEVELOPMENTALIST REGIMES

The distinctive feature of an authoritarian developmentalist regime is its capability of promoting both growth and welfare. The government is reform oriented and enjoys a high degree of autonomy from vested elite interests. It controls a state apparatus with the bureaucratic, organizational capacity for promoting development and is run by a state elite that is ideologically committed to boosting economic development in terms of growth as well as welfare. China is an example of a socialist authoritarian developmentalist regime. There is also a capitalist variety, with Taiwan under authoritarian rule (lasted from 1949 till the early 1990s) being an example. Taiwan, like China, pushed economic development through radical agrarian reform and the transfer of economic surplus from agriculture to industry. As in China, there has been a high degree of state involvement in the economy.

But there are also dissimilarities between the two countries, some of which account for the fact that Taiwan has in several respects been more successful than its socialist counterpart.[39] First, the starting point experiences of the countries when they began to pursue economic development (around 1949) were different. China was engaged in a vicious civil war during the first half of the twentieth century; in the same period, orderly Japanese rule in Taiwan provided a basis for advances in economic development. Second, centralized planning like that in China has not been employed in Taiwan; the regime there has never attempted to monopolize economic power. The path taken by Taiwan more closely resembles the Japanese model, with a combination of market forces and private property and with heavy state guidance of the market, than the Chinese model. Taiwan seems to have struck a sound balance between the stagnation problems of "too much state" and the ultraliberalism of uncontrolled market forces that do not automatically serve the goals of economic development. Third, Taiwan has experienced a smooth process of growth and productivity increases in both agriculture, with its system of family farms, and industry, with its emphasis on light, labor-intensive manufacturing supported by public enterprises. In this process of economic reform, Taiwan has not experienced the severe setbacks due to policy failures that characterize China. The entire process has been supported by significant economic aid from the United States. China, conversely, imitated a Stalinist model of industrial growth, which overemphasized heavy industry and left little room for growth in light industry and agriculture. It followed this policy until the late 1970s. In addition, China was internationally isolated for a long period, and its ties with the former Soviet Union during the 1950s did not yield much economic assistance compared to what Taiwan received from the United States. Taiwan's developmental success paved the way for its transition to democracy in the 1990s.

At one point it was hoped that the "four tigers" in Asia (i.e., Taiwan, South Korea, Hong Kong, and Singapore) represented an authoritarian developmentalist model of development that was relevant for other countries. This has not proved to be the case. Vietnam may be a current example of authoritarian developmentalism in that it appears to follow the Chinese model of economic liberalization and growth with some equity, but it is hard to find authoritarian developmentalism in other parts of the world.[40] This indicates that there is a special combination of economic, cultural, political, and other preconditions present in the case of Southeast Asia that cannot easily be replicated elsewhere.

AUTHORITARIAN GROWTH REGIMES

The second major type of authoritarian regime is the authoritarian growth regime, an elite-dominated government that promotes economic growth but not welfare. Brazil during military rule, from 1964 until the present period of redemocratization, is a good example of this form of rule. As an authoritarian growth regime, Brazil exhibited the following characteristics: It pursued economic growth objectives with the aim of building a strong national economy (which in turn could provide the basis for a strong military power), and it respected the long-term interests (but not necessarily the immediate interests) of the dominant social forces while it looked to the workers and peasants of the poor majority for the economic surplus needed to get growth under way.

The Brazilian regime was thus an explicitly elite-oriented model of development. It rested on an alliance between local private capital, state enterprises, and transnational corporations. The elite orientation of the model applies to the supply side of development (for the emphasis was on consumer durables) as well as to the demand side (for industrialization was capital intensive, with most benefits going to a small layer of skilled and white-collar employees and workers). The poor majority did not really benefit from the growth process; many had urgent needs in the areas of basic health, housing, education, and gainful employment.[41] Redistributive reform measures, including agrarian reform, could have helped push the welfare dimension of economic development, but what the regime undertook, especially in its early years, was exactly the opposite kind of redistribution. After cutting off popular organizations from political influence, the regime dramatically reduced real wages and took other measures that led to a substantial income concentration favoring the richest 20 percent of the population.[42]

The military regimes that imposed authoritarian rule in Uruguay, Chile, and Argentina in the early and mid-1970s attempted to implement models of economic growth with similar features. However, they were less successful than the Brazilian regime with regard to economic growth. In contrast to Brazil, these countries opened their economies to external shocks through the pursuit of ultraliberal economic policies, which, before corrective measures were taken, led to deindustrialization—a dismantling of the existing industrial base.[43] Even so, these cases have a basic feature in common: The authoritarian regimes attempted to one-sidedly pursue economic growth in an alliance with elite interests.

AUTHORITARIAN STATE ELITE ENRICHMENT REGIMES

The final major type of authoritarian rule, the authoritarian state elite enrichment (ASEE) regime, promotes neither growth nor welfare; its main aim is the enrichment of the elite that controls the state. It is often based on autocratic rule by a supreme leader. Although the leader's actions may not make sense when judged by the standards of formal development goals set up by the regime, they are perfectly understandable through the lenses of patronage and clientelistic politics. Several African regimes, with their systems of personal rule as described in Chapter 2, are candidates for this category of authoritarianism. One observer has described the system as one of clan politics: "The clan is a political faction, operating within the institutions of the state and the governing party; it exists above all to promote the interests of its members . . . and its first unifying principle is the prospect of the material rewards of political success: loot is the clan's totem."[44]

The surplus that comes into the hands of the leadership through its control of the state is distributed among the clan or a coalition of clans, which in turn provide political support for the leader. It is not, of course, an equal pattern of distribution; the lion's share of the benefits accrues to the supreme leader and a small elite around him. There is no clear distinction between politicians and civil servants; the latter are actively involved in efforts to gain personal advantage from their public posts.

Thus, despite official claims to the contrary, the ruling elite takes no real interest in economic development, be it in terms of growth or welfare. The main aim of the regime is self-enrichment. Attainment of this goal requires an act of balancing against potential opponents (who are paid off or held down by force) and, as mentioned, also requires the distribution of spoils. Both may have side effects in terms of promoting either welfare or growth, but again, this outcome is not the main aim.

Zaire (now Congo) under Mobutu may be the clearest example of an ASEE regime.[45] The inner circle of the Mobutu clan consisted of a few hundred people, Mobutu's "fraternity." The lucrative positions in the state, diplomatic corps, party, army, secret police, and the Presidence were reserved for clan members.[46] They directly claimed some 20 percent of the national budget, and their income was supplemented through smuggling (diamonds and gold) and private sales of copper. Mobutu himself had a personal share in all foreign undertakings operating in Zaire, and his family controlled 60 percent of the domestic trade net. The now late Mobutu accumulated enormous wealth and was recognized to be one of the richest people in the world.

Hence, the defining characteristic of the ASEE regime is simply that the elites who control the state are preoccupied with enriching themselves. Other examples from Africa that fit this description are the Central African Republic under Jean Bedel Bokassa and Uganda under Idi Amin. Examples of authoritarian regimes outside Africa that are also candidates for the ASEE category are Haiti under François and Jean-Claude Duvalier (Papa and Baby Doc), Nicaragua under Somoza, and Paraguay under Alfredo Stroessner.

What can be learned from this typology of authoritarian regimes? First, it is not possible to generalize across authoritarian systems in terms of their capacities for promoting economic development. Different authoritarian regimes vary greatly in this respect. In this chapter, I described three main categories of authoritarian systems: the authoritarian developmentalist regimes, capable of promoting both growth and welfare; the authoritarian growth regimes, which give priority to economic growth; and the ASEE regimes, which promote neither growth nor welfare. Second, authoritarianism does not automatically generate economic growth, order, and stability, as those advocating a trade-off between democracy and economic development contend. The authoritarian growth regime is perhaps the type closest to the mainstream view of authoritarian regimes held by those advocating the trade-off. Under this system, economic growth is promoted at the expense of the welfare of the majority of the population. Although proponents of this system seem to think that a long phase of growth can provide a good basis for improving welfare at a later stage, the case of authoritarian Brazil appears to demonstrate the opposite. In that country, a number of impediments prevented the expected trickle-down effect from making itself felt on a scale at which it could significantly contribute to welfare improvement.[47] One important reason was the specific elite orientation of the growth process.

Finally, the typology sets the trade-off debate in a new light by emphasizing the diversity of authoritarian regimes. If we examine the ASEE regime in Zaire, we find that authoritarianism is definitely worse for economic development than its rumor; if we study the authoritarian developmentalist regime in Taiwan, we find that authoritarianism is much better for economic development than its rumor.

Against this background, and with the knowledge that authoritarian developmentalist systems of the Taiwan type are few and far between, it is easy to reject the argument that there is a trade-off between democracy and economic development on the grounds that most authoritarian systems do not fare any better than democracies in the area of development. And then there is no reason to sacrifice the rights and liberties associated with democracy. Before we draw final conclusions, however, let us take a closer look at different types of democracies.

TYPES OF DEMOCRATIC SYSTEMS

It is difficult to create a typology of democratic systems simply because there are few relatively stable democracies in the developing world. In many cases these systems are elite-dominated democracies; in some cases they can transform themselves into welfare-orientated social democracies. More on these different regime types and their consequences for growth and welfare follows below.

ELITE-DOMINATED DEMOCRACIES
AND SOCIAL DEMOCRACIES

Indian democracy, in the vein of the current transitions toward democracy, was achieved by an elite-dominated coalition with three main groups: the urban professionals, who founded the Congress movement in 1885; the Indian business community in trade and industry; and the rural landowning elite. The masses of poor peasants supported the elite coalition's struggle for independence and democracy; they rallied behind Gandhi as the great leading figure who would be instrumental in welding this alliance between elite groups and the poor masses. Yet the support of the poor peasants did not really upset the rural elite. Gandhi's vision of the future of Indian villages included no threat to their position, and it was the rural elite, not the landless peasants, who controlled the Congress organization at the local level.[48]

We have already seen that the continued elite dominance in the Indian democracy shaped and set the limits of what could be achieved in terms of economic development. The process of economic development has mainly served the interests of the elite groups in the dominant coalition. Respect for elite interests has impeded the capacity of Indian democracy to mobilize resources for economic growth and welfare improvement through basic agrarian and other reforms.[49]

In Chapter 3, elite domination was set forth as a major characteristic of many of the current processes of regime change. One must fear that such regimes are unwilling to carry out substantive reforms that address the lot of the poor citizens. Against the background of the Indian experience with fifty-some years of elite-dominated democracy, such fears are well founded; there has been economic development in India both in terms of growth and welfare, but as a whole the process has offered little to the mass of poor people.

But it is important to emphasize another point raised in Chapter 2: Democracy introduces a degree of uncertainty in the political process. It opens channels for popular pressure on the rulers. Even elite-dominated democracies may be pushed in the direction of more effective reform measures; in other words, they can transform into social democracies. Social democracies are systems in which more broadly based political coalitions undertake welfare-oriented social reforms. Costa Rica is a case in point.

Costa Rican democracy is based on political pacts between elite factions. The three main groups in the dominant coalition in Costa Rica are the elites in export agriculture and industry (including foreign investors) and the members of the state bureaucracy.[50] They share the benefits of a development model that is based on export agriculture and promotes industrialization and a strong role for the state in certain areas. Thus export agriculture has received constant government support, the level of taxation has been quite modest, and the agrarian reform measures have been no threat. Although industrialists have had to accept that agriculture cannot be restructured according to the specific needs of industrialization, they have received ample support in terms of external protection, low tariffs for inputs, tax exemptions, and comprehensive infrastructural support from the public sector. The bureaucracy has grown stronger through the rapid expansion of a great variety of institutions in the public sector, which has provided a solid basis from which further benefits can be negotiated from the state.

In this sense, Costa Rican democracy may be seen as "a masked hegemony of competing elites who have explicitly agreed to respect one another's interests."[51] Policies are based on a balance between different elites respecting one another's basic interests. Thus welfare programs have been kept within limits acceptable to the dominant interests. Radical social programs of structural change have been avoided, as have economic policies that could pose a serious threat to any elite faction. As a result, welfare improvements in Costa Rica rest on the shaky basis of an agrarian export economy saddled with a heavy (and increasing) foreign debt.

Yet, within these limitations, the dominant coalitions in Costa Rica have supported governments that have promoted substantial welfare programs. As shown in Table 5.3, the overall achievements of the country are fairly impressive with respect to welfare, whereas the economic growth achievements have been more ordinary. It should be noted that the average figures given in Table 5.3 conceal the existence of a fairly large group of people at the bottom of the ladder that has made much less progress. Although there are very few at the level of actual starvation, one estimate from 2006 put the share of the population living at the subsistence level at 22 percent.[52] Most of these people belong to the rural landless or the urban populations from the city slums.

TABLE 5.3   **Welfare and growth in Costa Rica**

Life expectancy at birth, 2003 (years)	78.3
Adult literacy rate (% ages 15 and above)	94.9
Human Development Index, rank 2005[a]	0.838
Real GDP per capita (PPP dollars), 2003[b]	9.606
Annual growth rate, GDP per capita (%):	
1965–1980	3.5
1981–1995	0.7
1996–2006	2.1

[a]The Human Development Index (HDI) is composed of three indicators: life expectancy, education, and income. For each indicator, a worldwide maximum (1) and minimum (0) are identified, and each country is then ranked according to its position. The combined average of the three positions is the HDI; the closer it is to 1, the better the ranking. See United Nations Development Programme, *Human Development Report 1991* (New York: Oxford University Press, 1991), p. 106.

[b]PPP (purchasing power parities): An attempt to measure real GDP in terms of domestic purchasing powers of currencies, thereby avoiding the distortions of official exchange rates.

Source: United Nations Development Programme, *Human Development Report 2006*, http://hdr.undp.org/hdr2006/ and The World Bank, *World Development Indicators*.

Still, the elite-dominated democracy of Costa Rica has fared relatively well in terms of welfare. Several elements go into explaining this achievement. First, elite rule in Costa Rica during the nineteenth and early twentieth centuries differed from that in other Latin American countries. Costa Rica did not have a system with Indians and slaves under the control of a rural elite; there was an independent peasantry, and the rural working class was free from feudal ties binding it to rural patrons. Second, the dominant stratum of coffee barons supported liberal values of freedom of the press, religious freedom, and public education. A law for free, compulsory education was passed in 1884, and the educational level of the population combined with open public debate paved the way for the formation of a variety of groups and associations that fed demands into the political system.[53] Third, the democracy established after 1948 has a reputation for fair and honest elections in a political system geared toward negotiation and compromise. In dramatic contrast to its Central American neighbors, Costa Rica disbanded its army in 1949.

Costa Rica demonstrates that elite-dominated democracies need not fare as poorly as, for example, India has fared in welfare terms. They are capable of transforming toward a higher degree of responsiveness to mass demands. But the political background of Costa Rica contains unique features that allowed it to move in this direction. The egalitarian values of the dominant coalition led to a social and political environment that was conducive to the organization of popular forces at an early stage. These elements provided the basis for welfare policies and for the formation of "a system of stable liberal democracy without parallel in Latin America."[54]

As shown by this case study, elite-dominated democracies can address welfare issues. Unfortunately, few elite-dominated democracies in the Third World have conditions similar to those that were instrumental in producing this result for Costa Rica. In Eastern Europe, there are better prospects for social democracies, since popular groups are better organized and able to make themselves heard in the political process.[55]

MASS-DOMINATED DEMOCRACIES

Mass-dominated democracies are systems in which mass actors have gained the upper hand over traditional ruling classes. They push for reforms from below, attacking the power and privilege of the elites. A prominent example of this system of rule is the Unidad Popular (Popular Unity) government under Salvador Allende in Chile between 1970 and 1973. The government was elected on a program promising massive improvement for low-income and poor groups in terms of wage and salary increases and better social and housing conditions. It also promoted measures for making the economy more effective; policies would be geared to faster growth and increased popular control. It implemented policies for the redistribution of land through agrarian reform and for the nationalization of the mineral sector, something that it also foresaw for the largest enterprises in the private sector.[56]

Although successful during its first year in power, the Unidad Popular faced rapidly growing resistance from landowners, industrialists, and the middle sectors. A process of radicalization took place in which an increasingly united opposition faced a government that was divided internally over whether it should radically confront or moderately accommodate its political adversaries. In 1973 this situation culminated in the military coup led by Augusto Pinochet. This example underlines the fragility of mass-dominated democracies; they easily lead toward hostile confrontation, which may then result in a return to authoritarian rule.

A broader perspective gives a somewhat brighter picture. Mass-dominated democracies should be able to proceed more cautiously along the road of reform than did the Unidad Popular, for example, and thereby avoid the kind of all-encompassing showdown that took place in Chile. They would then become like the social democracies mentioned above. A government that has been successful in this way is the Left Front rule in West Bengal, India, which came to power in 1977.[57] Social democracies appear to be emerging in Eastern Europe, as mentioned above. At the same time, democracies have transformative capacities. The development of most Western European democracies since the nineteenth century can be seen as a process beginning with elite-dominated systems and then gradually transforming toward social democracies. The latter, in turn, are responsible for the welfare states built since the 1930s. The process of gradual transformation paved the way for elite acceptance of social reforms and equity policies.

Thus we can see that the economic development prospects of democratic systems, especially concerning the likelihood of improvements for the underprivileged, depend on the nature of the ruling coalitions behind the democracies. Highly restricted, elite-dominated democracies may be virtually **frozen** in that their room for maneuver in addressing welfare issues and also in promoting resources for economic growth is set within the narrow limits of continued support for the status quo. If, as was argued earlier, most of the current transitions toward democracy are from above (i.e., elite-dominated), the pessimistic projection that many of the current transitions will develop into frozen democracies remains rather convincing.

Mass-dominated democracies are not frozen in this way. They contain the potential for substantial reform going against vested elite interests. But such reform may lead to confrontation with elite forces and subsequently undermine democracy itself.

Yet there is a space between these extremes where relatively stable democracy and economic progress can go hand in hand. Social democracies demonstrate that possibility. The Scandinavian welfare states are examples of countries that have transformed from elite-dominated to social democracies.

ECONOMIC PERFORMANCE IN THE CURRENT DEMOCRATIC TRANSITIONS

So far we have focused on the long-term economic consequences of elite-dominated and mass-dominated democracies. But most of the current democratic transitions have conducted economic policies for a decade or more. What can we say about their economic policy performances during that time?

A research project has addressed this question through an analysis of twelve middle-income countries: Argentina, Bolivia, Brazil, Chile, Peru, Mexico, and Uruguay in Latin America; and South Korea, Taiwan, the Philippines, Thailand, and Turkey in Asia.[58] Some of these countries have been relatively successful in their economic policy, achieving economic stability and creating good conditions for economic growth. Others have been less successful. Given the fact that all of these countries are, in varying degrees, elite-dominated democracies, that factor alone cannot explain the differences in their economic policy performances. What, then, are the main conditions influencing economic policy performance in the short term?

In their study Haggard and Kaufman single out two types of structural factors—one economic and the other political—that help answer the above question. The economic factor considers the presence or absence of economic crisis at the time of democratic takeover; the political factor considers a country's ability to organize stable political rule.

Some of the new democracies examined in this study came to power amid severe economic crisis, characterized by high inflation and macroeconomic instability. Such was the case in Argentina, Brazil, Bolivia, Peru, and Uruguay. Economic crisis creates a difficult situation for new democratic administrations, which must deal with highly adverse economic conditions; there is, however, a strong public expectation that a democratic regime will substantially improve conditions and that economic benefits will quickly flow from democratization. This dilemma creates an incentive to move toward a form of "soft authoritarianism" with a strong executive and a weak parliament as in Peru, where President Fujimori closed congress and assumed dictatorial power in 1992. Yet this has not been the general pattern. In the other countries examined, policies of adjustment and macroeconomic stability were eventually implemented under democratic conditions; given the harsh economic conditions, the new democracies performed fairly well. "Democratization per se cannot, therefore, be considered the culprit for policy failures . . . regime change may have only a slight effect on policy, or even provide opportunities for new reform initiatives."[59]

In new democracies free from economic crisis (Thailand, South Korea, Chile, and Turkey), there has been a high degree of continuity in economic policy. Democratic administrations have essentially carried on the economic policy of their authoritarian predecessors. Although such policies may favor economic stability and growth in the short term, they also contain an inherent weakness of favoring those groups in the population that supported the authoritarian regime. As a result, the weaker and poorer groups that suffered most under authoritarianism continue to be disadvantaged under democracy. The consequence may be increasing polarization, with negative effects on democracy—a variant of the elite-dominated, frozen democracy identified earlier.

As described above, the political factor influencing economic policy performance in new democracies is the ability to organize stable political rule. This ability depends on political institutions, especially on the existence of a political party system that is not too fragmented or polarized (fragmentation increases with the number of competing parties; polarization increases with growing ideological distance among parties). In the cases examined by Haggard and Kaufman, "fragmented and polarized party systems have posed major impediments to sustained implementation of reform."[60]

Successful economic policy performance, then, depends heavily on a robust party system that is not seriously fragmented or polarized. Especially in Latin America (Uruguay is an exception), the lack of such a party system has led to "profound policy failures."[61] The worst cases of fragmentation and polarization of the party system in new democracies, however, are outside of the universe of cases examined by Haggard and Kaufman: They are in sub-Saharan Africa and parts of Eastern Europe, including Russia.

There is a connection, of course, between the short-term economic policy performance of new democracies discussed here and the long-term economic performance discussed earlier. New democracies capable of weathering severe economic crisis and able to formulate and implement sound economic policies leading to stability and growth will also have the best possibilities for addressing welfare issues and thus for improving conditions for large groups of poor people. Such democracies are also most likely to consolidate democratic rule and avoid authoritarian regress.[62]

DEMOCRACY AND ECONOMIC DEVELOPMENT IN PERSPECTIVE

Drawing on the typologies of authoritarian and democratic systems presented in this chapter and the comparative considerations discussed, we can now derive some general conclusions regarding the possible trade-off between democracy and economic development. First, there is no one-to-one relationship between the form of regime (democratic or authoritarian) and development outcomes for the simple reason that different types of democratic and authoritarian regimes have different developmental capacities. If we compare the elite-dominated type of democracy with the authoritarian developmentalist regime, as was done in the comparison between China and India, it is possible to argue that there is a trade-off between democracy and development because the authoritarian developmentalist regime performs better in development than the elite-dominated democracy does. This conclusion, however, is not strong enough to support the notion of a *general* trade-off between democracy and development; other types of authoritarian systems perform worse in economic development than the authoritarian developmentalist ones, and the democratic regimes may come out on top in comparisons with those systems.

Second, with regard to the relatively few authoritarian developmentalist systems that perform well in economic development, we need to demonstrate in precise terms how and to what extent the suspension of civil and political rights can be justified in order to promote economic development. For example, although socialist authoritarianism in China may well have provided the regime with a freedom of maneuver that paved the way for the radical redistribution of land to the benefit of the rural masses, the development benefits hardly justify a blanket trade-off between development and all types of civil and political rights. As one scholar has noted, such violations as "torture, disappearances, and arbitrary executions can almost always be eliminated with no costs to development; rights to nationality and to equality before the law would also seem to have very low development costs; due process is likely to be a bit more costly, but the burden seems bearable. . . . In other words, tradeoffs of civil and political rights must be selective, flexible, and rather specific if they are to be justified at all."[63] Therefore, even in cases that seem to justify the trade-off, it is necessary to examine which rights really require suspension in order to promote development.

I have stated that the theory of a general trade-off between democracy and development must be rejected. Yet democracy and economic development do not automatically go hand in hand, mutually reinforcing each other. Behind the rejected trade-off are other, equally serious dilemmas. First, a fairly large number of both authoritarian *and* democratic systems, for different reasons, do not perform well in terms of economic development. The ASEE regimes and the elite-oriented authoritarian growth regimes, together with the elite-dominated frozen democracies, hold out few promises for a process of economic development that will benefit the large masses of poor people.

Second, the main types of democracies seem to face a trade-off between stability, on the one hand, and the capacity for promoting rapid economic development, on the other. The elite-dominated democracies hold the best prospects for stability, as the Latin American experiences illustrate; at the same time, elite dominance often means support for the status quo and little development progress. Mass-dominated democracies promise more rapid economic advance through reforms attacking vested elite interests, but instability and reversion to authoritarianism may be the result. Earlier I argued that there is a space between these extremes, as exemplified by social democracies. The question is: How many of the current democratic openings are going to move in that direction?

DEMOCRACY AND HUMAN RIGHTS

Development is concerned not only with progress in material terms (food, housing, health service, education, and so forth); it also involves a nonmaterial aspect that has to do with human freedom, identity, and security.[64] The latter can be gathered under the umbrella of human rights, especially civil and political human rights.[65] They include such elements as the prohibition of torture, the right to a fair trial and equal protection under the law, freedom from arbitrary arrest, freedom of movement and residence, and freedom of thought, conscience, and religion.

What is the relationship between democracy and human rights? Does democracy promote human rights? On first impression, the answers seem to be straightforward. The definition of political democracy given in Chapter 1 involves civil and political rights: freedom of expression, freedom of the press, freedom of association, and the right of political participation. If civil and political rights are part of the definition of democracy itself, then democracies, one would think, must promote those rights. Democracies may not always promote, for example, economic development, but at least they provide for basic civil and political rights.[66] Indeed, democracy *is* a human right according to most human rights conventions.

Two scholars have tried to sort out the relationship between political democracy as measured by Freedom House and the pattern of human rights violations based on information from the U.S. State Department. As shown in Table 5.4, the democratic ("free") systems respect human rights to a much higher degree than the authoritarian ("not free") systems.

However, further scrutiny reveals problems at two points. First, the relationship between democracy and the promotion of human rights is not perfect. Many democracies promote the basic political freedoms associated with democracy while they violate other human rights. Such violations are monitored by Amnesty International. In recent years the measures many Western countries have taken in order to combat terrorism have been criticized for not sufficiently respecting human rights.[67]

If rights are defined in the very broad sense, even the most democratic countries may not provide all of them. Attempts to measure the quality of democracy introduced in Chapter 1 have helped draw attention to this.[68] Although this information may cast some democracies in an unfavorable light, it does not seem to break the general rule that democracies show higher respect for human rights than do authoritarian systems, even if this respect may not be complete.

But there is a second problem with the contention that democracy and human rights are two sides of the same coin. It has to do with the incom-

TABLE 5.4   Democracy and human rights, 2004: Percentage of states committing selected human rights violations[a]

	Not Free	Free
Disappearances	7	2
Political/extrajudicial killings	20	16
Political imprisonment	48	11
Torture	52	29

[a]The percentage of states where the human rights violations have occurred frequently (50 times or more). No data for Afghanistan, Iraq and Iran.

Sources: Cingranelli-Richards (CIRI) *Human Rights Database* (http://ciri.binghamton.edu/index.asp) and Freedom House, *Freedom in the World.*

pleteness of many of the transitions toward democracy. Most regimes are still restricted democracies in the gray zone with insufficient respect for civil and political rights. One recent analysis concluded that "authorities do not perceive any constraints on repression or alternatives to social control until the highest levels of democracy have been achieved; up to this point authorities are not deterred nor dissuaded from violating human rights."[69] In other words, respect for human rights depends heavily on democratic consolidation and most of the current (semi)democratic regimes are not consolidated.

In addition, some transitions provoke turbulence and instability, which can also have negative effects for human rights. In this context one scholar has emphasized that not only authoritarian rule but also the breakdown of authority involves major human rights violations.[70] The breakdown of authority means weakening a government's authority (democratic or authoritarian) to the point that it is on the verge of losing power or must employ harsh means to hold on to power.[71] Thus a high number of human rights violations can be seen in crisis-ridden transitions toward democracy, where weak civilian governments are struggling to stay in authority. Political freedoms (competition, participation) may indicate fairly democratic conditions, but the breakdown of authority leads to a high degree of (other) human rights violation. Many countries fall into this category, including Colombia, El Salvador, Paraguay, Peru, Bulgaria, Nicaragua, Panama, the Philippines, Turkey, and Sri Lanka.

In summary, democracies as a rule give higher respect to human rights in general than authoritarian regimes do. Viewing countries against a comprehensive list of human rights reveals that many democracies violate some of them. Furthermore, transitions toward democracy may lead to the breakdown of authority, which can result in even higher human rights violations than would be the case under stable authoritarian conditions. Thus stable and consolidated democracy correlates with a high respect for human rights in general, but the move toward democracy and the early phases of democratic opening that characterize the majority of the current transitions can produce situations with a high degree of human rights violation.

CONCLUSION

This chapter opened by asking whether democracy is really worth the trouble and whether it paves the way for improvements in areas other than those narrowly connected with political freedoms. A number of reasons were given for an affirmative answer to both questions. Not only is democracy a value in itself, but it helps promote other civil and political rights. Although democracies do not invariably perform better than authoritarian systems in terms of economic development, the notion of a general trade-off between democracy and development was rejected. Most authoritarian systems are oppressive and perform poorly in terms of economic development. At the same time, transitions toward democracy do not guarantee a promised land of rapid economic development and a vastly improved human rights situation. The elite-dominated frozen democracies hold out few promises for a process of economic development that would benefit the large groups of poor people.

The transitions themselves can lead to instability and breakdown that involve higher human rights violation than before. Democracy does not promise automatic improvement in areas of life that are not narrowly connected with political freedoms; it creates a window of opportunity, a political framework where groups struggling for development and human rights have better possibilities than before for organizing and expressing their demands. Democracy offers opportunity but does not guarantee success.

6

⟨○⟩

International Consequences
of Democracy

Peace and Cooperation?

Will the spread of democracy mean the end of war? Can we look forward to a peaceful world focused on cooperation and mutual gain instead of conflict and violence? This chapter examines the consequences for international relations of the spread of democracy. Democracy is again treated as the independent variable; my aim is to discover its effects on relations between states and on the international system.

The scholarly debate contains widely diverging views. One school of thought expects profoundly positive consequences from the spread of democracy; another rejects the importance of democracy for international relations. We shall see that these seemingly contrasting views are not incompatible, but first we need to review the main arguments in the theoretical debate.

THE DEBATE ON DEMOCRACY AND PEACE

The argument that democracy is an important force for peace has as its most forceful advocate the German philosopher Immanuel Kant. In *Perpetual Peace*, (1795), Kant developed his argument in stages.[1] First, he pointed to a natural tendency for states to organize in the form of liberal republics because that system of rule bestows legitimacy on the political leaders and promotes popular support for the state, making it well suited

131

to face foreign threats. In other words, states not organized as liberal republics will tend to be unsuccessful.

A "liberal republic" corresponds roughly to what is called a political
democracy in this book. The establishment of democracies in the world
is a natural tendency according to Kant, although there may be setbacks.
Once established, democracies will lead to peaceful relations because
democratic governments are controlled by the citizens, who are not willing to enter into violent conflict that may subject them to bloodshed and
war. In Kant's words,

> If the consent of the citizens is required in order to decide that war should
> be declared . . . nothing is more natural than that they would be very cau-
> tious in commencing such a poor game, decreeing for themselves all the
> calamities of war. Among the latter would be: having to fight, having to pay
> the costs of war from their own resources, having painfully to repair the
> devastation war leaves behind, and, to fill up the measure of evils, load
> themselves with heavy national debt that would embitter peace itself and
> that can never be liquidated on account of constant wars in the future.[2]

One of the great social scientists of the twentieth century, Joseph Schumpeter, has also supported the notion of peaceful democracies with reasoning similar to Kant's. Schumpeter has argued that imperialist expansion
and war benefit only a minority of profiteers, arms producers, and members of the military establishment. Therefore "no democracy would pursue
a minority interest and tolerate the high costs of imperialism."[3]

There is some empirical support for these views. A study by R. J. Rummel looked at libertarian states (meaning those emphasizing political
and economic freedom) and contrasted the involvement of these "free"
states in conflict at or above the level of economic sanctions with that of
"nonfree" and "partly free" states. Rummel concluded that only 24 percent of the free states were involved in violence between 1976 and 1980,
compared with 26 percent of the partly free and 61 percent of the nonfree states. In other words, the more libertarian a state, the less its involvement in foreign violence. Rummel further claimed that a number
of previous studies support this conclusion.[4]

However, several recent studies have rejected the idea that democracies are more peaceful than other regimes. Melvin Small and J. David

Singer studied wars between 1816 and 1965 and found no significant differences between democracies and other regimes in terms of frequency of war involvement. This conclusion was supported by Steve Chan in his study of wars between 1816 and 1980; it was also supported by Erich Weede's study of war involvement between 1960 and 1980. Rummel's study lends itself to criticism because it covers only the period between 1976 and 1980. The studies based on longer periods of observation have greater credibility. In addition, Rummel's way of surveying the literature can be criticized.[5] Indeed, there is an overwhelming consensus among scholars that democracies have gone to war as often as other types of regimes have. *But with whom do they go to war? Why?*

But the debate does not end there because the empirical studies have come up with a finding that revives the optimists' hopes for democracy as a road to peace. Although democracies are as prone to war as other regimes, democracies do not fight one another: "Even though liberal states have become involved in numerous wars with nonliberal states, constitutionally secure liberal states have yet to engage in war with each other."[6] The empirical investigations provide substantial support for this claim. The observation was first emphasized by Dean Babst in 1964, and it has been confirmed in numerous studies since then.[7] Indeed, one scholar has called the assertion that democracies do not fight each other "one of the strongest nontrivial or nontautological statements that can be made about international relations."[8]

This finding, then, is the basis of the present optimism among many scholars and policy makers. Their reasoning goes as follows: The number of democracies in the world has increased rapidly in recent years and democracies do not fight one another; therefore, we can look forward to a more peaceful world with international relations characterized by cooperation instead of conflict. If their assertion is true, it seems that realism, the dominant theoretical paradigm in international relations, needs profound revision. (In this context realism is a theoretical perspective on international relations that purports to analyze the world as it really is, not as it ought to be. According to this perspective, conflict in the real world is immanent due to forces inherent in human nature and due to the way the world's populations have chosen to organize in the form of independent, sovereign states that respect no authority outside or above themselves.) With realism, the major characteristic of the international

FIGURE 6.1   Elements of Kant's pacific union among
              democracies

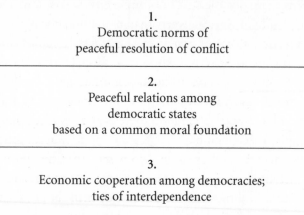

system is the lack of authority above the sovereign nation-states, which is
what makes the system an unsafe anarchy where states constantly fear violent conflict with other states. If we are to believe that democracies do
not fight one another, then a substantial modification of the notion of
anarchy leading to violent conflict is called for.

Before we move on with these issues, however, it is helpful to return to
Kant. Kant was well aware that democracy would not lead to the total
abolition of war but only to peace between democracies. His point of departure was outlined earlier: There are constitutional mechanisms in democracies that restrain them from going to war because of the burdens
war imposes on the population. Yet these restraints are effective only in
relations with other democracies. Why only there? Kant gave two reasons—one moral, the other economic. The moral reason has to do with
the common values of legitimate rights held by democracies and with
the mutual respect and understanding between democracies. These
bonds lead to what Kant called a pacific union, which is not a signed
treaty but a zone of peace based on the common moral foundation of
the democracies (see Fig. 6.1).

Peaceful ways of solving domestic conflicts are seen as morally superior to violent behavior, and this view is transferred to international relations between democracies. The beginning of cooperation starts a

virtuous circle of increasing cooperation: "As culture grows and men gradually move towards greater agreement over their principles, [these agreed-upon principles] lead to mutual understanding and peace."[9] The transparency of democracies is important for the whole process. Freedom of expression and free communication help establish mutual understanding internationally and help ensure that political representatives act in accordance with citizens' views domestically.

The economic reason is based on the benefits from international trade and investment. In the pacific union it is possible to focus on what Kant called "the spirit of commerce," the possibility for mutual gain for those involved in international economic cooperation. The development of economic interdependence that occurs when notions of autarky (self-sufficiency) are set aside and the pursuit of mutual economic gain is given priority further strengthens the pacific union.

In sum, there are three elements behind Kant's claim that democracy leads to peace. The first is the mere existence of democracies, with their culture of peaceful conflict resolution. Second, democracies hold common moral values, and the bonds they forge because of these values lead to the formation of a pacific union. Finally, the pacific union is strengthened through economic cooperation and interdependence. All three elements are necessary in order to make the connection between democracy and peace. But democracies continue to go to war with nondemocratic regimes, with which they have no common moral foundation. The peace among democracies is predicated on the existence of a pacific union with ties of economic interdependence. These elements do not come about automatically; they are formed in a process in which the early results of cooperation lead to further cooperative efforts. There can be backsliding toward the use of violence, warned Kant, but ultimately the pacific union will expand and provide perpetual peace among all democratic nations. As Kant also argued for the victory of democracy as the superior form of state, it follows that in the end, peace will prevail among all nations.

Such is the positive vision formulated by Kant. In order to evaluate its prospects in relation to the current processes of democratization, it is necessary to further examine each of the elements of Kant's vision in a contemporary context. We will look first at the domestic scene and then at international relations.

THE DOMESTIC SCENE:
FOREIGN POLICY IN DEMOCRACIES

Democracies show restraint in their relations with other democracies but not with nondemocratic regimes. Why the possible belligerence toward the latter? Although relations among the states within the pacific union are characterized by cooperation, outside the pacific union the power struggle for security, resources, and prestige continues, and the realist picture of an international system characterized by anarchy applies. Democracies have reasons to be skeptical in their relations with governments that cannot claim to represent their people. As one observer has written, "Because nonliberal governments are in a state of aggression with their own people, their foreign relations become for liberal governments deeply suspect. In short, fellow liberals benefit from a presumption of amity; nonliberals suffer from a presumption of enmity."[10] War as the outcome of conflict is always a possibility under these circumstances.

Further, democratic regimes can approach war as a crusade to promote democratic values in new areas. In this sense, "the very constitutional restraint, shared commercial interests, and international respect for individual rights that promote peace among liberal societies can exacerbate conflicts in relations between liberal and nonliberal societies."[11] This view helps explain the liberal democratic vigilance toward nondemocratic areas, especially the self-imposed "white man's burden" of bringing civilized government and order to the colonies. This ethnocentric orientation sees Western civilization as vastly superior to the "barbarian" ways of the indigenous peoples of the colonies; thus, it is only reasonable that the colonies are subject to Western leadership, by force if necessary. Later, the liberation movements of the colonies turned the argument against their Western masters. Self-government, so ran their claim, is a legitimate right according to democratic principles. This counterargument led many colonial masters to lose faith in their right to rule and provided an important impetus to the process of decolonization.[12]

Finally, it can be argued that democracy introduces an element of irrationality to foreign policy making. Instead of using prudence in international relations, democracies may succumb to whims of public opinion or moods of possible belligerence or appeasement that may result in confused, unwise policies. Walter Lippmann argued that public opinion has forced governments "to be too late with too little, or too long with too much, too pacifist in peace and too bellicose in war, too neutralist or appeasing in negotiation or too transient."[13]

This irrationality in foreign policy making introduces a dilemma in the way democracies conduct foreign affairs. The democratic framework of government is a cornerstone of the pacific union, but at the same time democracy can lead to imprudent, adventurous policies toward nondemocratic regimes. Removing this irrationality from policy making would seem to require an executive more unrestrained from the representative legislature than current executives are, but change in that direction would, in turn, threaten the basis for the pacific union. In other words, "completely resolving liberal dilemmas may not be possible without threatening liberal success."[14]

It is against the background of this dilemma that a long-standing debate is taking place about the proper amount of public influence on foreign policy in democracies. There are two main positions. Some agree with John Locke's argument that foreign policy should be left to the experts. He was supported in this view by Alexis de Tocqueville, who feared that foreign policy subjected to a democratic process would lead to poor results. A democracy, said Tocqueville in 1835, is "unable to regulate the details of an important undertaking, to persevere in a design, and to work out its execution in the presence of serious obstacles. It cannot combine its measures with secrecy, and will not await their consequences with patience."[15]

Others support the argument that a genuine democratic process in foreign policy will help secure peace. It was set forth by a British Member of Parliament, Arthur Ponsonby, in 1915, following the outbreak of World War I, which Ponsonby considered a demonstration of the failure of the elite model of decision making:

> When a small number of statesmen, conducting the intercourse of nations in secrecy, have to confess their inability to preserve good relations, it is not extravagant to suggest that their isolated action should be supplemented and reinforced by the intelligent and well-informed assistance of the peoples themselves.[16]

These views about public democratic influence in foreign policy are normative ones. What is the actual situation in the real world? There is no straightforward answer. Later in this section I shall describe some empirical studies, after first considering a possible incompatibility between democracy and the conduct of foreign policy.

One author listed three points in support of the argument that democracy and foreign policy are incompatible.[17] The first concerns the conditions involved in bargaining with outsiders. Democratic openness and the internal disunity associated with democracy can lead to poor results in a bargaining process. Furthermore, it seems wise to leave such negotiations in the hands of professionals, who are the experts in bargaining. There is also the need for secrecy, which is difficult to meet if foreign affairs are subjected to normal democratic debates and procedures.

The second point concerns the stakes involved in foreign policy. Foreign policy concerns the security of the nation, its survival. Therefore, citizens cannot afford, so runs the argument, to put such issues to open and free debates. It is critically important that they unite behind their leaders; opposition under such circumstances is not only disloyal but may imperil the safety of the nation.

Finally, there is the issue of remoteness. Foreign affairs are far removed from the bread-and-butter issues that dominate domestic politics, with their clear implications for individual citizens. It is not that foreign policy is unimportant. It is just more difficult for ordinary citizens to see the consequences that specific foreign policy options will have on their lives than it is for them to anticipate the outcome of domestic policies. It follows from this argument that foreign affairs should play an unobtrusive role in the political deliberations of the voters. The majority of voters prefer to leave such matters to the experts.[18]

An argument made against these three points is that they fail to differentiate between the various issue areas of foreign affairs. A common distinction is between the high politics of national security and the low politics of other foreign policy areas, such as those concerned with trade, finance, investment, the environment, and a host of other issues. Clearly the points concerning incompatibility between democracy and foreign policy pertain to high politics rather than low politics.[19] But even in the area of national security, it can be said that from a democratic viewpoint, it is simply unacceptable to leave issues isolated from the normal mechanisms of democracy. This normative debate, however, will not be pursued further here. In what follows, I shall focus on some empirical investigations concerning the actual degree of democratic influence on the high-politics area of foreign affairs.

One problem facing such investigations is the difficulty in determining what is actually meant in operational terms by more democracy and less democracy in foreign affairs. To what extent does public opinion influence the high-politics area of foreign policy? A study by Thomas Risse-Kappen compared the role of public opinion in the various responses of four countries—the United States, France, Germany, and Japan—to changes in Soviet foreign policy from Leonid Brezhnev (late 1970s) to Mikhail Gorbachev (late 1980s).[20] He concluded that mass public opinion does matter in each country; policy makers in liberal democracies do not decide against an overwhelming public consensus. However, the author went on to say that "there are discernible limits to the impact of the general public on foreign and security policies. Rarely does general public opinion directly affect policy decisions or the implementation of specific policies."[21] He argued that the major impact of the public is indirect, through its influence on elite groups. The elites have the final say, but elite groups whose opinions are in line with public preferences are likely to prevail. Finally, Risse-Kappen contended that variations in domestic structures in the four countries can explain the differences in policy outcomes that were sometimes seen even when there were similar public attitudes and similar influences from the international environment. Domestic structures encompass three elements: the degree of centralization of political institutions, the degree of state dominance over policy networks, and the degree of polarization between groups in society.

Other studies confirm the view that public opinion does matter in foreign affairs, albeit not in a direct manner but through influence on elite groups. Douglas Foyle's study found that the president's belief system about the value and significance of public opinion matters greatly for the ways in which the public influences foreign policy choices.[22] In sum, public opinion matters, but its importance varies according to political and policy context.

What light do these studies shed on the debate over the domestic aspect of democracy and peace? Kant asserted that democracies will be peaceful because citizens will see to it that governments stay out of bloodshed and war. It seems that the link between the views of citizens and the outcomes in terms of foreign policy decisions is much more indirect, blurred, and complex than indicated by Kant. The restraint shown by democracies in their relations with other democracies is not directly attributable to the influence of peace-loving citizens on the decision makers.[23] Thus it appears necessary to look for other factors that can help explain peace between democracies. One possibility that is consistent with Kant's general framework is that democracy promotes norms and expectations among citizens as well as among policy makers that support the peaceful resolution of conflicts with other democracies. Here the decisive element is not the constraining influence of citizens on elites; it is the democratic political culture, which holds that "states have the right to be free from foreign intervention. Since morally autonomous citizens hold rights to liberty, the states that democratically represent them have the right to exercise political independence. Mutual respect for these rights then becomes the touchstone of international liberal theory."[24] This democratic political culture rules out ideological motives for democracies to act in expansionist ways against one another and makes it extremely difficult for democratic elites to legitimate wars against other democracies.[25]

Furthermore, democracy helps remove some of the important reasons for expansionism and the quest for domination that characterized regimes before the advent of democracy. External belligerence could flow from the desire of nondemocratic rulers to bolster their domestic positions; it could also stem from the rulers' quest for recognition, not only from their own subordinates but from other states as well.[26] In democracies the recognition of leaders rests on a qualitatively different foundation. Democratic regimes may still go to war against states they regard as illegitimate, but the democratic political culture makes it difficult for them to wage war on regimes that are based on a democratic legitimacy.

The core of the matter is that democratic norms of peaceful conflict resolution and democratic norms recognizing other people's right to self-determination introduce an element of restraint or caution to the way in which democracies conduct international relations. These domestic elements of the democratic political culture help explain the peaceful relations between democracies. Below we will examine the international dimension, but first it is useful to consider this domestic element in relation to the current processes of democratization.

I have argued that the peaceful behavior of democracies is predicated on the existence of a democratic culture with well-defined norms concerning the peaceful resolution of conflict and the right of others to self-determination. If we wish to examine the prospects for a more peaceful world, a relevant question is therefore whether such a peaceful democratic culture can be found in the large number of democracies that are currently emerging.

In Chapter 2, I explained that the transition from a nondemocratic to a democratic regime is a long and complex process involving several over-lapping phases. The preparatory phase is characterized by a political strug- 3 *Phases* gle leading to the breakdown of the nondemocratic regime; the decision phase establishes clear-cut elements of a democratic order; and finally, the consolidation phase further develops the new democracy, with democratic practices eventually becoming an established part of the political culture.

The emergence of a democratic culture is a long-term process that oc- 4 curs as part of the consolidation phase. During this phase, democracy begins to be seen as "the only game in town" and both political actors and the population come to view democratic practices as the right and natural order of things. In Chapter 3, I argued that the new democracies cannot be seen as consolidated and claimed that "transition" has been replaced by "standstill," leaving most countries in the gray area between full democracy and outright authoritarianism.

It follows that the norms of a democratic culture for the peaceful resolution of conflict have not yet become characteristics of the new democracies. A closer look at some of the recent transitions confirms this view. In short, a democratic culture is beginning to emerge in the new democracies, but it is highly disputable whether this culture has grown strong enough to constitute the domestic basis for peaceful relations between democracies.

It is difficult to come up with a definite conclusion in this area because we do not know the precise extent to which a democratic culture has to be developed in order to provide the necessary basis for peaceful relations. Michael Doyle has indicated that a democratic culture (which he called "the pacifying effects of liberalism") has to be deeply ingrained before it can form the basis for peaceful relations. Bruce Russett has emphasized that "it is not clear what threshold of democratic norms and practices must be crossed to achieve peace."[27]

With the continuing high levels of domestic violence in several Latin American and African countries, there are good reasons for pessimism.

Perhaps the best one can say is that a substantial number of countries have adopted elements of a democratic culture. But it will certainly take some time before democratic culture becomes deeply ingrained, and there are no guarantees against setbacks or reversals.

The poor and institutionally feeble states in sub-Saharan Africa have experienced violent domestic conflict as a result of democratic openings.[28] As indicated in Chapter 3, it is extremely difficult to graft democracy onto weak states lacking the proper institutions as well as a level of trust and mutual acceptance among contending groups of the elite and of the population. Democratization means better possibilities for formulating demands and openly discussing conflicts; this situation can easily lead to sharper confrontations and conflicts that can potentially undermine frail democratic openings.

One such threat comes from secessionist movements, which are frequently based on ethnic groups and exist in most of the weak states in sub-Saharan Africa. When media liberalization and improved organization rights give more voice to these ethnic groups, the democratic openings can stumble into a partially self-made roadblock because a basic precondition of democracy is being questioned. That precondition concerns national unity, which, as noted in Chapter 2, means that "the vast majority of citizens in a democracy-to-be . . . have no doubt or mental reservations as to which political community they belong to." It is exactly this premise that is questioned by secessionist movements. They want their own independent political community. If that question is not resolved, democratization will most likely not proceed, and violent conflict will easily come back on the agenda.

Sadly, the two possible solutions to that question—secession and changing the minds of ethnic and other secessionist groups about which political community they want to belong to—are both difficult to translate into practice. Ethnic identities are malleable, but in many cases elite groups play on ethnic identities in ways that create more, not less, fragmentation and conflict. At the same time, the creation of a vast number of mini- or microstates is hardly a viable solution.

There may be other sources of conflict behind what appear as ethnic or nationalist demands. In weak states, political power is also economic power—the control of patron-client relationships based on the state apparatus. Control of the state means access to jobs, contracts, opportunities for illegal gain via import permits, business licenses, and so on. The elites have little incentive to create an independent market economy, and politically, democratization means a less secure control of the state apparatus and its clientelist networks. Therefore, "for the political elites of a state that is collapsing economically as well as politically, nationalism has greater rewards—it can create new, protected ponds for the fish in danger of being eaten in the larger one."[29]

In several instances early democratic openings have led to violent conflict and even state collapse. In Sudan, democratization gave political voice to the Muslim organizations of the north, leading to a sharpened conflict with the non-Muslim south. That situation led to state collapse, with warlords fighting each other for control of territory. In Angola, the 1993 elections provoked increased conflict; in Ethiopia, the Tigrean People's Liberation Front (TPLF), the dominant coalition party that took over after the Mengistu regime fell in 1991, attempted to avoid fragmentation by keeping ethnic parties out of the election. The effort did little to promote democracy but provoked a violent response from some of the ethnic groups.

In sum, stable, consolidated liberal democracy is the basis for the pacific union envisioned by Kant. But early processes of democratization and consolidated democracy are not the same. In weak states, early democratization often leads to more, not less, violent conflict. As a consequence, the process of democratization comes to a standstill or is rolled backward, and the pacific union remains a distant goal.

These considerations concern only the domestic basis for the pacific union envisaged by Kant. The possible zone of peace between democracies also contains an international dimension, which is the theme of the following section.

INTERNATIONAL RELATIONS:
COOPERATION BETWEEN DEMOCRACIES

The international dimension of Kant's vision of peace among democracies is dependent on two related elements, one moral, the other economic. I shall treat them separately in the sections that follow.

MORAL ASPECTS OF COOPERATION
AMONG DEMOCRACIES

According to Kant, the moral element that helps form the framework for peaceful relations between democratic states is based on the common principles of cooperation, mutual respect, and understanding. Such principles were emerging in Europe in the early nineteenth century, as the major European powers were expanding their territories in an attempt to achieve worldwide dominance. But it was also a time during which they worked out rules of behavior among themselves that can be seen as an important step toward the common standards envisaged by Kant.

The mutual understanding between the European powers rested on two basic principles: recognizing the absolute sovereignty of states and treating states as juridically equal.[30] On this basis, four principles came to form the framework for relations among the European states. The first was the balance of power, which has been called a systematic practice of antihegemonialism. The basic idea was that any state could be prevented from growing too powerful relative to the others as alliances shifted away from it, thereby hindering its rise to dominance. The second was the codification of a set of practices of interaction among states in order to form a body of international law. The third was the use of congresses for the purpose of settling the affairs of the European states; at the congresses, the states passed treaties to conclude wars and made additional agreements on general rules. The most important congresses were in Westphalia in 1648, in Utrecht in 1713, and in Vienna in 1815.

The fourth principle was diplomatic dialogue. The application of the first three principles—balance of power, international law, and congresses—took place through diplomatic dialogue. Taken together the four principles formed the basis of a consensus among the European states. As one observer stated, "In the eighteenth century Europe came to be regarded as a single diplomatic commonwealth made up of a number of independent states 'resembling each other in their manners, religion and degree of social improvement,' or in other words operating within the framework of a common culture."[31]

The European states never formed the full-fledged pacific union envisaged by Kant. The participating states were by no means full democracies, and the agreed-on standards of behavior did not actually rule out war between them. But Kant saw the pacific union as a long-term project, and many scholars view the standards of cooperation and common culture among the European states as an important first step. In recent scholarship, these relations between the European states have been looked on as the foundation for an international society. Hedley Bull and Adam Watson define an international society as

> a group of states (or more generally, a group of independent political communities) which not merely form a system, in the sense that the behavior of each is a necessary factor in the calculations of the others, but also have established by dialogue and consent common rules and institutions for the conduct of their relations, and recognize their common interest in maintaining these arrangements.[32]

If the relations between European states in the eighteenth and nineteenth centuries form the beginning of an international society, what is the present status of the international society? There is no uniform agreement about the common understanding that currently exists among the states in the world. Barry Buzan argues that the present international society is in fairly good shape by historical standards. He writes that we live in a "modestly cooperative, and ideologically liberal global international society."[33] Because the sovereign territorial state is nearly universally accepted as the fundamental unit of political legitimacy, diplomacy and international law continue to provide a framework for cooperative behavior.

Kant regarded free communication as an important means of establishing a common international understanding, but he could hardly have foreseen the extent to which television and other mass media have, in the words of one observer, "brought the entire world to the instant attention of any listener."[34] The possibilities for instantaneous relay of information about events that occur anywhere in the world have dramatically improved the possibility for mutual insight and understanding among peoples and leaders alike. Some scholars speculate that a new global culture is emerging on the basis of these and related developments.[35]

The collapse of the totalitarian regimes and planned economies in Eastern Europe seemingly paved the way for stronger adherence to the norms of liberal capitalism—the combination of political democracy and market economy. As stressed in Chapter 1, systems based on these principles can take many different forms. But there appears to be a higher consensus now regarding the adoption of the core features of liberal capitalism and the rejection of the two radical alternatives: fascism, on the one hand, and totalitarian communism, on the other. At the same time, global communication can also support antiliberal forces, as demonstrated by the "cartoon crisis" in Denmark or al Qaeda's use of the mass media. Countries and groups feeling threatened or marginalized by the advance of liberalism may strengthen their support of antiliberal actions.[36]

How do these developments relate to prospects for peaceful relations among democracies that are bound by a common understanding? Following Kant's logic, we would expect the general trends described here to be especially strong in relationships between democracies with a common moral foundation. Consequently we should expect norms to have developed between the democracies (especially the consolidated ones) that secure their devotion to the peaceful resolution of conflict.

This seems to be the case when we look at relations among well-established democracies in the industrialized West (including Japan). Western Europe, North America, Japan, Australia, and New Zealand have developed into a security community, which means that they constitute a group of states that do not prepare for, expect, or fear the use of military force in their relations with one another.[37] Several other factors have been important in the development of this security community, including economic cooperation and interdependence (on which I have more to say below) and the cooperation between the Western powers in the alliance against the Eastern bloc. Yet, according to Kant's reasoning, the decisive element in the development of a security community between the partners in the Western alliance would not be the negative characteristic of a common enemy, but the positive shared foundation of democracy and cooperation.[38] There have been disagreements across the Atlantic in recent years about the best ways of confronting the threat from international terrorism, but the security community has not been endangered by them; it is too deeply rooted for that to happen.[39]

However, the peaceful relations among the Western industrialized democracies have not been extended in equal measure to democracies in the developing world. Relations between the United States and some democracies in Latin America provide an illustration. On a rhetorical level, the U.S. posture has been in perfect harmony with Kant's view of democracies seeking to promote democratic values in relations with other countries ever since Woodrow Wilson set forth the rules for his administration's relationship with Latin America:

> We hold, as I am sure all thoughtful leaders of republican government everywhere hold, that just government rests always upon the consent of the governed, and that there can be no freedom without order based upon law and upon the public conscience and approval. We shall look to make these principles the basis of mutual intercourse, respect and helpfulness between our sister republics and ourselves.[40]

In recent times as well, the promotion of democratic values has been a guiding principle of U.S. policy. Yet other elements of perceived national interest continue to compete with the goal of promoting democracy. Since 1945, an important issue has been the struggle against communism and Soviet influence in Latin America; another concern has been the protection of U.S. economic interests in the region. Both of these issues have been allowed to override concerns for the promotion of democracy on several occasions. A situation that occurred in the Dominican Republic in the early 1960s provides an instructive example. At that time a democratically elected leadership under Juán Bosch set out to promote economic development through nationalist economic policies that went against certain American economic interests in the country. When Bosch faced the prospect of a military coup, Washington decided to opt for the authoritarian military dictatorship. John F. Kennedy formulated the alternatives as follows: "There are three possibilities, in descending order of preference, a decent democratic regime, a continuation of the Trujillo regime [a military dictatorship], or a Castro regime. We ought to aim at the first, but we can't really renounce the second until we are sure we can avoid the third."[41] Thus, fearing that the democratic Bosch regime would develop into a Castro regime, the United States found it safest to back a military dictatorship. This action aided the struggle against communism and protected U.S. economic interests, but it hardly promoted democracy or economic welfare policies in the Dominican Republic.

A situation in Chile provides another example. In 1970, Chile already had a record as one of the most stable and long-lasting democracies in Latin America. The elections in 1970 brought Salvador Allende, a candidate backed by the left-wing Popular Unity coalition, to power. His economic policies that aimed at redistributive reforms went against vested elite interests, including U.S. economic interests in Chile. Washington had attempted to prevent Allende's election by supporting rival candidates; after his election the United States actively supported the opposition in politics, the Chilean military, and elsewhere.[42] The confrontation culminated in the military coup led by Augusto Pinochet in 1973, which paved the way for more than fifteen years of harsh military dictatorship in Chile. It is not that the United States went to war with Allende's Chile; in that sense, Kant has not been disproved. Yet, as events in Central America in the 1980s show, covert involvement with economic, military, and expert support for opposition forces can develop to a point where the distinction between such activities and open war becomes academic.

Some observers fear that attempts to promote democracy or a capitalist market economy in the context of a war on terror can lead to illiberal and nondemocratic results.[43] Chapter 4 includes a discussion of the current problems in promoting democracy from the outside.

In any case, these and other examples are hardly evidence of democracies developing peaceful relations based on a common understanding and a shared moral foundation. How will relations between the dominant democracies in the north and the democracies in the south develop in the future? Optimistically, because Soviet communism is no longer a threat, the dominant liberal democracies led by the United States ought to be able to accept and support a broad variety of democratic openings in the south. They no longer need be viewed as prospective allies of a world communist movement because no such movement exists. On the other hand, post–cold war developments also give reason for concern. Perceived national security or economic interests may help preserve the existence of "standstill" regimes in the gray zone, and that would not be supportive of a democratic peace.

What about the new democracies in Eastern Europe? Even though the leading Western democracies would clearly prefer liberal democratic systems in Eastern Europe, the scenario of Western support for an Eastern European Trujillo is not likely. The countries of Eastern Europe share a common past with Western Europe and are in the process of reviving old relationships and building new ones. If the process of democratization proceeds successfully, most of the East European countries can become full members of the security community that has developed in Western Europe.

Bulgaria, Estonia, Latvia, Lithuania, Poland, Hungary, the Czech Republic, Romania, Slovakia, and Slovenia are already members of the European Union; Macedonia, Croatia, and Turkey are candidates for membership. Most of these countries are also now NATO members. The future may well see the North Atlantic Treaty Organization transformed into a Democratic Europe Treaty Organization.[44]

At present, the major problem in Eastern Europe is Russia. Continued democratization in Russia ought to facilitate its full incorporation into the community of liberal democracies, but we saw in Chapter 3 that such as process is not automatically forthcoming. In the best possible scenario, further democratization in Russia and the expansion of ties with the West will resolve the problem. In the worst-case scenario, democratization in Russia will suffer setbacks and the threat of a new cold war will develop.[45]

In this section we have considered Kant's vision of peaceful cooperation between democracies based on their common moral foundation. I argued that such cooperation has indeed developed among the consolidated democracies of the north. In regard to relations with democracies in the Third World, the picture is less clear. In Eastern Europe, several countries have good prospects for joining a larger European security community, but the relationship between such a community and Russia is much less certain.

ECONOMIC COOPERATION BETWEEN DEMOCRACIES

The final element on which Kant's pacific union among democracies rests is economic cooperation. When countries focus on the spirit of commerce, they develop mutually beneficial ties of trade and investment as well as other economic relations. These ties in turn strengthen the bonds of peace among them.

The flow of goods and money, as well as of people, messages, and other forms of intercourse between countries, has increased by leaps and bounds since the time of Kant's writing. As early as 1975, one scholar argued that "recent decades reveal a general tendency for many forms of human interconnectedness across national boundaries to be doubling every ten years."[46] Since the early 1980s, world trade has consistently grown faster than world economic output, and international financial flows have grown even faster than trade.

According to Kant's reasoning, economic exchange should be especially well developed among democracies. This premise also appears to hold true when we look at the Western industrialized democracies, but clearly other factors, such as the size of the national economy, the level of economic development, and the nature of economic policies, may play an even larger role than the presence of democracy in determining levels of economic intercourse. Thus a country with a large national economy, like the United States or India, has a relatively smaller share of its total economic activity crossing its borders than countries with small economies, like Costa Rica and Denmark. Countries with high levels of economic development, like Japan and Sweden, have much greater external trade than countries with low levels of development, such as Nepal and Bangladesh. Finally, countries with development policies aimed at the international market, for example, Taiwan and the Netherlands, have greater levels of external activity than countries with more inward strategies, such as Syria and North Korea.

In any case, there is a high degree of mutual economic dependence, or economic interdependence, among the Western industrialized democracies in Europe, North America, Japan, Australia, and New Zealand. These countries not only meet the third of Kant's conditions for a pacific union—economic cooperation—but also the other two discussed earlier, namely, a developed democratic culture with norms of peaceful conflict resolution and a common moral understanding cultivated on this basis. As indicated above, they constitute a security community, which can be described as a contemporary version of Kant's pacific union. Karl Deutsch defined a security community as follows:

A *security community* is a group of people which has become "integrated." By *integration* we mean the attainment, within a territory, of a *"sense of* _community_" and of institutions and practices strong enough and wide-spread enough to assure . . . dependable expectations of "peaceful change" among its population. By sense of community we mean a belief . . . that common social problems must and can be resolved by processes of "peaceful change."[47]

Although there may be problems within security communities that require change, and there may also be economic and other areas of conflict between the members, the groups within the security communities are determined to promote change and solve conflicts through peaceful means.

In Eastern Europe, the countries that have been or are on the way to being admitted to the EU will benefit in economic terms. In contrast, the less developed Eastern European countries with looser ties to the community will have more of a dependent status in the realm of economic relations.

North-south relations are characterized by the south's unilateral dependence on the north, not by a mutually beneficial interdependence. Some southern countries actually benefit from economic cooperation with the north. An example of the first situation is the weak states, many of which are in sub-Saharan Africa. Exports from these countries consist of one or a few primary products, and the economies are highly dependent on imports of technology-intensive products. Foreign direct investment (FDI) is not interested in coming into these countries because stability and attractive conditions of operations are lacking; less that 2 percent of total FDI goes to sub-Saharan Africa. [48] And when investment does come in, it has monopolistic control over pockets of the economy with few or no links to local undertakings. Under such conditions, FDI produces little economic development; and sure enough, the "investors" coming in are often arms dealers, gold and diamond traders, drug smugglers, and so on. This is dependence more than interdependence.

Compare this situation to the more advanced states in East Asia and to some extent in Latin America. Taiwan is a good example. Economic development in Taiwan has proceeded in three stages: import substitution in the 1950s, export of manufactured consumer nondurables (toys, shoes, and so on) in the 1960s, and a process of industrial upgrading with emphasis on producer goods and some consumer durables (electronic equipment and computers) beginning in the mid–1970s. When FDI started coming in on a larger scale, Taiwan had already built an industrial base—a local industrial capacity that could benefit from relationships with outside investors and upgrade its capacity in the process.[49] Participating in economic globalization via FDI helped Taiwan produce economic development. In sum, mutually beneficial economic ties, the third pillar of the democratic peace, have developed in some parts of north-south relations; in other parts, one-sided dependence persists.

In this section we have focused on Kant's third basic pillar of a pacific union, mutually beneficial economic cooperation between democracies. Such economic cooperation has indeed developed between the stable, industrialized democracies—Western Europe, North America, Japan, Australia, and New Zealand. Economic relations are mixed in the south, however; the weak states are highly dependent while the more developed and capable states benefit from economic interdependence. The weak fledgling democracies in the south have not developed the mutually beneficial ties of economic cooperation with the leading democracies in the north that in Kant's view constitute the third necessary element of a pacific union. Prospects for some parts of the south, and for Eastern Europe, are better, especially for the countries that join, or have already joined, the European Union.

PEACE AS A RESULT OF DEMOCRACY?

In the past, democracies have not gone to war against one another, and the number of countries in the world with some measure of democracy has increased rapidly in recent years. Will the spread of democracy bring a bright future with peace among nations? The theoretical foundation for expecting peace to flow from democracy is set forth by Kant. His pacific union of democracies rests on three pillars: (1) the mere existence of democracies with their culture of peaceful conflict resolution, (2) the moral bonds that are forged between democracies on the basis of their common moral foundations, and (3) the democracies' economic cooperation toward mutual advantage.

This chapter has analyzed each of these conditions in the light of recent processes of democratization. It is evident that a democratic culture with norms of peaceful conflict resolution has not yet developed in the new democracies. Democratic norms must be ingrained before the domestic basis of the pacific union becomes secure, and such development of the political culture will take some time. Setbacks toward nondemocratic forms of rule may occur.

The second condition is the existence of common moral bonds between democracies. Such relations have indeed developed among the consolidated democracies of the West. Furthermore, there is reason to believe that the security community made up of stable Western democracies can be extended to include the new democracies in Eastern Europe, provided there are no severe setbacks in their further democratization. The democracies in the south may or may not be included. In the past, the United States sometimes turned against democracies in the south to protect its perceived economic or security interests. And there are fears that attempts at democracy promotion can lead to illiberal or nondemocratic results. In that case the pacific union would not be strengthened.

The final condition is the existence of mutually beneficial economic cooperation between democracies. Such economic interdependence is highly developed among the consolidated democracies in the West. Several of the new democracies in Eastern Europe are set to be integrated into these economic networks through their anticipated membership in the European Union. For the weakest countries in the south, however, continued one-sided economic dependence rather than interdependence is the order of the day, even after the end of the cold war.

In short, the emergence of a global pacific union embracing new and old democracies cannot be taken for granted. The pacific union with its zone of peace is a long-term project. For the project to be successful, the three basic conditions laid down by Kant must be met by all of the democracies. Presently a pacific union is a reality among the industrialized democracies in the west, and it may expand to include new democracies in the east. Yet many of the democracies in the south fail to meet at least two of Kant's conditions. And instead of exhibiting further progress, they may backslide toward authoritarian rule.

What are the consequences of the existence and expansion of a pacific union for the dominant theoretical paradigm in international relations—realism? In the next section of this chapter, we will examine the realist critique of Kantian visions.

PEACEFUL DEMOCRACIES AND REALIST THOUGHT

Kant's vision of a peaceful world of democracies belongs to a liberal school of thought; critics prefer "idealism" because they view liberal claims with skepticism and/or are doubtful about the claims made. The basic notion of liberal thinking is that conflict and violence can be overcome if the world is organized according to liberal principles. With regard to Kant, the right principle would be democracy. This notion is rejected by *realist* thought, which claims to analyze the world as it really is, not as it ought to be. In the real world, conflict is inherent in human nature; moreover, the world's populations have chosen to organize in the form of independent, sovereign states that respect no authority outside or above themselves. Early realist thought stressed the quest for power and dominance stemming from human nature as the basic reason for conflict; more recent contributions, often termed neorealist, emphasize the structure of the state system as the reason. Sovereign states respect no higher authority than themselves. There is no world government. In that sense, *anarchy* is the basic feature of the state system. With anarchy conflict is imminent. States cannot really trust one another, and one state's attempt to increase its safety by increasing its weaponry is a threat to the security of other states. In short, as long as there are sovereign nation-states, there will be a state system characterized by anarchy. As long as there is anarchy, there is a threat of violent conflict. In such a system, perpetual peace as envisaged by Kant is impossible.

It is not surprising, therefore, that according to many neorealists, "the theory of peace-loving democracies is unsound."[50] In this section I shall discuss the neorealist critique of Kant's visions of democracy and peace. I argue that the distance between an analysis based on Kant, on the one hand, and neorealist thought, on the other, is much smaller than implied by the critique. Anarchy need not have the dreadful consequences claimed by Mearsheimer and others; the results described in the discussion of democracy and peace are, to a considerable extent, compatible with neorealist analysis.

Mearsheimer started by attacking the logic of Kant's theory linking democracy and peace.[51] The first point, as already noted, concerns the assertion that democracies are more peaceful than authoritarian systems because the people are more hesitant to go to war. Mearsheimer noted that democracies are as likely to fight wars as are other systems and that the public may be no less prone to war than authoritarian leaders are. His arguments do not contradict Kant; the general propensity for war among democracies has already been noted, as well as the fact that the restraint democracies show in their relations with other democracies is not directly attributable to the influence of peace-loving citizens on the decision makers. The suggestion offered here was that a democratic culture of peaceful conflict resolution introduces an element of restraint in the ways in which democracies conduct international relations. This element alone is not enough to explain the existence of a pacific union among democracies, but it is one of the three basic pillars of the pacific union.

The next point made by Mearsheimer criticizes the notion of a common moral foundation between democracies—the second pillar of a pacific union. He claimed that moral bonds compete with other factors that are drawing toward conflict instead of peace, such as nationalism and religious fundamentalism. However, Kant did not deny the existence of these countervailing elements. He claimed, quite simply, that in relations between democracies with ingrained democratic cultures the competing factors likely will *not* override the common moral foundation.

We now reach the central point in Mearsheimer's attack on the logic of the theory. His argument is worth quoting in full:

> The possibility always exists that a democracy will revert to an authoritarian state. This threat of backsliding means that one democratic state can never be sure that another democratic state will not change its stripes and turn on it sometime in the future. Liberal democracies must therefore worry about relative power among themselves, which is tantamount to saying that each has an incentive to consider aggression against the other to forestall future trouble. Lamentably, it is not possible for even liberal democracies to transcend anarchy.[52]

Kant was well aware of the possibility of reversals toward authoritarian rule. That countries may backslide does not invalidate the notion of a pacific union. The decisive point in Mearsheimer's argument is his inference that because there can be setbacks, anarchy remains the basic feature of the system regardless of the form of regime of the state.

In a system of independent states (i.e. in an anarchy) one state must always fear what the other state is going to do and what the dangerous consequences can be. This is what neorealists mean when they speak of an unbreakable link between anarchy and self-help: Anarchy prevails with all its dreadful but unavoidable consequences of imminent conflict and risk of war.

A system of independent states is indeed characterized by anarchy. But must anarchy always lead to self-help, competition, power balancing, rivalry, and possibly open war, as neorealists claim? Alexander Wendt has argued that anarchy need not necessarily have such consequences. Independent states can be friends as well as rivals. There are different "cultures of anarchy"; Wendt suggests three major ideal types of anarchy: Hobbesian, Lockean, and Kantian.[53] In the Hobbesian culture, states view each other as enemies; the logic of Hobbesian anarchy is "war of all against all." States are adversaries and war is endemic because violent conflict is a way of survival; this corresponds to the neorealist image of self-help. But there are other possibilities. In a Lockean culture, states are rivals; in a Kantian culture of anarchy, states view each other as friends, settle disputes peacefully, and support each other in the case of threat by a third party.[54]

This line of thinking is supported by the notion of a pacific union. Friendly anarchy rests on the three forces discussed above: (1) the culture of peaceful conflict resolution in consolidated democracies, (2) the moral bonds that are forged between democracies on the basis of their common moral foundations, and (3) the democracies' economic cooperation toward mutual advantage. And it has certainly developed among a group of consolidated democracies.

Mearsheimer would object that such security communities may not endure; there can be backsliding toward raw forms of anarchy. He is right; Kant also feared such developments. But on the one hand, neorealist predictions about increasing rivalry in Europe and across the Atlantic after the end of the cold war (because the common enemy ceased to exist) have not held up.[55] On the other hand, friendly anarchies can also develop toward further integration, as is currently happening, according to many observers, in the European Union. The EU has taken over political functions that earlier were the prerogative of the single member states; if the process of integration continues along that path, the result will be a European federation, a new state, and a new unitary international actor. Anarchy between the old member states would be ruled out for good because they would have accepted a new central authority above the old nation-states. Contrary to Mearsheimer's argument, it thus appears that it *is* possible for liberal democratic states to completely transcend anarchy. It must be emphasized, however, that the process of integration in the EU has not yet reached this point.

This takes us to the second path of criticism brought forward by Mearsheimer. He claimed that history provides no clear test of the theory that democracies do not fight one another. He raised the objection that several democracies have come close to fighting, for example, the United States and Allende's Chile. If Wilhelmine Germany is classified as a democracy or a quasi-democracy, then World War I becomes a war among democracies. But these examples stem from the misunderstanding that the pacific union springs into existence between countries as soon as they meet a minimum definition of democracy. It does not. The pacific union is built on a domestic foundation of democratic culture as well as two international pillars. All three must be in place for the pacific union to be effective, which is not the case in these examples.

Mearsheimer's other complaints concern the lack of a proper test of the theory of peaceful democracies. He pointed to the fact that democracies have been few in number over the past two centuries, and thus there have not been many situations in which two democracies have been in a position to fight each other. When there actually have been such situations, Mearsheimer claims that "there are other persuasive explanations for why war did not occur. . . . These competing explanations must be ruled out before the peace loving democracies theory can be accepted."[56]

If a proper test of the theory must meet Mearsheimer's requirement that all other competing explanations be ruled out, then there will never be a proper test of the theory. In international relations, as well as in other branches of social science, there is no possibility for laboratory experiments. One cannot in a clinical fashion isolate one single factor, such as democracy, from all other possibly relevant factors in the relationships between countries. Even so, the preservation of the security community in Western Europe after the end of the cold war can be seen as a strong test in favor of the pacific union. The security community rests on the three pillars discussed above. Those pillars are not affected by the presence or absence of a Soviet threat. Thus Kant's theory would predict that the security community will remain intact and perhaps even expand due to the process of democratization in Eastern Europe. This is exactly what appears to be going on.[57]

CONCLUSION

Kant's theory of a pacific union between democracies is basically sound. But it is a mistake to think that a pacific union automatically extends to include countries that are in the early stages of a long and tenuous process of democratization or countries that have not developed moral bonds and economic interdependence. The current processes of democratization increase the possibilities for a larger pacific union but do not guarantee its realization. In particular, the prospects are poor for the inclusion of the new democracies of the south in the pacific union. Critics argue that proponents of the theory have a problem because it is not sufficiently clear.[58] They have a point; on the one hand, it is no easy task to specify exactly when the culture of peaceful conflict resolution is in place, or when the moral bonds between democracies have developed. Nor is it easy to pinpoint the exact mechanisms that lead from democracy to peace. On the other hand, the general claim of a relationship between consolidated democracy and peace appears difficult to reject.

Conclusion
The Future of Democracy and Democratization

At the end of 2006, ninety countries were free according to the Freedom House rating. This is great progress since the cold war days; in 1972 only forty-three countries were free.[1] Today, popular support for democratic ideals is strong, even in societies once thought to embrace different values.[2] There appears to be only one major ideological opponent to the dominant idea of political democracy—Islam. But even if Islam is strong in several Asian and African countries, the current Islamic revival must be set against the quest for modernization that is also at work in the heartland of Islam. In Saudi Arabia, the process of modernization has given democratic ideas a much stronger foothold.[3] At the same time, Algeria and Iraq demonstrate the paradoxical situation that democratic openings can bring forward less democratic Islamic forces at elections, which had been suppressed during earlier periods of authoritarian rule. But there would not appear to be a general incompatibility between Islam and democracy as demonstrated by the cases of Indonesia and Turkey. In sum, the idea of democracy is robust at the global ideological level. Few authoritarian rulers would actively defend traditional, authoritarian modes of rule.

At the same time, there are numerous unconsolidated and fragile democracies in the gray zone, and in most of these countries the prospects for further democratic advance are not good. Chapter 2 explained how frail elections, lack of "stateness," and elite domination have helped replace "transition" with "standstill." Chapter 5 demonstrated that economic development and a general improvement of human rights are not necessarily forthcoming from the regimes in the gray zone. Chapter 6 stressed that a more peaceful world will not necessarily be secured as a result of the present processes of democratization; the inclusion of all democratic openings in a pacific union is a long-term project with no guarantee of success.

Against this background, the immediate challenge is not so much one of imminent authoritarianism as it is of democratic consolidation—of pushing forward with the many institutional, economic, and social changes that will help develop and deepen democracy in the shallow systems in the gray zone. The process of deepening democracies is one aspect of consolidation; the other aspect is the change whereby democracy becomes a firmly embedded element of the political culture.

There is no theory that identifies the most important factors influencing the consolidation of democracy. One line of analysis argues that the level of economic development is a crucial factor in whether a country will sustain democracy: "Once a country is sufficiently wealthy, with per capita income of more than $6,000 a year, democracy is certain to survive, come hell or high water."[4] Yet the vast majority of recent democratic openings are below this economic level. What are the relevant factors for evaluating their chances for democratic consolidation? Scholars addressing that question have come up with a number of different factors, some of which were introduced in the discussion of typical features of the current democratic transitions (Chap. 3).[5] The most important factors are:

- The legitimacy of political rule
- Institutionalized political parties
- The strength of civil society

Consolidated democracies are based on a type of legitimacy that Max Weber called "rational-legal": The population accepts the authority of rulers, not because of their individual personalities but because the system under which these rulers won and now hold office is accepted and supported. For this type of legitimacy to prevail, the source and the agent of legitimacy must be separated. This separation is especially difficult in systems in which the regime's legitimacy rests on people's faith in a personal leader—what Weber called charismatic legitimacy. The personal rule systems in Africa, for example, are based on charismatic legitimacy, which makes democratic consolidation in these countries especially difficult because the whole basis for legitimate rule has to be changed. The more such nonrational-legal forms of legitimacy are entrenched, the higher the difficulties for democratic consolidation become.[6]

Political parties are crucially important for democratic consolidation. As mentioned in Chapter 2, democracy introduces an element of uncertainty into the political process. Democratic institutions, especially a stable party system, help reduce uncertainty because "actors know the rules and have some sense of how to pursue their interests. . . . Democracy has generally thrived when party systems have been institutionalized."[7] Institutionalization of political parties means that they emerge as valued and stable elements in the political process.[8] Many countries in Africa, Asia, and Latin America do not have institutionalized party systems; such a situation hinders the process of democratic consolidation for these countries. In contrast, countries possessing such a system (e.g., Uruguay and Chile) have much better prospects for democratic consolidation.

Political parties are part of the larger system of nonstate institutions called **civil society**. An effective civil society—a dense network of associations, interest groups, civil rights groups, and so forth—is the best basis for the consolidation of democracy. In a number of new democracies, including those in Eastern Europe and Russia as well several in the south, an effective civil society is only in the process of being established; these countries thus face additional problems for democratic consolidation.

In sum, there are numerous unconsolidated democratic openings in the world with differing prospects for further consolidation. The three factors mentioned above are among the most important determinants of those prospects. In countries where those factors are favorable, we should expect a high success rate for democratic consolidation, and vice versa. In several countries, all three factors mitigate against democratic consolidation; in others, the picture is mixed. Few, if any, countries present optimal prospects for democratic consolidation on all three counts—hence the current skepticism regarding prospects for democratic consolidation.

The previous considerations concern prospects for the new democracies. One final item important to the future of democracy must be considered: the possibilities for continued democratic vitality in established industrialized democracies. Robert Putnam has argued that there is currently a loss of "social capital" in the United States, which has negative implications for the quality of democracy. Social capital is defined as "features of social organization, such as trust, norms, and networks, that can improve the efficiency of society by facilitating coordinated actions."[9] The leading indicator of social capital is the rate of membership in voluntary associations such as amateur soccer clubs, choral societies, hiking clubs, and literary circles. But the rate of membership in the United States has dwindled. Bowling clubs experienced a 40 percent decrease in membership between 1980 and 1993, yet the number of bowlers during the same period increased by 10 percent. Putnam argues that a decrease in social capital will undermine the vitality of democracy in many established, wealthy democracies.

Although critics see theoretical and empirical problems in Putnam's analysis, his contribution makes the important point that democracy cannot be taken for granted; indeed, it is a process that requires continued input to remain vital and vigorous.[10] One crucial element in maintaining a democracy, therefore, is the active participation and support of a large majority of the population. With the decline in social capital, the conditions for such popular participation and support are increasingly adverse.

The other great challenge to established democracies comes from globalization. As indicated earlier, globalization may undermine democracy because national governments have less and less control over what happens within their own borders. National leaders may be elected according to democratic principles, but what does that mean if they are powerless to manage national affairs because economic and other developments are decided by outside factors beyond their control?

In approaching this question, we should keep in mind that the extent to which globalization challenges a country's democracy remains a highly debated issue. Some scholars argue that the negative effects of globalization are exaggerated—that there is still much scope for democratic governments to influence national development. Some politicians use globalization as an excuse to do nothing, to be passively reactive rather than actively regulate and manage national affairs.[11] Other scholars emphasize that globalization profoundly affects conditions for national policy making by limiting the maneuvering room of national governments.[12]

How can democracy face the challenge of globalization? To resort to isolation—an attempt to shut off the country from outside influence—is hardly a way out. Globalization involves cooperating with others for mutual benefit; the industrialized democracies, for example, reap great welfare benefits from globalization. In an increasingly interdependent world, isolation does not benefit a nation's welfare, as demonstrated by North Korea and a few other countries.

One way to proceed is via regional integration, as in the case of the European Union. The EU cooperation can be understood as an attempt by member countries to reclaim some of the influence they lost at the national level due to globalization. Intense cooperation means an opportunity to influence policies in other countries and thereby directly affect the external environment at the European level.

From a democratic point of view, however, EU cooperation has two problems. First, while in gaining influence over others, countries must in turn allow other countries increased influence over them. But how much can small countries decide in regional and international forums? Are they not forced to follow the lead of the big and strong? Second, the European Union's supranational governance structures are in some ways less democratic than those of national parliaments and governments. Some have identified a "democratic deficit" in the EU, since many decisions are left to bureaucrats with no clear democratic mandates or to divisions such as the Commission, whose deliberations are not sufficiently open to democratic scrutiny. One solution is to proceed to a more genuine federal structure in EU cooperation, but member countries are not ready to go that far.

The case of the European Union demonstrates the difficulty of constructing supranational levels of governance that live up to the demands of democracy we have learned to expect from our experiences at the national level. If such regional organizations have problems with democracy, we must expect even larger problems in attempts to construct global structures of governance. Some scholars have begun to contemplate a "cosmopolitan democracy with global reach," in which countries respond to the challenge of globalization by constructing a new democratic framework based not on the nation-state but on a democratic structure with global reach.[13] David Held, for example, envisions a cosmopolitan democracy in which people have multiple citizenships: "They would be citizens of their immediate political communities, and of the wider regional and global networks which impacted upon their lives."[14]

The idea of multiple citizenship indicates the magnitude of the challenge to democracy contained in processes of globalization. Remember the precondition for democracy spelled out by Rustow in Chapter 2: People must have no doubt or mental reservation about which political community they belong to. Contrast this with the notion of multiple citizenship, in which people are citizens of local, national, regional, and supraregional communities. Cosmopolitan democracy is different from the democracy in an independent country. In that sense, globalization presents a profound challenge to democracy, especially in the developed, industrialized parts of the world—which are also the most touched by processes of globalization. In short, the process of democratization must continually face and respond to new problems. A democracy can never be taken for granted, not even in those parts of the world where it appears to be the most firmly entrenched.

The discussion of the meaning of democracy in Chapter 1 formed the basis for our assessment of the processes of democratization under way in many countries and for our examination of the possible domestic and international consequences of democracy. A basic dilemma was identified at the beginning: The democratic openings we have seen are a mere beginning; by no means do they ensure further democratization or additional benefits in the form of economic development, peace, and cooperation. Each of the main chapters in this book has focused on a particular aspect of this dilemma. If the final assessment leans toward the pessimistic scenario, bear in mind that the future is not predetermined; expected patterns of development can be fundamentally changed by the actions of individuals and groups on both the local, the national, and the global level. It is the sum of these actions that determines whether democracy will prevail. At any rate, ways must be found to deepen and strengthen democratic processes. Today's fragile democracies are a step ahead compared to yesterday's authoritarian systems, but real, sustained progress will require further democratic consolidation.

Discussion Questions

Chapter 1

1. Give a broad and a narrow definition of democracy. What are the arguments in favor of each?
2. According to Julius Nyerere, the former president of Tanzania, the struggle for freedom in the third world is primarily a struggle for freedom from hunger, disease, and poverty, and not so much a struggle for political rights and liberties. Is that true?
3. In 1968, a progressive military junta took power in Peru and did away with the democratic political system. The military government went on to launch far-reaching measures against poverty and poor living conditions for the mass of people than had been seen under the previous, democratic government, which was dominated by an elite. Which regime is more democratic: the one that upholds a democratic political system that serves mainly an elite or the one that does away with the democratic political system in order to promote the struggle for freedom from hunger, disease, and poverty?
4. Discuss the assertion that only a capitalist system can provide the necessary basis for democracy. Which elements in capitalism can promote democracy and which can impede it?

Chapter 2

1. Some conditions favor the rise of democracy more than others. What are the most favorable economic, social, and cultural conditions for democracy? Why is it that democracy may emerge in places where the conditions for it are adverse?
2. Are there common factors that help explain the recent surge toward democracy in many countries, or must democratization in different parts of the world be explained in different ways?
3. Outline the phases in the transition toward democracy according to the model described in this chapter and apply the model to your own country. Is your country a consolidated democracy? How much time has passed since the move toward democracy began in your country? What light does the experience of your own country shed on the process of transition to democracy in other countries?

4. What arguments can you make for and against the assertion that democracy has made great progress in the world during the past decade?

Chapter 3

1. What is the role of elections in a process of democratization. Are elections a certain indicator that democratization is under way? Why or why not?
2. Define the concepts of "delegative democracy," "illiberal democracy," "feckless pluralism," and "dominant power politics." Are they similar or different concepts?
3. What is a weak state and why is democratization in weak states difficult to achieve?
4. Discuss popular mobilization in the struggle for democracy. Is it always helpful for furthering democratization?

Chapter 4

1. Is democracy promotion from the outside a contradiction in terms? Discuss pros and cons.
2. What is "low-intensity democracy"? Is this a version of democracy supported by the United States?
3. Costly elections are a problem, say Ottaway and Chung, but low-budget elections are also a problem. Discuss.
4. Look at the findings of the democracy audit in Box 4.9. Can these problems be solved in the short and medium run?
5. Will democratization succeed in Iraq? Why or why not?

Chapter 5

1. What arguments have been made in support of the view that there is a trade-off between political democracy and economic development? What arguments have been made against this view? Is it possible to settle this debate on the basis of empirical analysis?
2. This chapter identifies three types of authoritarian systems: authoritarian developmentalist regimes, authoritarian growth regimes, and authoritarian state elite enrichment regimes. Which of these types is the most common today? How do elite-dominated and mass-dominated democracies differ?
3. Sometimes the early process of democratization brings neither welfare improvement nor a better human rights situation. Is this an argument against democracy?

Chapter 6

1. What are the arguments in favor of the contention that the spread of democracy will lead to the creation of a peaceful world? Democracies have not gone to

war with one another in the past, but they have been few in number and have not had many opportunities to fight one another. Is this knowledge about the past a reliable guide to the actions of democracies in a future world where, possibly, a large number of democracies can come into conflict?

2. Do you think that a more peaceful world will result from the current processes of democratization? Why or why not?

3. Evaluate current developments in the European Union in light of the debate between a Kantian view and Mearsheimerian neorealism. Which of these views, if either, is correct?

Notes

Chapter 1

1. David Held, *Models of Democracy*, 3rd ed. (Cambridge: Polity, 2006), pp. 1–2.

2. Held, *Models of Democracy*, pp. 23–28. See also Arne Naess et al., *Democracy, Ideology, and Objectivity* (Oslo: Oslo University Press, 1956), p. 78 n.

3. Held, *Models of Democracy*, p. 26.

4. C. B. Macpherson, *The Life and Times of Liberal Democracy* (Oxford: Oxford University Press, 1977), p. 13.

5. Isaiah Berlin, "On the Pursuit of the Ideal," *New York Review of Books*, March 17, 1988, p. 15.

6. Held, *Models of Democracy*, p. 59.

7. Goran Therborn, "The Rule of Capital and the Rise of Democracy," *New Left Review* 103 (1977): 3.

8. Macpherson, *Life and Times*; see also Held, *Models of Democracy*.

9. Macpherson, *Life and Times*, pp. 35–39; Held, *Models of Democracy*, p. 77.

10. Held, *Models of Democracy*, p. 77.

11. F. A. Hayek, *The Constitution of Liberty* (London: Routledge & Kegan Paul, 1960), p. 103.

12. Held, *Models of Democracy*, pp. 201–206.

13. Quoted from Held, *Models of Democracy*, p. 204.

14. Held, *Models of Democracy*, p. 79.

15. Held, *Models of Democracy*, p. 86.

16. Macpherson, *Life and Times*, pp. 60–64; Held, *Models of Democracy*, pp. 88–93.

17. Quoted from Held, *Models of Democracy*, p. 46.

18. Macpherson, *Life and Times*; Carole Pateman, *Participation and Democratic Theory* (Cambridge: Cambridge University Press, 1970); Pateman, *The Problem of Political Obligation: A Critique of Liberal Theory* (Cambridge: Polity, 1985).

19. Pateman, *Participation and Democratic Theory*, p. 110.

20. See the discussion of Marx in Held, *Models of Democracy*, pp. 96–122.

21. Robert A. Dahl, *A Preface to Economic Democracy* (Cambridge: Polity, 1985), p. 60.

22. See, for example, Carol C. Gould, *Rethinking Democracy* (New York: Cambridge University Press, 1988).

23. For a summary of the debate, see Charles F. Andrain, "Capitalism and Democracy Revisited," *Western Political Quarterly* 37, no. 4 (1984): 652–664. See also David Beetham, *Democracy and Human Rights* (Cambridge: Polity, 1999).

24. Joseph Schumpeter, *Capitalism, Socialism, and Democracy* (1942; London: Allen & Unwin, 1976), p. 260.

25. Held, *Models of Democracy,* p. 264.

26. Held, *Models of Democracy,* p. 278.

27. Carl Cohen, *Democracy* (New York: Free Press, 1971), p. 109 n.; see also Gavin Kitching, *Rethinking Socialism: A Theory for a Better Practice* (London: Methuen, 1983), p. 49; and Beetham, *Democracy and Human Rights,* chap. 1.

28. Francis Fukuyama, "The End of History?" *National Interest* 16 (1989): 3–18.

29. Robert A. Dahl, *Democracy and Its Critics* (New Haven: Yale University Press, 1989), p. 221.

30. Dahl prefers the term "polyarchy." In an early contribution, he noted that there is no country in which these conditions are perfectly satisfied; Robert A. Dahl, *Polyarchy* (New Haven: Yale University Press, 1971), p. 3. In *Democracy and Its Critics* he further extends the definition of democracy so that the conditions of polyarchy are necessary but not sufficient for the fullest democracy.

31. Larry Diamond, Juan J. Linz, and Seymour Martin Lipset, eds., *Democracy in Developing Countries,* vol. 2, *Africa* (Boulder: Lynne Rienner, 1988), p. xvi.

32. For attempts at differentiation in African and Latin American countries, respectively, see Richard Sklar, "Democracy in Africa," *African Studies Review* 26, no. 3–4 (1983): 11–25; and Karen L. Remmer, "Exclusionary Democracy," *Studies in Comparative International Development* 20, no. 4 (1985–1986): 64–86. See also note 44.

33. Dahl, *Polyarchy,* p. 4.

34. Tatu Vanhanen, *Prospects of Democracy: A Study of 172 Countries* (London: Routledge, 1997).

35. Freedom House, *Freedom in the World 2006* (Lanham, Md.: Rowman & Littlefield, 2006). For another comprehensive survey, see the Polity IV dataset at www.cidcm.umd.edu/icr/polity/polreg.htm. For a general survey of attempts to measure democracy, see *Studies in Comparative International Development* 25, no. 1 (1990).

36. Freedom House, *Freedom in the World 2006.*

37. See the list of questions in Freedom House, *Freedom in the World 2005,* pp. 780–782.

38. Gerardo L. Munck and Jay Verkuilen, "Conceptualizing and Measuring Democracy: Evaluating Alternative Indices," *Comparative Political Studies* 35, no. 1 (2002): 5–34.

39. Mark Gasiorowski, "The Political Regimes Project," *Studies in Comparative International Development* 25, no. 1 (1990): 112 n.

40. UNDP, *Human Development Report 2006* (New York: Oxford University Press, 2006). This report is published annually.

41. Kitching, *Rethinking Socialism,* p. 48.

42. UNDP, *Human Development Report 2006.*

43. David Beetham, "Freedom as the Foundation," *Journal of Democracy* 15, no. 4 (2004): 61–75.

44. Larry Diamond, "The Quality of Democracy: An Overview," *Journal of Democracy* 15, no. 4 (2004): 20–31. See also other articles on the same theme in that issue of

the journal as well as Guillermo O'Donnell et al., eds., *The Quality of Democracy* (Notre Dame, Ind.: University of Notre Dame Press, 2004).

45. Therborn, "Rule of Capital."

46. Robert O. Keohane and Joseph S. Nye Jr., *Power and Interdependence: World Politics in Transition,* 3rd ed. (New York: Longman, 2001).

47. Dahl, *Democracy and Its Critics,* p. 319.

48. Quoted from John Loxley, "The Devaluation Debate in Tanzania," in Bonnie K. Campbell and John Loxley, eds., *Structural Adjustment in Africa* (London: Macmillan, 1989), p. 15.

49. J. R. Scott, *Comparative Political Corruption* (Englewood Cliffs, N.J.: Prentice Hall, 1972), p. 137.

50. For an example of such a program, see O. M. Prakash and P. N. Rastogi, "Development of the Rural Poor: The Missing Factor," *IFDA Dossier* 51 (1986); see also Georg Sørensen, *Democracy, Dictatorship, and Development: Economic Development in Selected Regimes of the Third World* (London: Macmillan, 1991), chap. 2.

51. See Mark Blecher, *China: Politics, Economics, and Society* (London: Frances Pinter, 1986), p. 104.

52. Blecher, *China,* p. 25 n.

53. Blecher, *China,* p. 26.

Chapter 2

1. Seymour Martin Lipset, "Some Social Requisites of Democracy: Economic Development and Political Legitimacy," *American Political Science Review* 53 (1959): 75. See also Lipset, "The Social Requisites of Democracy Revisited," *American Sociological Science Review* 59 (1994): 1–22; and Seymour Martin Lipset and Jason M. Lakin, *The Democratic Century* (Norman: University of Oklahoma Press, 2004).

2. Samuel P. Huntington, "Will More Countries Become Democratic?" *Political Science Quarterly* 99, no. 2 (1984): 199.

3. Robert A. Dahl, *Polyarchy: Participation and Opposition* (New Haven: Yale University Press, 1971), p. 65. See also Barbara Geddes, "What Do We Know About Democratization After Twenty Years?" *Annual Review of Political Science* 2 (1999): 129–148.

4. Guillermo O'Donnell, *Modernization and Bureaucratic-Authoritarianism: Studies in South American Politics* (Berkeley: University of California, Institute of International Studies, 1973).

5. F. Limongi and A. Przeworski, "What Makes Democracies Endure?" *Journal of Democracy* 7, no. 1 (1997): 39–55. See also A. Przeworski and F. Limongi, "Modernization: Theories and Facts," *World Politics* 49, no. 2 (1997): 155–183. The question is whether economic development "causes" democracy or the other way around. Scholars do not agree on the issue. See, for example, Ross E. Burkhart and Michael S. Lewis-Beck, "Comparative Democracy. The Economic Development Thesis," *American Political Science Review* 88, no. 4 (1994): 903–910; and Yong U. Glasure et al., "Level of Economic Development and Political Democracy Revisited," *International Advances in Economic Research* 5, no. 4 (1999): 466–477.

6. Fareed Zakaria, "Islam, Democracy, and Constitutional Liberalism," *Political Science Quarterly* 119, no. 1 (2004): 1–20.

7. Huntington, "Will More Countries Become Democratic?" p. 209. See also Samuel P. Huntington, *The Third Wave: Democratization in the Late Twentieth Century* (Norman: University of Oklahoma Press, 1991).

8. Terry Lynn Karl, "Dilemmas of Democratization in Latin America," *Comparative Politics* 23, no. 1 (1990): 4.

9. Barrington Moore Jr., *Social Origins of Dictatorship and Democracy: Lord and Peasant in the Making of the Modern World* (Boston: Beacon, 1966), p. 418. A part of this debate concerns the precise definition of the term "bourgeoisie."

10. Goran Therborn, "The Rule of Capital and the Rise of Democracy," in David Held et al., eds., *States and Societies* (Oxford: Martin Robertson, 1983), p. 271.

11. Huntington, "Will More Countries Become Democratic?" p. 206.

12. For example, Fernando Henrique Cardoso, "Dependent Capitalist Development in Latin America," *New Left Review* 80 (1973): 83–95.

13. Dahl, *Polyarchy,* pp. 202–208.

14. Larry Diamond, Juan J. Linz, and Seymour Martin Lipset, eds., *Democracy in Developing Countries,* vol. 2, *Africa* (Boulder: Lynne Rienner, 1988), pp. ix–xxix.

15. In Juan J. Linz and Alfred Stepan, eds., *The Breakdown of Democratic Regimes: Crisis, Breakdown, and Reequilibration* (Baltimore: Johns Hopkins University Press, 1978), p. 5. See also Dankwart A. Rustow, "Transitions to Democracy," *Comparative Politics* 2, no. 3 (1970): 337–365.

16. For a similar view, see Karl, "Dilemmas of Democratization."

17. Terry Lynn Karl, "From Democracy to Democratization and Back: Before *Transitions from Authoritarian Rule*," CDDRL Working Paper 45 (Stanford, 2005); Adam Przeworski, Michael E. Alvarez, Jose Antonio Cheibub, and Fernando Limongi, *Democracy and Development: Political Institutions and Well-Being in the World* (Cambridge: Cambridge University Press, 2000); Sunil Bastion and Robin Luckham, *Can Democracy Be Designed? The Politics of International Choice in Conflict-Torn Societies* (London: Zed, 2003); Robert J. Barro, "Determinants of Democracy," *Journal of Political Economy* 107, no. 6 (1999): 158–183.

18. Adam Przeworski, "Democracy as a Contingent Outcome of Conflicts," in Jon Elster and Rune Slagstad, eds., *Constitutionalism and Democracy* (Cambridge: Cambridge University Press, 1988), pp. 59–81.

19. Przeworski, "Democracy as a Contingent Outcome," p. 71.

20. Guillermo O'Donnell and Philippe C. Schmitter, *Transitions from Authoritarian Rule: Tentative Conclusions About Uncertain Democracies* (Baltimore: Johns Hopkins University Press, 1986), p. 19.

21. Richard Sandbrook, "Liberal Democracy in Africa: A Socialist-Revisionist Perspective," *Canadian Journal of African Studies* 22, no. 2 (1988): 253.

22. Sandbrook, "Liberal Democracy in Africa," p. 254.

23. Przeworski, "Democracy as a Contingent Outcome," p. 69.

24. Przeworski, "Democracy as a Contingent Outcome," p. 79.

25. In 2004 "President Vladimir Putin took further steps toward the consolidation of executive authority by increasing pressure on opposition political parties and civil

society, strengthening state control over national broadcast media, and pursuing politically driven prosecutions of independent business leaders and academics" (Freedom House, *Freedom in the World 2005*, p. 519).

26. Huntington, "Will More Countries Become Democratic?" p. 197.

27. Donald Share, "Transitions to Democracy and Transition Through Transaction," *Comparative Political Studies* 19, no. 4 (1987): 545. See also Kenneth Medhurst, "Spain's Evolutionary Pathway from Dictatorship to Democracy," *West European Politics* 7, no. 2 (1984): 30–50; P. Nikiforos Diamandouros, "Transition to, and Consolidation of, Democratic Politics in Greece, 1974–83: A Tentative Assessment," *West European Politics* 7, no. 2 (1984): 50–72; Thomas C. Bruneau, "Continuity and Change in Portuguese Politics: Ten Years After the Revolution of 25 April 1974," *West European Politics* 7, no. 2 (1984): 72–83.

28. Francisco C. Weffort, quoted from Hélgio Trindade, "Presidential Elections and Political Transition in Latin America," *International Social Science Journal* 128 (1991): 301–314.

29. Fernando Henrique Cardoso, "Democracy in Latin America," *Politics and Society* 15, no. 1 (1986–1987): 32.

30. Timothy Garton Ash, "Eastern Europe: The Year of Truth," *New York Review of Books*, February 15, 1990, pp. 17–22.

31. Quoted from Ole Nørgaard, "De post-stalinistiske samfund og demokratiet" [The post-Stalinist societies and democracy], *Politica* 23, no. 3 (1991): 246.

32. Ash, "Eastern Europe," p. 19.

33. Nørgaard, "De post-stalinistiske samfund," pp. 241–259.

34. Adam Przeworski, "The 'East' Becomes the 'South'? The 'Autumn of the People' and the Future of Eastern Europe," *PS: Political Science and Politics* 24, no. 1 (1991): 21.

35. Samuel Decalo, "The Process, Prospects, and Constraints of Democratization in Africa" (paper delivered at the 15th World Congress of the International Political Science Association, Buenos Aires, July 21–25, 1991), p. 2.

36. Decalo, "Process, Prospects and Constraints," p. 8.

37. Jacques-Mariel Nzouankeu, "The African Attitude to Democracy," *International Social Science Journal* 128 (1991): 374.

38. Quoted from Decalo, "Democratization in Africa," p. 11.

39. Karl D. Jackson, "The Philippines: The Search for a Suitable Democratic Solution, 1946–86," in Larry Diamond, Juan J. Linz, and Seymour Martin Lipset, eds., *Democracy in Developing Countries*, vol. 3, *Asia* (Boulder: Lynne Rienner, 1989), pp. 231–267.

40. Niranjan Koirala, "Nepal in 1990: End of an Era," *Asian Survey* 31, no. 2 (1991): 134–140.

41. Rustow, "Transitions to Democracy."

42. Rustow, "Transitions to Democracy," p. 350.

43. W. Ivor Jennings, quoted in Rustow, "Transitions to Democracy," p. 351.

44. Rustow, "Transitions to Democracy," p. 354.

45. Alfred Stepan, "Paths Toward Redemocratization: Theoretical and Comparative Considerations," in Guillermo O'Donnell, Philippe C. Schmitter, and Laurence White-

head, eds., *Transitions from Authoritarian Rule: Comparative Perspectives* (Baltimore: Johns Hopkins University Press, 1988), pp. 64–85.

46. O'Donnell and Schmitter, *Transitions from Authoritarian Rule*.

47. See Nørgaard, "De post-stalinistiske samfund," p. 14.

48. Rustow, "Transitions to Democracy," p. 355.

49. O'Donnell and Schmitter, *Transitions from Authoritarian Rule*, pp. 21–23.

50. Karl, "Dilemmas of Democratization," p. 9.

51. Karl, "Dilemmas of Democratization," p. 8.

52. Terry Lynn Karl and Philippe C. Schmitter, "Modes of Transition in Latin America, Southern and Eastern Europe," *International Social Science Journal* 128 (1991): 269–284.

53. Linz, "Transitions to Democracy," p. 158.

54. Linz, "Transitions to Democracy." For some observers, a democracy is never fully consolidated because there is always room for a process of further democratic deepening; see Andreas Schedler, "What Is Democratic Consolidation?" in Larry Diamond and Marc F. Plattner, eds., *The Global Divergence of Democracies* (Baltimore: Johns Hopkins University Press, 2001), pp. 149–164.

55. Jose Nun, "Democracy and Modernization, Thirty Years After" (paper delivered at the 15th World Congress of the International Political Science Association, Buenos Aires, July 21–25, 1991), p. 23.

56. Wolfgang Merkel, "The Consolidation of Post-Autocratic Democracies," *Democratization* 5, no. 3 (1998): 33–67. For a case study, see Thomas R. Rochon and Michael J. Mitchell, "Cultural Components of the Consolidation of Democracy in Brazil" (paper delivered at the annual meeting of the American Political Science Association, Washington, D.C., August 28–31, 1991). Schedler, "What Is Democratic Consolidation?" Juan J. Linz and Alfred Stepan, "Toward Consolidated Democracies," in Larry Diamond and Marc F. Plattner, eds., *The Global Divergence of Democracies* (Baltimore: Johns Hopkins University Press, 2001), pp. 93–112.

57. See Jørgen Elklit and Andrew Reynolds, "A Framework for the Systematic Study of Election Quality," *Democratization* 12, no. 2 (2005): 147–162.

Chapter 3

1. Terry Lynn Karl, "From Democracy to Democratization and Back: Before *Transitions from Authoritarian Rule*," CDDRL Working Paper 45 (Stanford, 2005), p. 9.

2. Ghia Nadia, "How Different Are Postcommunist Transitions," *Journal of Democracy* 7, no. 4 (1996): 15–29.

3. Karl, "From Democracy to Democratization," p. 9. On the poor quality of many elections, see Thomas Carothers, *Aiding Democracy Abroad: The Learning Curve* (Washington, D.C.: Carnegie Endowment for International Peace, 1999).

4. Robert A. Dahl, "Democracy and Human Rights Under Different Conditions of Development," in Asbjørn Eide and Bernt Hagtvet, eds., *Human Rights in Perspective: A Global Assessment* (Oxford: Blackwell, 1992), p. 246.

5. Andreas Schedler, "The Menu of Manipulation," *Journal of Democracy* 13, no. 2 (2002): 39–40.

6. Guillermo O'Donnell, "Delegative Democracy," *Journal of Democracy* 5, no. 1 (1994): 55–70.

7. Ivan Krastev, "Democracy's 'Doubles,'" *Journal of Democracy* 17, no. 2 (2006): 52–62.

8. Fareed Zakaria, "The Rise of Illiberal Democracy," *Foreign Affairs* 76, no. 6 (1997): 22–43; Zakaria, *The Future of Freedom: Illiberal Democracy at Home and Abroad* (New York: Norton, 2003).

9. Zakaria, "Rise of Illiberal Democracy," p. 1.

10. In 1997 Zakaria found that half of the countries in the gray zone performed better on political liberties than on civil ones. Almost ten years later, most countries performing badly on civil liberties also have problems with political liberties. Freedom House, *Freedom in the World 2006*.

11. Thomas Carothers, "The End of the Transitions Paradigm," *Journal of Democracy* 13, no. 1 (2002): 5–21.

12. Carothers, "End of the Transitions Paradigm," p. 9.

13. Carothers, "End of the Transitions Paradigm," pp. 9–10.

14. Carothers, "End of the Transitions Paradigm," p. 18.

15. This procedure follows the one suggested by Larry Diamond in "Thinking About Hybrid Regimes," *Journal of Democracy* 13, no. 2 (2002): 21–35. See also Jørgen Møller, "The Gap Between Liberal and Electoral Democracy Revisited: Some Conceptual and Empirical Clarifications," EUI Working Papers 1 (2006).

16. Robert A. Dahl, *Democracy and Its Critics* (New Haven: Yale University Press, 1989), p. 314. See also the section on preconditions for democracy in Chapter 2 of this volume.

17. Some of what follow draws on Georg Sørensen, *Changes in Statehood: The Transformation of International Relations* (Basingstoke, U.K.: Palgrave Macmillan, 2001); and Sørensen, *The Transformation of the State: Beyond the Myth of Retreat* (Basingstoke, U.K.: Palgrave Macmillan, 2001).

18. Peter B. Evans et al., eds., *Bringing the State Back In* (London: Cambridge University Press, 1985), p. 50.

19. Gordon White, "Developmental States and Socialist Industrialization in the Third World," *Journal of Development Studies* 21, no. 1 (1984): 100.

20. S. N. Ndegwa, "Citizenship and Ethnicity: An Examination of Two Transition Moments in Kenyan Politics," *American Political Science Review* 91, no. 3 (1997): 601.

21. See, for example, Earl Conteh-Morgan, *Democratization in Africa: The Theory and Dynamics of Political Transitions* (Westport, Conn.: Praeger, 1997).

22. Marina Ottaway, "Democratization in Collapsed States," in W. I. Zartman, ed., *Collapsed States: The Disintegration and Restoration of Legitimate Authority* (Boulder: Lynne Rienner, 1995), p. 235.

23. H. Bienen and J. Herbst, "The Relationship Between Political and Economic Reform in Africa," *Comparative Politics* 29, no. 1 (1996): 35.

24. Francis Fukuyama, "'Stateness' First," *Journal of Democracy* 16, no. 1 (2005): 84.

25. Francis Fukuyama, *State Building: Governance and World Order in the Twenty-First Century* (London: Profile, 2004).

26. Some of what follows draws on Georg Sørensen, "Democracy and the Developmental State," mimeograph (Institute of Political Science, University of Aarhus, 1991).

27. Frances Hagopian, "'Democracy by Undemocratic Means?': Elites, Political Pacts, and Regime Transition in Brazil," *Comparative Political Studies* 23, no. 2 (1990): 154–157.

28. Hagopian, "Democracy by Undemocratic Means?" p. 157.

29. Hagopian, "Democracy by Undemocratic Means?" p. 159.

30. Karl, "From Democracy to Democratization and Back," p. 28.

31. Terry Lynn Karl and Philippe C. Schmitter, "Modes of Transition in Latin America, Southern and Eastern Europe," *International Social Science Journal* 128 (1991), pp. 269–284.

32. Lucan Way, "Authoritarian State Building and the Sources of Regime Competitiveness in the Fourth Wave," *World Politics*, January 2005, pp. 231–261.

33. Richard Sandbrook, *The Politics of Africa's Economic Stagnation* (Cambridge: Cambridge University Press, 1985); Richard Sandbrook, "The State and Economic Stagnation in Tropical Africa," *World Development* 14, no. 3 (1986): 319–332; Goran Hyden, *No Shortcuts to Progress: African Development Management in Perspective* (London: Heinemann, 1983); Robert Jackson and Carl G. Rosberg, *Personal Rule in Black Africa: Prince, Autocrat, Prophet, Tyrant* (Berkeley: University of California Press, 1982).

34. Sandbrook, "The State and Economic Stagnation," p.324.

35. Ibid.

36. Ruth Berins Collier, *Regimes in Tropical Africa: Changing Forms of Supremacy, 1945–75* (Berkeley: University of California Press, 1975), p. 22.

37. For an instructive overview of the situation in Africa, see Nicolas van de Walle, "Africa's Range of Regimes," *Journal of Democracy* 13, no. 2 (2002): 66–80.

38. Anne Applebaum, "Central Europe: Nice Guys Finish Last," in Roger Kaplan et al., eds., *Freedom in the World: The Annual Survey of Political Rights and Civil Liberties, 1995–1996* (New York: Freedom House, 1996), pp. 24–30.

39. Applebaum, "Central Europe: Nice Guys Finish Last," p. 27.

40. Quoted from Ivan Krastev, "Democracy's 'Doubles,'" *Journal of Democracy* 17, no. 2 (2006): 52–62.

41. Burhan Ghalioun, "The Persistence of Arab Authoritarianism," *Journal of Democracy* 15, no. 4 (2004): 129.

42. Linz, "Transitions to Democracy," p. 152. See also Peter Von Doepp, "Political Transition and Civil Society: The Cases of Kenya and Zambia," *Studies in Comparative International Development* 31, no. 1 (1996): 24–47; Patricia L. Hipsher, "Democratization and the Decline or Urban Social Movements in Chile and Spain," *Comparative Politics* 28, no. 3 (1996): 273–297; J. Cherry et al., "Democratization and Politics in South African Townships," *International Journal of Urban and Regional Research* 24, no. 4 (2000): 889–905.

43. Guillermo O'Donnell and Philippe C. Schmitter, *Transitions from Authoritarian Rule: Tentative Conclusions About Uncertain Democracies* (Baltimore, Md.: Johns Hopkins University Press, 1986), p. 54.

44. David Lehmann, *Democracy and Development in Latin America* (Cambridge: Polity, 1990), p. 150.

45. Naomi Chazan, "The New Politics of Participation in Tropical Africa," *Comparative Politics* 14, no. 2 (1982): 172.

46. Sandbrook, *Politics of Africa's Economic Stagnation*, p. 148.

47. Sandbrook, "Liberal Democracy in Africa," p. 262.

48. Rochon and Mitchell, "Cultural Components," p. 17.

49. Ralf Dahrendorf, lecture on Eastern Europe, University of Oslo, 1990.

50. Terry Lynn Karl, "Dilemmas of Democratization in Latin America," *Comparative Politics* 23, no. 1 (1990): 17.

Chapter 4

1. Woodrow Wilson, "Address to Congress Asking for Declaration of War," 1917; quoted in John A. Vasquez, *Classics of International Relations* (Upper Saddle River, N.J.: Prentice Hall, 1996), pp. 35–40.

2. A major inspiration for this view is the analysis by Walt W. Rostow, *The Stages of Economic Growth: A Non-Communist Manifesto* (Cambridge: Cambridge University Press, 1960). See also the section on preconditions for democracy in Chapter 2 of this book.

3. Quoted from Thomas Carothers, *Aiding Democracy Abroad* (Washington: Carnegie Endowment for International Peace, 1999), p. 31. The comprehensive analysis by Carothers is a major source of inspiration for this chapter.

4. Kristian Skrede Gleditsch and Michael D. Ward, "Diffusion and the International Context of Democratization," *International Organization* 60, no. 4 (2006): 911–933; John O'Loughlin, Michael D. Ward, Corey L. Lofdahl, Jordin S. Cohen, David S. Brown, David Reilly, Kristian S. Gleditsch and Michael Shin, "The Diffusion of Democracy, 1946–1994," *Annals of the Association of American Geographers* 88 (1998): 545–574.

5. William I. Robinson, *Promoting Polyarchy: Globalization, US Intervention, and Hegemony* (Cambridge: Cambridge University Press, 1996); Gorm Rye Olsen, "Europe and the Promotion of Democracy in Post Cold War Africa: How Serious Is Europe and for What Reason?" *African Affairs* 97 (1998): 343–367; and Michael McFaul, "Democracy Promotion as a World Value," *Washington Quarterly* 28, no. 1 (2004): 147–163.

6. See, for example, Carothers, *Aiding Democracy Abroad.*

7. Robinson, *Promoting Polyarchy.*

8. Celestin Monga, "Eight Problems with African Politics," *Journal of Democracy* 8, no. 3 (1997): 156–170.

9. *National Security Strategy of the United States of America,* sec. 2 (Washington: Office of the President, 2002).

10. Jennifer L. Windsor, "Promoting Democratization Can Combat Terrorism," *Washington Quarterly* 26, no. 3 (2003): 48. The particularly hard cases in this regard are Iraq and Afghanistan.

11. Windsor, "Promoting Democratization," p. 54.

12. Carothers, *Aiding Democracy Abroad*, p. 125.

13. Carothers, *Aiding Democracy Abroad*, p. 128.

14. Marina Ottaway and Theresa Chung, "Toward a New Paradigm," *Journal of Democracy* 10, no. 4 (1999): 99–113, quote from p. 100.

15. Ottaway and Chung, "Toward a New Paradigm," p. 100.

16. Robert Kaplan, "Was Democracy Just a Moment?" *Atlantic Monthly,* December 1997.

17. See, for example, World Bank, *Adjustment in Africa: Reforms, Results, and the Road Ahead* (Oxford: Oxford University Press, 1994).

18. Douglas W. Payne, "Latin America and the Caribbean: Storm Warnings," in Roger Kaplan et al., eds., *Freedom in the World: The Annual Survey of Political Rights and Civil Liberties* (New York: Freedom House, 1996), pp. 77–84.

19. Merilee Grindle, *Challenging the State: Crisis and Innovation in Latin America and Africa* (Cambridge: Cambridge University Press 1996); see also World Bank, *World Development Report 1997: The State in a Changing World* (Oxford: Oxford University Press, 1997).

20. Promotion of the rule of law, for example, involves reforming institutions, rewriting laws, upgrading the legal profession, and increasing legal access and advocacy, cf. Carothers, *Aiding Democracy Abroad*, p. 168.

21. Carothers, *Aiding Democracy Abroad*.

22. Paddy Ashdown, inaugural speech, May 27, 2002, quoted from David Chandler, "Back to the Future? The Limits of Neo-Wilsonian Ideals of Exporting Democracy," *Review of International Studies* 32, no. 3 (2006): 480.

23. Chandler, "Back to the Future?" p. 480.

24. Jiri Pehe, "Consolidating Free Government in the New EU," *Journal of Democracy* 15, no. 1 (2004): 36–47.

25. Barbara Wake Carroll and Terrance Carroll, "State and Ethnicity in Botswana and Mauritius: A Democratic Route to Development?" *Journal of Development Studies* 33, no. 4 (1997): 464–486.

26. Carroll and Carroll, "State and Ethnicity," p. 473.

27. Göran Hydén, *Governance and Politics in Africa* (Boulder: Lynne Rienner), p. 23.

28. Carroll and Carroll, "State and Ethnicity," p. 479.

29. Ottaway and Chung, "Toward a New Paradigm," p. 106.

30. Joan Bloch Jensen, "American Democracy Promotion in Africa," manuscript, Department of Political Science, Aarhus, 2006; in Danish.

31. Christopher Clapham, "Governmentality and Economic Policy in Sub-Saharan Africa," *Third World Quarterly* 17, no. 4 (1996): 809–824.

32. Pamela Paxton and Rumi Morishima, "Does Democracy Aid Promote Democracy?" working paper, Ohio State University, 2006. See also Jensen, "American Democracy Promotion in Africa."

33. Carl Gershman and Michael Allen, "The Assault on Democracy Assistance," *Journal of Democracy* 17, no. 2 (2006): 36–51. See also Thomas Carothers, "The Backlash Against Democracy Promotion," *Foreign Affairs* 85, no. 2 (2006): 55–68.

34. Summarized from Gershman and Allen, "Assault on Democracy Assistance."

35. Gershman and Allen, "Assault on Democracy Assistance," pp. 46–51.

Chapter 5

1. See the overview in Atul Kohli, "Democracy and Development: Trends and Prospects," in Atul Kohli, Chun-in Moon, and Georg Sørensen, eds., *States, Markets, and Just Growth* (Tokyo: UN University Press, 2003): 39–64. See also Larry Sirowy and Alex Inkeles, "The Effects of Democracy on Economic Growth: A Review," *Studies in Comparative International Development* 25, no. 1 (1990): 125–157; A. Brunetti, "Political Variables in Cross-Country Growth Analysis," *Journal of Economic Surveys* 11, no. 2 (1997): 163–190; Yi Feng, *Democracy, Governance, and Economic Performance* (Cambridge: MIT Press, 2003); Robert J. Barro, *Determinants of Economic Growth: A Cross-Country Empirical Study* (Cambridge: MIT Press, 1997); Charles Kurzman, Regina Werum, and Ross E. Burkhart, "Democracy's Effect on Economic Growth: A Pooled Time-Series Analysis, 1951–1980," *Studies in Comparative International Development* 37, no. 1 (2002): 3–33; Jagdish N. Bhagwati, "Democracy and Development: Cruel Dilemma or Symbiotic Relationship?" *Review of Development Economics* 6, no. 2 (2002): 151–162; and David Gillies, "Democracy and Economic Development," *International Democratic Development* 6 (2005): 8–28. Some of what follows draws on Georg Sørensen, *Democracy, Dictatorship, and Development: Economic Development in Selected Regimes of the Third World* (London: Macmillan, 1991).

2. B. K. Nehru, "Western Democracy and the Third World," *Third World Quarterly* 1, no. 2 (1979): 57 n. See also V. Rao, "Democracy and Economic Development," *Studies in Comparative International Development* 19, no. 4 (1984–1985): 67–82; Robert J. Barro, *Determinants of Economic Growth*, 49; and Erich Weede, "Political Regime Type and Variation in Economic Growth Rates," *Constitutional Political Economy* 7 (1996): 167–176.

3. Samuel P. Huntington, *Political Order in Changing Societies* (New Haven: Yale University Press, 2006).

4. David E. Apter, *The Politics of Modernization* (Chicago: University of Chicago Press, 1965).

5. Dieter Senghaas, *The European Experience: A Historical Critique of Development Theory* (Leamington Spa/Dover: Berg, 1985); and Dieter Senghaas, "China 1979," in J. Habermas, ed., *Stichworte zur "Geistigen Situation der Zeit"* vol. 1 (Frankfurt Main: Suhrkamp, 1979), p. 435.

6. J. A. Hall, *Powers and Liberties: The Causes and Consequences of the Rise of the West* (Harmondsworth, U.K.: Penguin, 1986), p. 222.

7. Gabriel Almond and G. Bingham Powell, *Comparative Politics: A Developmental Approach* (Boston: Little, Brown, 1978), p. 363. See also Samuel P. Huntington,

"The Goals of Development," in Myron Weiner and Samuel P. Huntington, eds., *Understanding Political Development* (Boston: Little, Brown, 1987), p. 19; and Irene Gendzier, *Managing Political Change: Social Scientists and the Third World* (Boulder: Westview, 1985), chap. 6.

8. Hollis Chenery et al., *Redistribution with Growth* (London: Oxford University Press, 1974); and Paul Streeten et al., *First Things First: Meeting Basic Human Needs in Developing Countries* (New York: Oxford University Press, 1981).

9. Grace Goodell and John P. Powelson, "The Democratic Prerequisites of Development," in Raymond Gastil, ed., *Freedom in the World: Political Rights and Civil Liberties* (New York: Freedom House, 1982), pp. 167–176; and Atul Kohli, "Democracy and Development," in John Lewis and Valeriana Kallab, eds., *Development Strategies Reconsidered* (New Brunswick, N.J.: Transaction, 1986), pp. 153–182.

10. Richard Claude, "The Classical Model of Human Rights Development," in Richard Claude, ed., *Comparative Human Rights* (Baltimore: Johns Hopkins University Press, 1976), pp. 6–50; Feng, *Democracy, Governance, and Economic Performance*; Dani Rodrik, "Institutions for High-Quality Growth: What They Are and How to Acquire Them," *Studies in Comparative International Development* 35, no. 3 (2000): 3–31.

11. Georg Sørensen, "Democracy and the Developmental State," mimeograph, Institute of Political Science, University of Aarhus, 1991.

12. See the works mentioned in note 1. For a critical review of the research designs and contradictory results of previous studies, see Jonathan Krieckhaus, "The Regime Debate Revisited: A Sensitivity Analysis of Democracy's Economic Effect," *British Journal of Political Science* 34 (2004): 635–655.

13. Robert M. Marsh, "Does Democracy Hinder Economic Development in the Latecomer Developing Nations?" *Comparative Social Research* 2 (1979): 244.

14. Youssef Cohen, "The Impact of Bureaucratic-Authoritarian Rule on Economic Growth," *Comparative Political Studies* 18, no. 1 (1985): 123–136.

15. Dirk Berg-Schlosser, "African Political Systems: Typology and Performance," *Comparative Political Studies* 17, no. 1 (1984): 143.

16. Berg-Schlosser, "African Political Systems," p. 121. See also Gizachew Tiruneh, "Regime Type and Economic Growth in Africa: A Cross-National Analysis," *Social Science Journal* 43, no. 1 (2006): 3–18; Nicolas van de Walle, "Economic Reform in Democratizing Africa," *Comparative Politics* 32 (1999): 21–41.

17. Dwight Y. King, "Regime Type and Performance: Authoritarian Rule, Semi-Capitalist Development and Rural Inequality in Asia," *Comparative Political Studies* 13, no. 4 (1981): 477.

18. G. William Dick, "Authoritarian Versus Nonauthoritarian Approaches to Economic Development," *Journal of Political Economy* 82, no. 4 (1974): 823.

19. Kohli, "Democracy and Development"; Sirowy and Inkeles, "Effects of Democracy on Economic Growth"; Brunetti, "Political Variables in Cross-Country Growth Analysis;" Kurzman et al., "Democracy's Effect on Economic Growth."

20. Some of these considerations draw on Sørensen, *Democracy, Dictatorship, and Development*.

21. See Jean Drèze and Amartya Sen, *Hunger and Public Action* (Oxford: Clarendon, 1989), p. 206 n.

22. See C. Ka and M. Selden, "Original Accumulation, Equity, and Late Industrialization: The Cases of Socialist China and Capitalist Taiwan," *World Development* 14, no. 10–11 (1986): 1300 n.

23. See, for example, Francine Frankel, "Is Authoritarianism the Solution to India's Economic Development Problems?" in Atul Kohli, ed., *The State and Development in the Third World* (Princeton: Princeton University Press, 1986), pp. 154–161.

24. Barrington Moore Jr., *Social Origins of Dictatorship and Democracy: Lord and Peasant in the Making of the Modern World* (Boston: Beacon, 1966), p. 355.

25. Pranab Bardhan, *The Political Economy of Development in India* (Delhi: Oxford University Press, 1984), p. 56. See also Rajni Kothari, *Politics in India* (Delhi: Orient Longman, 1982), p. 352 n.; and K. Subbarao, "State Policies and Regional Disparity in Indian Agriculture," *Development and Change* 16, no. 4 (1985): 543.

26. A. Piazza, *Food Consumption and Nutritional Status in the PRC* (Boulder: Westview, 1986), p. 36.

27. Carl Riskin, *China's Political Economy: The Quest for Development Since 1949* (Oxford: Oxford University Press, 1987), p. 276.

28. Ka and Selden, "Original Accumulation," p. 1301.

29. Clemens Stubbe Østergaard and Christina Petersen, "Official Profiteering and the Tiananmen Square Demonstrations in China" (paper delivered at the Second Liverpool Conference on Fraud, Corruption, and Business Crime, Liverpool, April 17–19, 1991).

30. World Bank, *World Development Report 2006*.

31. G. Etienne, *India's Changing Rural Scene, 1963–79* (New Delhi: Oxford University Press, 1982), pp. 152–158; J. Breman, "I Am the Government Labour Officer . . . State Protection for Rural Proletariat of South Gujarat," *Economic and Political Weekly* 20, no. 4 (1985): 1043–1056.

32. Bardhan, *Political Economy of Development in India*, p. 4.

33. The following analysis draws heavily on Bardhan, *The Political Economy of Development in India*.

34. A. Rudra, "Political Economy of Indian Non-Development," *Economic and Political Weekly* 20, no. 21 (1985): 916.

35. Riskin, *China's Political Economy*, p. 235.

36. Piazza, *Food Consumption and Nutritional Status*, p. 176.

37. Drèze and Sen, *Hunger and Public Action*, p. 209. The authors underline that democracies always take action in cases of famine.

38. Drèze and Sen, *Hunger and Public Action*, p. 215.

39. See, for example, Thomas B. Gold, *State and Society in the Taiwan Miracle* (New York: Sharpe, 1986).

40. The "tigers" experienced economic crisis in the late 1990s; see, for example, Robert Garran, *Tigers Tamed: The End of the Asian Miracle* (Honolulu: University of Hawaii Press, 1998); K. S. Jomo, ed., *Southeast Asian Paper Tigers? From Miracle to Debacle and Beyond* (New York: Routledge Curzon, 2003).

41. Peter T. Knight, "Brazilian Socio-Economic Development: Issues for the Eighties," *World Development* 9, no. 11–12 (1981).

42. Sylvia Ann Hewlett, *The Cruel Dilemmas of Development: Twentieth-Century Brazil* (New York: Basic, 1980).

43. C. Ominami, "Déindustrialisation et restructuration industrielle en Argentine, au Brésil et au Chili," *Problemas D'Amerique Latine* 89 (1988): 55–79.

44. D. Cruise O'Brien, quoted in Goran Hyden, *No Shortcuts to Progress: African Development Management in Perspective* (London: Heineman, 1983), p. 37.

45. David Gould, "The Administration of Underdevelopment," in Guy Gran, ed., *Zaire: The Political Economy of Underdevelopment* (New York: Praeger, 1979), pp. 87–107; Salua Nour, "Zaire," in Dieter Nohlen and Franz Nuscheler, eds., *Handbuch der Dritten Welt* (Hamburg: Hoffmann und Campe), 4:468–522. See also Mabiengwa Emmanuel Naniuzeyi, "The State of the State in Congo-Zaire: A Survey of the Mobuty Regime," *Journal of Black Studies* 29, no. 5 (1999): 669–683.

46. Nour, "Zaire," p. 512.

47. Hewlett, *The Cruel Dilemmas of Development;* and Knight, "Brazilian Socio-Economic Development."

48. Sørensen, *Democracy, Dictatorship, and Development*, chap. 2.

49. For the view that Indian democracy may be changing in the direction of what is called "social democracy" here, see Susanne and Lloyd Rudolph, "New Dimensions of Indian Democracy," *Journal of Democracy* 13, no. 1 (2002): 52–66.

50. Charles D. Ameringer, *Democracy in Costa Rica* (New York: Praeger, 1982); John A. Peeler, *Latin American Democracies: Colombia, Costa Rica, Venezuela* (Chapel Hill: University of North Carolina Press, 1985).

51. Peeler, *Latin American Democracies*, p. 129.

52. "Costa Rica," in Freedom House, *Freedom in the World 2006.*

53. Ameringer, *Democracy in Costa Rica*, p. 19.

54. J. A. Booth, "Costa Rica," in Larry Diamond, Jonathan Hartlyn, Juan J. Linz, and Seymour Martin Lipset, eds., *Democracy in Developing Countries: Latin America*, 2nd ed. (Boulder: Lynne Rienner, 1999), p. 462.

55. Nick Crook, Michael Dauderstädt, and André Gerrits, eds., *Social Democracy in Central and Eastern Europe* (Bonn: Friedrich Ebert, 2002); Detlef Pollack, Jörg Jacobs, Olaf Müller, and Gert Pickel, eds., *Political Culture in Post-Communist Europe: Attitudes in New Democracies* (Aldershot, U.K.: Ashgate, 2003).

56. The remarks on Chile are based on Jakob J. Simonsen and Georg Sørensen, *Chile 1970–73: Et eksempel på Østeuropæisk udviklingsstrategi?* (Aarhus: University of Aarhus, Institute of Political Science, 1976).

57. Atul Kohli, *The State and Poverty in India: The Politics of Reform* (Cambridge: Harvard University Press, 1987).

58. Stephan Haggard and Robert R. Kaufman, *The Political Economy of Democratic Transitions* (Princeton: Princeton University Press, 1995). The following remarks are based on this contribution.

59. Haggard and Kaufman, *Political Economy*, p. 227.

60. Haggard and Kaufman, *Political Economy*, p. 370.

61. Haggard and Kaufman, *Political Economy*, p. 371.

62. For the view that there is variation across regions on the relationship between democratization and economic reform, see Valerie Bunce, "Democratization and Economic Reform," *Annual Review of Political Science* 4 (2001): 43–65.

63. Jack Donnelly, "Human Rights and Development: Complementary or Competing Concerns?" *World Politics* 36, no. 2 (1984): 281 n.

64. See, for example, Johan Galtung, "Why the Concern with Ways of Life?" in Council for International Development Studies, *The Western Development Model and Life Style* (Oslo: University of Oslo, 1980).

65. Jack Donnelly, *Human Rights and World Politics* (Boulder: Westview, 1993). See also Jack Donnelly, *Universal Human Rights in Theory and Practice* (Ithaca: Cornell University Press, 2002); David Forsythe, *Human Rights in International Relations* (Cambridge University Press, 2002).

66. David Beetham, *Democracy and Human Rights* (Cambridge: Polity, 1999), pp. 89–95.

67. Amnesty International, *Amnesty International Report 2005*; web version at http://web.amnesty.org/repo005/index-eng; Michael Welch, "Trampling Human Rights in the War on Terror: Implications to the Sociology of Denial," *Critical Criminology* 12 (2004): 1–20; Richard Ashby Wilson, ed., *Human Rights in the War on Terror* (New York: Cambridge University Press, 2005).

68. Freedom House, *Freedom in the World 2005* (Lanham, Md.: Rowman & Littlefield, 2006); web version at www.freedomhouse.org; David Beetham, Sarah Bracking, Iain Kearton, Nalini Vittal, and Stuart Weir, eds., *The State of Democracy: Democracy Assessments in Eight Nations Around the World* (The Hague: Kluwer Law International, 2002); Larry Diamond, "The Quality of Democracy. An Overview," *Journal of Democracy* 15, no. 4 (2004): 20–31.

69. Christian Davenport and David A. Armstrong II, "Democracy and the Violation of Human Rights: A Statistical Analysis from 1976 to 1996," *American Journal of Political Science* 48, no. 3 (2004): 551.

70. See Richard Falk, *Human Rights and State Sovereignty* (New York: Holmes & Meier, 1981), pp. 63–124.

71. See Stephen Marks, "Promoting Human Rights," in Michael T. Klare and Daniel C. Thomas, *World Security: Trends and Challenges at Century's End* (New York: St. Martin's, 1991), p. 303.

Chapter 6

1. An English version of Kant's *Perpetual Peace* can be found in Hans Reiss, ed., *Kant's Political Writings* (Cambridge: Cambridge University Press, 1970). My summary of Kant's ideas relies heavily on three articles by Michael W. Doyle: "Kant, Liberal Legacies, and Foreign Affairs," *Philosophy and Public Affairs* 12, no. 3 (1983): 205–235; "Kant, Liberal Legacies, and Foreign Affairs, Part 2," *Philosophy and Public Affairs* 12, no. 4 (1983): 323–354; and "Liberalism and World Politics," *American Political Science Review* 80, no. 4 (1986): 1151–1169. See also Michael W. Doyle, "Three Pillars of the Liberal Peace," *American Political Science Review* 99, no. 3 (2005): 463–466. For studies critical of Doyle's interpretation of Kant, see John MacMillan, "Beyond the

Separate Democratic Peace," *Journal of Peace Research* 40, no. 2 (2003): 233–243; and John MacMillan, "Liberalism and the Democratic Peace," *Review of International Studies* 30, no. 2 (2004): 179–200.

2. Quoted from Reiss, *Kant's Political Writings*, p. 100.

3. Quoted from Doyle, "Liberalism and World Politics," p. 1153.

4. Rudolph J. Rummel, "Libertarianism and International Violence," *Journal of Conflict Resolution* 27, no. 1 (1983): 27–71.

5. Melvin Small and J. David Singer, "The War-Proneness of Democratic Regimes," *Jerusalem Journal of International Relations* 1, no. 4 (1976): 50–69; Steve Chan, "Mirror, Mirror on the Wall . . . Are the Freer Countries More Pacific?" *Journal of Conflict Resolution* 28, no. 4 (1984): 617–648; Erich Weede, "Democracy and War Involvement," *Journal of Conflict Resolution* 28, no. 4 (1984): 649–664. Studies such as Chan's (cited in this note), which are based on long periods of observation, face other difficulties because, as demonstrated in Chapter 1, the concrete content of the entity called "democracy" changes over time.

6. Doyle, "Kant, Liberal Legacies, and Foreign Affairs," p. 213.

7. Dean Babst, "Elective Governments: A Force for Peace," *Wisconsin Sociologist* 3, no. 1 (1964): 9–14; see also Small and Singer, "War-Proneness of Democratic Regimes"; Chan, "Mirror, Mirror"; Bruce Russett, "Democracy and Peace," in B. Russett, H. Starr, and R. J. Stoll, eds., *Choices in World Politics: Sovereignty and Interdependence* (New York: Freeman, 1989), pp. 245–261; Fred Chernoff, "The Study of Democratic Peace and Progress in International Relations," *International Studies Review* 6, no. 1 (2004): 49–79; Bruce Russett and John Oneal, *Triangulating Peace: Democracy, Interdependence, and International Organizations* (London: Norton, 2001). There are numerous recent studies; see the bibliography at the website by Rummel: www.hawaii.edu/powerkills/BIBLIO.HTML.

8. Russett, "Democracy and Peace," p. 245.

9. Reiss, *Kant's Political Writings*, p. 114.

10. Doyle, "Liberalism and World Politics," p. 1161.

11. Doyle, "Kant, Liberal Legacies, and Foreign Affairs, Part 2," p. 324 n. This quotation was italicized in the original. For a contemporary analysis of the liberal quest for promotion of liberal values, see Georg Sørensen, "Liberalism of Restraint and Liberalism of Imposition: Liberal Values and World Order in the New Millennium," *International Relations* 20, no. 3 (2006): 251–272.

12. Russett, "Democracy and Peace," p. 250.

13. Walter Lippmann, *Essays in the Public Philosophy* (Boston: Little, Brown, 1955), p. 20. For studies of the role of the media in foreign policy, see Matthew Baum, *Soft News Goes to War: Public Opinion and American Foreign Policy in the New Media Age* (Princeton: Princeton University Press, 2003); and Yehudith Auerbach and Yaeli Bloch-Elkon, "Media Framing and Foreign Policy: The Elite Press vis-à-vis US Policy in Bosnia, 1992–5", *Journal of Peace Research* 42, no. 1 (2005): 83–99.

14. Doyle, "Kant, Liberal Legacies, and Foreign Affairs, Part 2," p. 344.

15. Quoted from Kjell Goldmann, "'Democracy Is Incompatible with International Politics: Reconsideration of a Hypothesis," in K. Goldmann, S. Berglund, and G. Sjöstedt, eds., *Democracy and Foreign Policy* (Aldershot, U.K.: Gower, 1986), p. 2.

16. Goldmann, Berglund, and Sjöstedt, eds., *Democracy and Foreign Policy*, p. 2. There are several modern versions of Ponsonby's argument. See, for example, Jørgen Christensen, *Demokratiet og sikkerhedspolitikken*, vols. 1–2 (Aarhus: University of Aarhus, Institute of Political Science, 1990).

17. Goldmann, "Democracy Is Incompatible with International Politics," pp. 5–8.

18. Goldmann, "Democracy Is Incompatible with International Politics," p. 7 n.

19. Further distinctions have been made that focus the argument concerning incompatibility primarily on diplomatic security policy. They are outlined in Goldmann, "Democracy Is Incompatible with International Politics," pp. 27–31.

20. Thomas Risse-Kappen, "Public Opinion, Domestic Structure, and Foreign Policy in Liberal Democracies," *World Politics* 43, no. 4 (1991): 479–513. See also Douglas C. Foyle, *Counting the Public In: Presidents, Public Opinion, and Foreign Policy* (New York: Columbia University Press, 1999); and Richard Sobel, *The Impact of Public Opinion on U.S. Foreign Policy Since Vietnam* (New York: Oxford University Press, 2001).

21. Risse-Kappen, "Public Opinion, Domestic Structure, and Foreign Policy," p. 510.

22. Foyle, *Counting the Public In*. See also Douglas Foyle, "Leading the Public to War? The Influence of American Public Opinion on the Bush Administration's Decision to Go to War in Iraq," *International Journal of Public Opinion Research* 16, no. 3 (2004): 269–294.

23. The public may favor military action as often as it doesn't; Miroslav Nincic, *Democracy and Foreign Policy: The Fallacy of Political Realism* (New York: Columbia University Press, 1992).

24. Doyle, "Kant, Liberal Legacies, and Foreign Affairs," p. 213.

25. Stephen Van Evera, "Primed for Peace: Europe After the Cold War," *International Security* 15, no. 3 (1990–1991): 26 n.

26. Evera, "Primed for Peace," p. 25.

27. Doyle, "Kant, Liberal Legacies, and Foreign Affairs," p. 213; Russett, "Democracy and Peace," p. 260. See also Bruce Russett, *Grasping the Democratic Peace* (Princeton: Princeton University Press, 1993).

28. Some of what follows draws on Georg Sørensen, "Individual Security and National Security: The State Remains the Principal Problem," *Security Dialogue* 27, no. 4 (1996): 371–386.

29. Marina Ottaway, "Democratization in Collapsed States," in William I. Zartmann, ed., *Collapsed States: The Disintegration and Restoration of Legitimate Authority* (Boulder: Lynne Rienner, 1995), p. 243.

30. Adam Watson, "European International Society and Its Expansion," in Hedley Bull and Adam Watson, eds., *The Expansion of International Society* (Oxford: Clarendon, 1988), p. 23.

31. Watson, "European International Society," p. 24 n.

32. Watson, "European International Society," p. 1.

33. Barry Buzan, *From International to World Society? English School Theory and the Social Structure of Globalisation* (Cambridge: Cambridge University Press, 2004), p. 233.

34. Daniel Bell, *The Coming of Post-Industrial Society: A Venture in Social Forecasting* (New York: Basic, 1973), p. 317.

35. See, for example, James N. Rosenau, *Turbulence in World Politics: A Theory of Change and Continuity* (Princeton: Princeton University Press, 1990), pp. 416–443; James Lull, *Media, Communication, Culture: A Global Approach*, 2nd ed. (New York: Columbia University Press, 2000).

36. Georg Sørensen, "What Kind of World Order? The International System in the New Millennium," *Cooperation and Conflict* 41, no. 4 (2006). The "cartoon crisis" arose when a Danish newspaper published caricatures of the Prophet Muhammad in 2005.

37. Karl Deutsch and S. A. Burrell, *Political Community and the North Atlantic Area* (Princeton: Princeton University Press, 1957).

38. For a recent analysis along these lines, see Daniel Deudney and G. John Ikenberry, "The Nature and Sources of the Liberal International Order," *Review of International Studies* 25, no. 2 (1999): 179–197.

39. For the argument that structural changes in (liberal) statehood create a strong foundation for the transatlantic security community, see Georg Sørensen, *Changes in Statehood: The Transformation of International Relations* (Basingstoke, U.K.: Palgrave Macmillan, 2001).

40. Speech printed in the *New York Times*, March 12, 1913, p. 1, quoted from Cole Blasier, "The United States and Democracy in Latin America," in James M. Malloy and Mitchell A. Seligson, eds., *Authoritarians and Democrats: Regime Transition in Latin America* (Pittsburgh: University of Pittsburgh Press, 1987), pp. 219–233.

41. Quoted from Doyle, "Kant, Liberal Legacies, and Foreign Affairs, Part 2," p. 335.

42. See, for example, James Petras and Morris Morley, *How Allende Fell* (Nottingham, U.K.: Spokesman, 1974).

43. William Robinson, "Promoting Capitalist Polyarchy: The Case of Latin America," in M. Cox, G. J. Ikenberry, and T. Inoguchi, eds., *American Democracy Promotion* (New York: Oxford University Press, 2000), pp. 308–325, as well as the other contributions to the volume. See also Edward Rhodes, "American Grand Strategy: The Imperial Logic of Bush's Liberal Agenda," *Policy*, Summer 2003–2004, pp. 1–14.

44. Timothy Garton Ash, "Ten Thoughts on the New Europe," *New York Review of Books*, June 14, 1990; see also Timothy Garton Ash, *History of the Present* (London: Penguin, 2000).

45. Graeme Gill, "A New Turn to Authoritarian Rule in Russia?" *Democratization* 13, no. 1 (2006): 58–77; and Roger E. Kanet, ed., *The New Security Environment: The Impact on Russia, Central and Eastern Europe* (Aldershot, U.K.: Ashgate, 2005).

46. Alex Inkeles, "The Emerging Social Structure of the World," *World Politics* 27, no. 4 (1975): 479.

47. Deutsch and Burrell, *Political Community*, p. 5.

48. World Bank, *World Development Report 2000* (New York: Oxford University Press, 2000), p. 38.

49. The argument is further developed in Georg Sørensen, *The Transformation of the State: Beyond the Myth of Retreat* (Basingstoke, U.K.: Palgrave Macmillan, 2004).

50. John J. Mearsheimer, "Back to the Future: Instability in Europe After the Cold War," *International Security* 15, no. 1 (1990): 49; see also Christopher Layne, "Kant or Cant: The Myth of the Democratic Peace," *International Security* 19, no. 2 (1994): 5–49; David E. Spiro, "Give Democratic Peace a Chance? The Insignificance of the Liberal Peace," *International Security* 19, no. 2 (1994): 50–86; Sebastian Rosato, "The Flawed Logic of the Democratic Peace Theory," *American Political Science Review* 97, no. 4 (2003): 585–602.

51. Mearsheimer, "Back to the Future," pp. 49–51.

52. Mearsheimer, "Back to the Future," p. 50.

53. Alexander Wendt, *Social Theory of International Politics* (Cambridge: Cambridge University Press, 1999). The notion of different degrees of anarchy is supported by several analyses based on versions of neorealist theory; see, for example, Barry Buzan, *People, States, and Fear,* 2nd ed. (Hemel Hempstead, U.K.: Harvester Wheatsheaf, 1991). See also Barry Buzan and Ole Wæver, *Regions and Powers: The Structure of International Security* (Cambridge: Cambridge University Press, 2003).

54. Wendt, *Social Theory,* pp. 246–313.

55. Sørensen, "Liberalism of Restraint and Liberalism of Imposition," pp. 252–253.

56. Mearsheimer, "Back to the Future," p. 50.

57. Thomas Risse, "Beyond Iraq: The Crisis of the Transatlantic Security Community," pp. 181–213; in David Held and Mathias Kosnig-Archibugi, eds., *American Power in the 21st Century* (Cambridge: Polity, 2004). See also Sørensen, *Changes in Statehood;* Michael Cox, "Beyond the West: Terrors in Transatlantia," *European Journal of International Studies* 11, no. 2 (2005): 203–233; Gregory Flynn and Henry Farrell, "Piecing Together the Democratic Peace: The CSCE, Norms, and the 'Construction' of Security in Post–Cold War Europe," *International Organization* 55, no. 3 (1999): 505–535.

58. See the contributions in note 50. See also Halvard Buhaug, "Dangerous Dyads Revisited: Democracies May Not Be That Peaceful After All," *Conflict Management and Peace Science* 22 (2005): 95–111.

Conclusion

1. Arch Puddington, "Freedom in the World," 2007, freedomhouse.org/essays.

2. Ronald Inglehart and Pippa Noris, "The True Clash of Civilizations," *Foreign Affairs* 81, no. 5 (2004): 49–60.

3. See, for example, Rebekka Sylvest, *Værdier og udvikling i Saudi-Arabien* [Values and development in Saudi Arabia] (Aarhus: University of Aarhus, Institute of Political Science, 1991). For the role of Islam as a carrier of anti-Western sentiment, see Barry Buzan, "New Patterns of Global Security in the Twenty-First Century," *International Affairs* 67, no. 3 (1991): 441 n.

4. Adam Przeworski et al., "What Makes Democracies Endure?" *Journal of Democracy* 7, no. 1 (1996): 49.

5. The following remarks draw on Larry Diamond, "Is the Third Wave Over?" *Journal of Democracy* 7, no. 3 (1996): 20–38; Scott Mainwaring and Timothy R. Scully,

eds., *Building Democratic Institutions: Party Systems in Latin America* (Stanford: Stanford University Press, 1995); Seymour Martin Lipset, "The Social Requisites of Democracy Revisited," *American Sociological Review,* February 1994, pp. 1–22; and Arend Lijphart and Carlos H. Waisman, eds., *Institutional Design in New Democracies: Eastern Europe and Latin America* (Boulder: Westview, 1996).

6. Lipset, "Social Requisites of Democracy."

7. Mainwaring and Scully, eds., *Building Democratic Institutions,* p. 27.

8. Mainwaring and Scully, eds., *Building Democratic Institutions,* p. 5. Mainwaring and Scully identify four conditions for institutionalization: (1) the rules and the nature of interparty competition are both stable, (2) parties have somewhat stable roots in society, (3) the major political actors accord legitimacy to the electoral process and to parties, and (4) party organizations play an independent role in the political process and are not completely controlled by powerful leaders.

9. Robert D. Putnam, *Making Democracy Work: Civic Traditions in Modern Italy* (Princeton: Princeton University Press, 1993); see also Robert D. Putnam, "Bowling Alone: America's Declining Social Capital," *Journal of Democracy* 5, no. 1 (1995): 65–78.

10. Sidney Tarrow, "Making Social Science Work Across Space and Time: A Critical Reflection on Robert Putnam's *Making Democracy Work,*" *American Political Science Review* 90, no. 2 (1995): 389–397.

11. For this argument, see Paul Hirst and Grahame Thompson, *Globalization in Question: The International Economy and the Possibilities of Government* (Cambridge: Polity, 1996).

12. See, for example, Philip G. Cerny, "Globalisation and the Erosion of Democracy" (paper presented at ECPR workshop, Berne, 1997); and David Held, *Democracy and the Global Order* (Cambridge: Polity, 1995).

13. Held, *Democracy and the Global Order,* p. 232.

14. Held, *Democracy and the Global Order,* p. 233.

Suggested Readings

Ake, Claude. *Democracy and Development in Africa*. Washington, D.C.: Brookings Institution, 1996.

Bastion, Sunil, and Robin Luckham. *Can Democracy Be Designed? The Politics of International Choice in Conflict-Torn Societies*. London: Zed, 2003.

Beetham, David. *Democracy and Human Rights*. Cambridge: Polity, 1999.

Bull, Hedley, and Adam Watson, eds. *The Expansion of International Society*. Oxford: Clarendon, 1988.

Carothers, Thomas. *Aiding Democracy Abroad*. Washington, D.C.: Carnegie Endowment for International Peace, 1999.

Chernoff, Fred. "The Study of Democratic Peace and Progress in International Relations." *International Studies Review* 6, no. 1 (2004): 49–79.

Dahl, Robert A. *Democracy and Its Critics*. New Haven: Yale University Press, 1989.

_____. *Polyarchy: Participation and Opposition*. New Haven: Yale University Press, 1971.

Diamond, Larry. *Developing Democracy: Toward Consolidation*. Baltimore: Johns Hopkins University Press, 1999.

Diamond, Larry, Juan J. Linz, and Seymour Martin Lipset, eds. *Democracy in Developing Countries*. Vol. 1, *Persistence, Failure, and Renewal*. Vol. 2, *Africa*. Vol. 3, *Asia*. Vol. 4, *Latin America*. Boulder: Lynne Rienner, 1988, 1989.

Diamond, Larry, and M. F. Plattner, eds. *The Global Resurgence of Democracy*. Baltimore: Johns Hopkins University Press, 1993.

Donnelly, Jack. *International Human Rights*. 3rd ed., Boulder: Westview 2002.

Doyle, Michael W. "Kant, Liberal Legacies, and Foreign Affairs." *Philosophy and Public Affairs* 12, no. 3 (1983): 205–235.

_____. "Liberalism and World Politics." *American Political Science Review* 80, no. 4 (1986): 1151–1169.

_____. "Three Pillars of the Liberal Peace." *American Political Science Review* 99, no. 3 (2005): 463–466.

Elklit, Jørgen, and Andrew Reynolds. "A Framework for the Systematic Study of Election Quality." *Democratization* 12, no. 2 (2005): 147–162.

Fukuyama, Francis. "The End of History?" *The National Interest* 16 (1989): 3–18.

Gills, Barry, et al., eds. "The Developmental State? Democracy, Reform, and Economic Prosperity in the Third World in the Nineties." *Third World Quarterly* 17, no. 4 (1996): 585–855.

Haggard, Stephan, and Robert R. Kaufman. *The Political Economy of Democratic Transitions*. Princeton: Princeton University Press, 1995.

Haggard, Stephan, and Robert R. Kaufman, eds. *The Politics of Economic Adjustment.* Princeton: Princeton University Press, 1992.

Held, David. *Democracy and the Global Order: From the Modern State to Cosmopolitan Governance.* Cambridge: Polity, 1995.

_____. *Models of Democracy.* 3rd ed. Cambridge: Polity, 2006.

_____. *Prospects for Democracy. North, South, East, West.* Stanford: Stanford University Press, 1993.

Huntington, Samuel P. *The Third Wave: Democratization in the Late Twentieth Century.* Norman: University of Oklahoma Press, 1993.

Journal of Democracy. This quarterly journal provides wide coverage of current processes of democratization as well as in-depth background analyses.

Karl, Terry Lynn. "Dilemmas of Democratization in Latin America." *Comparative Politics* 23, no. 1 (1990): 1–21.

_____. "From Democracy to Democratization and Back: Before *Transitions from Authoritarian Rule.*" CDDRL Working Paper no. 45. Stanford, 2005.

Kohli, Atul, ed. *The Success of India's Democracy.* Cambridge: Cambridge University Press, 2001.

Lee Ray, James. *Democracy and International Conflict: An Evaluation of the Democratic Peace Proposition.* Columbia: University of South Carolina Press, 1995.

Linz, Juan J. "Transitions to Democracy." *Washington Quarterly* 13, no. 3 (1990): 143–164.

Lipset, Seymour Martin, ed. *The Encyclopedia of Democracy.* 4 vols. Washington, D.C.: Congressional Quarterly; London: Routledge, 1995.

Lipset, Seymour Martin, and Jason M. Lakin. *The Democratic Century.* Norman: University of Oklahoma Press, 2004.

Macmillan, John. "Liberalism and the Democratic Peace." *Review of International Studies* 30, no. 2 (2004): 179–200.

Macpherson, C. B. *The Life and Times of Liberal Democracy.* Oxford: Oxford University Press, 1977.

Mansfield, Edward, and Jack Snyder. "Democratization and War." *International Security* 20, no. 1 (1995): 5–38.

O'Donnell, Guillermo. "Delegative Democracy." *Journal of Democracy* 5, no. 1 (1994): 55–70.

O'Donnell, Guillermo, and Philippe C. Schmitter. *Transitions from Authoritarian Rule: Tentative Conclusions About Uncertain Democracies.* Baltimore: Johns Hopkins University Press, 1986.

O'Donnell, Guillermo, Philippe C. Schmitter, and Laurence Whitehead, eds. *Transitions from Authoritarian Rule: Comparative Perspectives.* Baltimore: Johns Hopkins University Press, 1988.

O'Donnell, Guillermo, et al., eds. *The Quality of Democracy.* Notre Dame, Ind.: University of Notre Dame Press, 2004.

Pinkney, Robert. *The Frontiers of Democracy: Challenges in the West, the East, and the Third World.* Aldershot, U.K.: Ashgate, 2005.

Pridham, Geoffrey, and Tatu Vanhanen, eds. *Democratization in Eastern Europe: Domestic and International Perspectives.* New York: Routledge, 1994.

Przeworski, Adam. *Democracy and the Market: Political and Economic Reforms in Eastern Europe and Latin America.* Cambridge: Cambridge University Press, 1991.

Putnam, Robert D. *Making Democracy Work: Civic Traditions in Modern Italy.* Princeton: Princeton University Press, 1993.

Reiss, Hans, ed. *Kant's Political Writings.* Cambridge: Cambridge University Press, 1970.

Risse, Thomas. "Beyond Iraq: The Crisis of the Transatlantic Security Community." In David Held and Mathias Kösnig-Archibugi, eds., *American Power in the 21st Century,* pp. 181–213. Cambridge: Polity, 2004.

Risse-Kappen, Thomas. "Public Opinion, Domestic Structure, and Foreign Policy in Liberal Democracies." *World Politics* 43, no. 4 (1991): 479–513.

Rosato, Sebastian. "The Flawed Logic of Democratic Peace Theory." *American Political Science Review* 97, no. 4 (2003): 585–602.

Rueschemeyer, Dietrich, Evelyne Huber Stephens, and John D. Stephens. *Capitalist Development and Democracy.* Cambridge: Polity, 1992.

Rummel, Rudolph J. "Libertarianism and International Violence." *Journal of Conflict Resolution* 27, no. 1 (1983): 27–71.

Russett, Bruce, and John Oneal. *Triangulating Peace: Democracy, Interdependence, and International Organizations.* London: Norton, 2001.

Rustow, Dankwart A. "Transitions to Democracy." *Comparative Politics* 2, no. 3 (1970): 337–365.

Singer, Max, and Aaron Wildawsky. *Zones of Peace/Zones of Turmoil.* Chatham N.J.: Chatham House, 1993.

Sirowy, Larry, and Alex Inkeles. "The Effects of Democracy on Economic Growth and Inequality: A Review." *Studies in Comparative International Development* 25, no. 1 (1990): 126–157.

Sobel, Richard. *The Impact of Public Opinion on U.S. Foreign Policy Since Vietnam.* New York: Oxford University Press, 2001.

Sørensen, Georg. "Democracy, Authoritarianism, and State Strength." *European Journal of Development Research* 5, no. 1 (1993): 6–34.

_____. *Democracy, Dictatorship, and Development: Economic Development in Selected Regimes of the Third World.* London: Macmillan, 1991.

_____. "Liberalism of Restraint and Liberalism of Imposition: Liberal Values and World Order in the New Millennium." *International Relations* 20, no. 3 (2006): 251–272.

Van Evera, Stephen. "Primed for Peace: Europe After the Cold War." *International Security* 15, no. 3 (1990–1991): 7–57.

Glossary

Absolute poverty indicates the minimum level of subsistence in a specific country. Basic human needs are not met; disease, malnutrition, and illiteracy are common.

Anarchy is the absence of political authority. The international system is anarchic because there is no central political authority above the sovereign states.

An **authoritarian developmentalist regime** is a reform-oriented system that enjoys a high degree of autonomy from vested elite interests. The regime controls a state apparatus with the bureaucratic capacity for promoting development and is run by a state elite ideologically committed to boosting economic development in terms of growth and welfare.

An **authoritarian growth regime** is an elite-dominated system focused on building a strong national economy. The long-term interests of the dominant social forces are respected, whereas the workers and peasants of the poor majority are looked to for providing the economic surplus needed to get growth under way.

The **authoritarian state elite enrichment regime** has as its main aim the enrichment of the elite who control the state. Neither economic growth nor welfare is an important goal. This type of regime is often based on autocratic rule by a supreme leader. Mobutu's Zaire is an example.

Civil society is the realm of social relations not regulated by the state. It includes all nonstate institutions, such as interest groups, associations, civil rights groups, and youth movements. In a totalitarian system, the state attempts to absorb civil society; all types of organizations are under state control.

A **consociational democracy** is a type of democratic system that is characterized by mechanisms serving to promote compromise and consensus among the groups in society. Such mechanisms include federalist systems, special legislative practices, and state agencies that facilitate intergroup compromise.

A **consolidated democracy**, according to Juan Linz, is one in which none of the major political actors recognize an alternative to democratic processes to gain power, and no political institution or group has a claim to veto the action of democratically elected decision makers. In short, democracy is seen as the "only game in town."

Delegitimation must be understood against the background of legitimacy, which indicates a government's right to govern based on such criteria as popular acceptance, the constitutional process, or economic or other achievements. Delegitimation sets in when the government can no longer point to a basis for its right to govern.

Democratic autonomy is the very broad concept of democracy set forth by David Held. It includes direct participation in local community institutions, active

193

control of elected politicians through the party system, and social as well as economic rights to ensure adequate resources for citizens' political activity. It also foresees self-management of cooperatively owned enterprises.

Democratization refers to the process of change toward more democratic forms of rule. The first phase involves the breakdown of the nondemocratic regime. In the second phase, the elements of a democratic order are established. During the third phase, consolidation, the new democracy is further developed; eventually democratic practices become an established part of the political culture.

Elite domination marks the presence of elite groups whose members reserve the right to interfere in the democratic process in order to protect their interests.

The **end of history** is a phrase coined by Francis Fukuyama to describe the end point of humankind's ideological evolution and the universalization of Western liberal democracy as the final form of human government.

External factors are the economic, political, ideological, and other elements that constitute the international context for the processes that take place in single countries. They often have a profound influence on those processes.

Francophone Africa is the name used to describe the countries in Africa that were once under French colonial rule and retain special ties with France. The countries making up Francophone Africa are Mauritania, Senegal, Mali, Côte d'Ivoire, the Central African Republic, Burkina Faso, Congo, Gabon, and Cameroun.

Founding elections are competitive, free, and fair, marking a distinctive shift in the roles of the political game toward new democratic practices.

Frozen democracies is Terry Lynn Karl's label for restricted, elite-dominated democracies that are unwilling to carry out substantive reforms addressing the lot of the poor.

Globalization is the intensification of economic, social, political, and cultural relations across borders.

The **Group of Seven (G7)** includes the seven most economically and militarily powerful capitalist nations: the United States, Japan, Germany, Great Britain, France, Italy, and Canada. The group meets periodically to discuss global issues.

Horizontal accountability is defined by Robert Johansen as the ability of citizens to influence the decisions that are made in neighboring societies and that directly affect them. It is achieved through democratic international institutions that guarantee rights for global minorities as well as majorities.

Illiberal democracy is the term suggested by Fareed Zakaria to designate systems where the liberal side of democracy is underdeveloped; the rule of law, the separation of powers, and basic rights of speech, assembly, and religion and property are not in force even though elections may be held.

Idealism, in the context of this book, is the view that conflict and violence can be overcome if the world is organized according to certain ideas or principles. Harmony is possible if priority is given to the "right" ideas.

The degree of **inclusiveness** (or participation) describes the number of citizens in a society who enjoy political rights and liberties. Nondemocratic regimes may exclude the large majority of the population from participation. In democratic regimes the entire adult population enjoys the full range of rights and liberties.

Interdependence is a word used to describe situations characterized by mutual dependence between countries or among actors in different countries.

An **international society,** according to Hedley Bull and Adam Watson, is a group of states that establish by dialogue and consent common rules and institutions for the conduct of their relations, and they recognize their common interest in maintaining these arrangements.

Intrafirm trade refers to trade across national borders but between different units of the same corporation.

Liberalization is the process of increasing the possibilities for political opposition and competition for government power. Often the first steps involve improving the possibilities for open public debate, allowing criticism of the authoritarian regime, and allowing open oppositional activity.

Mass-dominated democracies are systems in which mass actors have gained the upper hand over traditional ruling classes.

Neopatrimonialism must be understood against the background of patrimonialism, a term Max Weber coined to describe any type of government that originated from a royal household and has a ruler who treats matters of state as his or her personal affair. Present-day systems of this type, such as the system of personal rule in Africa, are examples of neopatrimonialism.

Nomenklatura is the name of the privileged class (i.e., the political, economic, and ideological elite) under the communist system. In the former Soviet Union, the *nomenklatura* numbered about 75,000 people.

Pacific union is the name Immanuel Kant used to describe his vision of a peaceful world of democracies. The pacific union would be based on three elements: (1) the mere existence of democracies with their culture of peaceful conflict resolution, (2) the common moral bonds that are forged between democracies, and (3) the democracies' economic cooperation toward mutual advantage.

In **patron-client relationships,** a patron provides services, rewards, or protection to a number of clients in return for their personal allegiance. The patron controls the resources; the clients are thus in a relationship of dependence.

Personal rule is the name given to the African system of government based on personal loyalty toward the leading figure of the regime, the strongman. The important positions in the state are filled by followers of the strongman. Their allegiance is reinforced by their share of the spoils of office.

In a system with **plural voting,** some members of the electorate have more votes than others. J. S. Mill suggested that the "wiser and more talented" should have more votes than the "ignorant and less able."

Political culture, following Samuel Huntington's definition, refers to the system of values and beliefs that defines the context and meaning of political action.

Political pacts are agreements between elite groups that restrict democracy by defining vital areas of interest for the elites. Often the elite groups will not support the new democracy unless it respects these pacts.

Polyarchy is a word used by Robert Dahl to describe systems that are called democracies in this book. Dahl outlines eight conditions that must be met in order for a system to qualify as democratic. No country satisfies all of these conditions perfectly. Therefore, Dahl uses the term "polyarchy" for these systems.

Realism, as used in the context of this book, is a theoretical perspective on international relations that purports to analyze the world as it really is, not as it ought to be. In the real world, conflict is immanent due to forces inherent in human nature and due to the way the world's populations have chosen to organize in the form of independent, sovereign states that respect no authority outside or above themselves.

Restricted democracies are political systems with some democratic elements but also with restrictions on competition, participation, and liberties.

A **security community,** according to Karl Deutsch, is made up of groups of people having attained a sense of community, and it has institutions and practices strong enough and widespread enough to assure dependable expectations of peaceful exchange among its populations. "Sense of community" is a belief that common social problems must and can be resolved by processes of peaceful exchange.

Security complex is the name used by Barry Buzan to describe a group of states whose primary security concerns are linked. Examples of security complexes are Europe, the Persian Gulf, and South Asia.

Soft authoritarian is Chalmers Johnson's label for Japanese democracy, which has retained some mildly authoritarian features in its governmental institutions, including single-party rule, which has been a part of the system for more than three decades, and an extremely strong and comparatively unsupervised state administration.

A **totalitarian** system is an authoritarian form of regime in which the state controls every aspect of citizens' lives.

Weak states are deficient in three basic respects. First, the economy is defective; second, there is a lack of coherent national community; third, there is a lack of effective, responsive state institutions.

About the Book and Author

When the Berlin Wall crumbled, the world experienced a "springtime for democracy" as many formerly communist states reconfigured their governments and economies. Countries in the developing world experienced democratic openings as well. But is democracy developing in a sustainable fashion? What pitfalls are there in recent trends toward democratization?

This book examines the prospects for democracy in the world today and frames the central dilemma confronting all states touched by the process of democratization. The author clarifies the concept of democracy, shows its application in different contexts, and questions whether democratic advancement will continue—and if so, at what price. The consequences of democracy for economic development, human rights, and peaceful relations among countries are illuminated in both their positive and negative aspects.

Professor Sørensen is uniquely qualified to give students and general readers a sense of the long, slow process that democratization entails—both from the inside out (at national and local levels) and from the outside in (international causes and effects). He draws on a wealth of case studies, examples, and anecdotes to illustrate historical as well as contemporary instances of democratic transition.

Democracy, as he convincingly portrays it, is a value in itself as well as a potential promoter of peace, prosperity, and human well-being. But democracy is not inevitable, and actions at every level—from the individual to the international—are necessary to ensure that frail or "frozen" democracies do not founder and that established democracies flourish.

Georg Sørensen is professor of international politics and economics at the University of Aarhus, Denmark. He has written numerous books and articles on international relations and development issues.

Index